The Urban Masterplanning Handbook

Eric Firley and Katharina Grön

The Urban Masterplanning Handbook

Eric Firley and Katharina Grön

WILEY

A John Wiley and Sons, Ltd, Publication

FRONTISPIECE: A famous example of 19th century urban renewal: Avenue de l'Opéra and its surroundings, Paris, France.

PAGE 6: A square in the Jianwai SOHO district, part of Beijing's new CBD.

ISBN 978-0-470-97225-0 (hardback)
ISBN 978-1-118-49464-6 (ebk)
ISBN 978-1-118-49465-3 (ebk)

Executive Commissioning Editor: Helen Castle
Project Editor: Miriam Swift
Assistant Editor: Calver Lezama
Cover design by Kate Ward
Front cover photos © Eric Firley
Drawings © 2013 Katharina Grön and Eric Firley
Page design and layouts by Maggi Smith
Printed in Italy by Printer Trento Srl

FSC
MIX
Paper from
responsible sources
FSC® C015829
www.fsc.org

For Louise
Eric Firley

For Lea and David
Katharina Grön

Acknowledgements

We would like to thank our sponsors who have made possible the realisation of this book not only through their financial contribution, but also through their continuous and personal interest in the subject:

Dominique Boré and her team from EPADESA, La Défense Seine Arche

Steve Tomlinson and Mark Brearley from Design for London

Charles Walford and Ron German from Stanhope plc

Thierry Laget and Julie Sanchez from SERM-Montpellier

Steve Tomlinson deserves special mention, his support including considerable input in establishing the book's structure, the choice of case studies and the revision of the introduction.

The numerous purpose-made plans and diagrams are a key feature of this work. Conceived by Katharina Grön herself, we would like to show our gratitude to Jennifer Margitan, Axel Eitel and David Zink who contributed to their production.

During our long research and travel period we have been in touch with hundreds of people. Without their help the following material could not have been gathered. Space dictates that we can only mention some of them (in alphabetical order): Bill Addis (Buro Happold); Sharif Aggour (Pelli Clarke Pelli Architects); Thomas Albrecht (Hilmer & Sattler und Albrecht); Diego Ardiaca; Larry Beasley, Alain Beauregard (APUR); Professor Roberto Behar; Marie Beirne; Neil Bennett (Farrells); Peter Bishop; Barbara Bottet (Atelier Christian de Portzamparc); Reinhard Böwer (Böwer Eith Murken); Marlies Britz (City of Potsdam); Steve Brown (Buro Happold); Professor Ricky Burdett; Stefania Canta (Renzo Piano Building Workshop); Björn Cederquist (City of Stockholm); James KM Cheng; Emma Cobb (Pei Cobb Freed & Partners); Catherine Coquen-Creusot (SEMAPA); Alexander Cooper (Cooper, Robertson & Partners), Craig Copeland (Pelli Clarke Pelli Architects); Daniel Day (Metropolitan Life); Michel Dionne; Sir Philip Dowson; Professor François Dufaux; Mats Egelius (White Architects); Eveline van Engelen (OMA); William Fain (Johnson Fain); Mads Farsø; Kathryn Firth; Stellan Fryxell (Tengbom); Hiroaki Fuji (MEC); Alfredo Garay (CAPMSA); Stephanie Gelb (Battery Park City Authority); Fenella Gentleman (Grosvenor Estates); Mieke de Geyter (EMAAR); Caroline Giezeman (City of Rotterdam); Michael Gordon (City of Vancouver); Laure Gosselin (EPADESA); Nathalie Grand (SEMAPA); Len Grundlingh (DSA Architects); Professor Sharon Haar; Professor Christoph Hadrys; Meinhard Hansen (Hansen Architekten); Eric Heijselaar (City Archives Amsterdam); Philippe Honnorat (WSP); Nigel Hughes (Grosvenor Estates); Christine Huvé (BHVP), Susanne Klar (Freie Planungsgruppe Berlin GmbH); William Kelly; Christoph Kohl (Krier Kohl Architekten); Sven Kohlhoff; Adrián Kraisman (CAPMSA); Kengo Kuma; Thierry Laget (SERM Montpellier); Rob Latham (WSP); Pacal Le Barbu (TGT); François Leclerc (Agence François Leclerc); Anu Leinonen (OMA); Xie Li; Sir Stuart Lipton; Weiming Lu; Neill Maclaine (Broadgate Estates); Professor Lars Marcus; Erik Mattie; Yves Nurit (Montpellier Agglomération); Malin Olsson (City of Stockholm); Adrian Penfold (British Land); Professor Elizabeth Plater-Zyberk; Christian de Portzamparc; Wang Qingfeng (CBD Authority Beijing); Margit Rust (City of Berlin); Keiichiro Sako (SAKO Architects); Suzan Samaha (EMAAR); Russell Sharfman (DSA Architects); Brian Shea (Cooper, Robertson & Partners); Malcolm Smith (Arup Associates); Sebastian Springer (City of Freiburg); Gerhard Stanierowski (City of Berlin); Marinke Steenhuis (Steenhuismeurs bv); Hans Stimmann; Professor Vladimir Stissi; Isamu Sugeno (MEC); Yvonne Szeto (Pei Cobb Freed & Partners); Manuel Tardits (Mikan); Koji Terada (Mitsubishi Jisho Sekkei); Jérôme Treuttel (TGT); Peter Udzenija (Concord Pacific); Professor Arnold van der Valk; Professor Laura Vaughan; Roland Veith (City of Freiburg); Christophe Vénien (EPADESA); Serena Vergano (Taller de Arquitectura); Sharon Wade (Battery Park City Authority); David Wauthy (SAEM Euralille); Sarah M Whiting; Barry Winfield; Norio Yamato (Mori); Christina du Yulian (CBD Authority Beijing); Kentaro Yusa (MEC); Sérida Zaïd (APUR); Ruoli Zhou.

Thanks also to Timea Hopp who performed a language check of the book before the handover to the publisher.

Last but not least, we would like to express our gratitude to Helen Castle, Calver Lezama and Miriam Swift from John Wiley & Sons.

Contents

Introduction

Blueprints for urban life

From a philosophical early history traceable back to utopian visions and ideas, masterplanning today is internationally recognised as a planning method that is embedded in political, social and economic frameworks. It responds to the needs of architects, urban designers, planners, developers and other construction professionals to participate in major urban expansion and regeneration projects that cross the boundaries of their own roles and promise to transform the quality of city life. Vast in scope, such initiatives demand extensive preparatory research in order to identify an effective approach for the site in question. Following on from the first two books in Wiley's 'Urban Handbook' series – *The Urban Housing Handbook* (2009) and *The Urban Towers Handbook* (2011) – this manual sets out to equip professionals for the task.

Rather than to test or discuss a particular hypothesis in the field of planning, our aim is to enable an organisational and visual comparative approach. We have selected 20 masterplans from around the world, historic and recent, each of which is analysed in turn. Project descriptions and key data are complemented by specially custom-made diagrams that outline each masterplan's physical nature and development. Each study includes four analysis drawings of the current site – highlighting separately green spaces, the street network, public transport connections and building uses – a further four graphics illustrate the development process, putting special emphasis on the notions of cadastral subdivisions and of public or private ownership.

Images and figure-ground diagrams of Avenue de l'Opéra in Paris (opposite and below left) and Stuyvesant Town in New York City (below).

One of the main aims of this book is to examine the ways in which the diversity of these urban artefacts has been influenced by non-formal parameters.

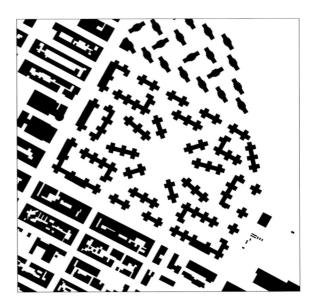

Images and figure-ground
diagrams of False Creek
North in Vancouver (below)
and Hammarby Sjöstad in
Stockholm (below right and
opposite).

With public buildings and plots shown in pink and private ones in blue, they explain the change of landownership that occurred in most of the cases during the development process, as well as suggesting a conceptual reading of the masterplan's prescriptions for the creation of blocks and building masses. Potsdamer Platz in Berlin is hence an example of a plan that focused, from the city's point of view, on the clear delimitation of urban blocks and the street space; while New York's Stuyvesant Town represents a contrasting type of urbanism, the tower-in-park configuration, in which there is no intermediate scale between the buildings themselves, their footprints and the rest of the plot. At the end of the book, the appendices provide not only comparative tables, but also a scale comparison of all project perimeters in their entirety, and a timeline that facilitates the understanding of each project's development frame. Finally, to highlight the impressive diversity of built results, we have assembled all 20 of the figure-ground diagrams featured in the case studies. By focusing on the relationship between built and unbuilt spaces, these reveal a broad range of urban patterns employed in masterplanning.

   Before moving on to the case studies themselves, some background information on the evolution of masterplanning as a concept, and on our own approach to it, will be useful. This introductory essay prepares the ground for our hands-off project presentations and clarifies our point of view in relation to several fundamental issues of planning.

A BRIEF HISTORY OF MASTERPLANNING

Historically, in its more figurative sense, the notion of the masterplan was primarily linked less to the built environment than to political, philosophical or religious affairs. In signifying a blueprint, long-term strategy or divine plan, it has been interpreted as the equivalent of the Greek *logos*,

Platon

FAR LEFT: Portrait of the
Greek philosopher Plato.

LEFT: Woodcut by
Ambrosius Holbein
for a 1518 edition of
Thomas More's *Utopia*.

schema or *kosmos* which can be found in the epistemological writings of the philosopher Plato
around the early 4th century BC. These evoke the concept of a divine plan as something the
average human – due to the physical world's and his own imperfection – is not able to decipher.
In contrast to the expression's most common current use, it hence alluded to something
fundamentally out of reach, rather than something under human control.

It was through the theoretical description of ideal societies that these philosophical ideas
indirectly found an application in the world of architecture. The earliest and most influential
such source is Plato's *The Republic*, which was meant as an allegory of the human soul's inner
workings. This was adopted and elaborated in 1516 by the English Renaissance humanist
Thomas More in his vision of the hypothetical island country Utopia. Over the following centuries,
the notion of an ideal community and its masterplan in the sense of a blueprint became a
recurring theme in the history of architecture and urbanism. Sometimes explicitly, but mostly
not, it led to built and unbuilt projects such as French philosopher Charles Fourier's early-19th-
century Phalanstère concept, Robert Owen's New Harmony in Indiana (founded 1814) and
Ebenezer Howard's Garden Cities in the UK (late 19th and early 20th centuries). Modernist
versions of Utopia include Ludwig Karl Hilberseimer's Hochhausstadt (High-Rise City, 1924),
Le Corbusier's Plan Voisin (1925) and Frank Lloyd Wright's Broadacre City (1932). In this context,
the masterplan can be understood as the key to happiness, sometimes in the form of a specific
intervention, and sometimes as an abstract model.

If these insights deal with the notion of 'masterplanning' in the widest possible sense, a more
technical and literal application of the word can be traced back to the beginnings of modern
comprehensive planning in the early 20th century. The Netherlands played a pioneering role:
the Dutch Housing Act of 1902 not only provided new building regulations and guidelines for
the creation of housing associations, but also prescribed the establishment of comprehensive

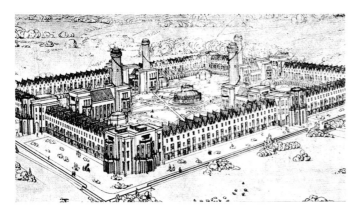

Charles Fourier's unbuilt Phalanstère, conceived in the early 19th century. Its revolutionary claim is expressed through the architectural similarity with the Chateau of Versailles, symbol of a very different type of society. Autarkic and utopian, the Phalanstère figures as a precedent for Le Corbusier's Unité d'Habitation in Marseilles (1947–52).

Illustration by the architect Thomas Stedman Whitwell for Robert Owen's New Harmony in Indiana (1825). As a vision of a new type of community, it explicitly referred back to Plato's and More's utopian writings.

BELOW: Ludwig Hilberseimer's influential vision of a Hochhausstadt (high-rise city) for one million inhabitants (1924). The diagrammatic and hypothetical proposal is almost contemporaneous with Le Corbusier's Ville Contemporaine (1922) and Plan Voisin for Paris (1925).

plans for all municipalities above 10,000 inhabitants (see Spangen case study) which – importantly – had to be reviewed and adjusted every 10 years. Similar laws were adopted in Britain with the two consecutive Town Planning Acts of 1909 and 1919, and in France in 1919 and 1924. In the USA, the City Beautiful Movement – an aesthetically driven vision of social cohesiveness achieved through the reform of architecture and urbanism, which began to flourish in the 1890s – paved the way for the development of broader planning frameworks. Edward M Bassett, whose 1938 book *The Master Plan* links the origin of masterplans to the creation of planning commissions in the USA of the 1920s, proved a key figure. Often referred to as 'the father of zoning', he believed that control had to be exerted through the establishment of seven planning elements: streets; parks; sites for public buildings; public reservations; zoning districts; routes for public utilities; and pierhead and bulkhead lines.

The essential element of this rather administrative definition of masterplanning is the development of national or state legislations as an institutional practice. Such a view allows us to draw a (still blurred) separation line between the modern conception of masterplanning and scattered cases of 19th-century urbanism, notably the Ringstrasse in Vienna, the Castro Plan for Madrid or Baron Haussmann's works in Paris. These plans and many others can certainly also be understood as masterplans – one of Haussmann's breakthroughs even figuring in this book (see Avenue de l'Opéra case study). However, they were essentially one-off interventions and not yet the result of a binding and recurring planning culture. Similar statements could be made about Frederick Law Olmsted's visionary work in the USA, using vast networks of green infrastructure – New York's Central Park (1850s) and Boston's Emerald Necklace (1860s) being the most prominent examples – in order to sustain the long-term growth of a conurbation. It should not be forgotten that the initiative for most of these late 19th- and early 20th-century plans was forced on by the swift spread of diseases and the subsequent danger of political unrest. The exploding cities of the post-Industrial Revolution era were threatening to escape the control of the decision-makers.

THE POST-WAR CHANGE IN PARADIGM

An awareness of the early ideological connotations of masterplanning is necessary in order to understand the word's evolving and increasingly fragmented interpretations in the post-war era. An illustrious critique of the relation between utopianism and masterplanning can be found in Colin Rowe and Fred Koetter's *Collage City* (1978). Among many other sources quoted in their book is the British philosopher Karl Popper, whose works – including *The Open Society and its Enemies* (1945) – scrutinise the logical and inevitable relation between a utopian vision of the ideal society and the emergence of totalitarian regimes. While Popper's findings were purely political, conceived against the background of the rise of fascism and Stalinism, the architects Rowe and Koetter apply them to Modernism and its often dogmatic expression in the built environment.

Though not explicitly mentioned, the 'masterplan' becomes the blueprint that everybody has to follow. Ideal by definition, it cannot be adjusted and cannot be the result of a collaborative design effort, leading to a tragic and never-ending spiral of tabula-rasa interventions. In contrast to More's allegorical and ironic notion of Utopia, or Fourier's and Owen's elaborate social and political agenda, the Modernist urban versions of Hilberseimer or Le Corbusier convey the idea of universal finality, generated on the basis of formal convictions rather than scientific findings. As a reaction, Rowe and Koetter explore in their book the notion of the urban *bricoleur*, not only working on the basis of what already exists – therefore including tradition – but also refusing a scientific claim for a discipline that cannot solely function according to scientific rules. Popper's own philosophical counterproposal – similar, but not equal to the notion of the bricoleur – consists of 'piecemeal social engineering', a concept that aims for the fragmentary and consecutive abolishment of defects, rather than for the ad-hoc installation of an ideal state.

Eventually, it was the comprehensive and holistic claim of the early 20th-century understanding of 'masterplanning', and its belief in the possibility to plan for a fixed future in detail and over a long period of time, that led to a shift not only in the terminology of planning, but in the whole understanding of planning as a discipline. Since the 1960s, as claimed by Peter Hall in his book *Urban and Regional Planning* (1975), the notion of masterplanning has been considered to symbolise an outdated and static process involving survey, analysis and plan. It has been opposed to a set of proposals for systems planning, in which the understanding of the system's dynamics and the constant review and adjustment of objectives is meant to avoid the application of planned actions that can only have a partial and potentially destructive effect on the system as a whole. Interestingly, this fairly technical and iterative view is – translated into the political realm – analogous to Popper's own concept of 'piecemeal social engineering'.

The critique of modern design and planning principles has hence led to a scale-shift of the word's terminology, rather than to an abolition of its use. If the addition of the word 'master' in the early 20th century described the largest possible size of a plan's application in the form of regional zoning plans, it would later increasingly be applied to the smaller scale of neighbourhoods and grouped architectural interventions. Today, masterplans tend to be used in the realm of urban design rather than planning, and therefore define the relation between built form and public realm more than that between infrastructural networks and land uses.

The use of the word 'master', with its ultimately elitist background, can be the source of a certain malaise in contemporary planning practice. The crux of the matter is in the end not the plan itself as a product, but the authority and (potential lack of) flexibility that it evokes, justified by a blueprint of higher (moral) order. For this reason, in the UK the word 'masterplan' tends to be avoided by public bodies in favour of gentler terms, not only for the largest-scale planning documents like the current 'London Plan – A Spatial Development Strategy', but even for smaller-scale design proposals. When the public OPLC (Olympic Park Legacy Company) was formed, in charge of steering the development of the Olympic site after the London 2012 Games, the 'Legacy Masterplan Framework' was hence rebranded as 'Legacy Communities Scheme'. Concurrently, elsewhere in the world the term 'masterplan' continues to be freely employed, such as for Delhi's 'Master Plan 2021'. Its use or otherwise strongly depends on the cultural background of each planning system, and can be considered as a symptom of each country's relation to the principles and ideological origins of modern planning.

In view of the word's connotations, it is perhaps not surprising that in the Western world 'masterplanning' is increasingly used for private developments, in which the suggested notion of control is considered to be a marketable quality rather than a potential challenge for democratic decision-making. It not only expresses confidence in the professional implementation of a large investment, but also evokes – in the City Beautiful tradition – memories of a grand design and its utopian claim for the creation of a better environment. The fact that it often describes plans for private residential communities is, however, also a statistical consequence of the increasing withdrawal of public authorities from the practice of urban planning. The case study of the Kirchsteigfeld project in Potsdam, as just one example, highlights how the planning monopoly of the German state is partly undermined by the practice of asking developers to finance the establishment or modification of communal development plans which pertain to their own projects. The planning initiative for most activities under the regional zoning level hence heavily depends on the private sector.

The sites of Kirchsteigfeld (Potsdam), Hammarby Sjöstad (Stockholm) and Euralille (Lille) before or during intervention. In each of these cases the starting position in terms of ownership structure and type was entirely different.

'MASTERPLANNING': OUR OWN DEFINITION

Having established the ambiguity and inconsistent application of masterplanning as a concept both historically and in a contemporary context, it should be explained that our use of the term throughout the book and in the title is entirely intuitive. It is used here as it is currently and most widely applied and understood in professional practice: as a framework that provides more or less detailed design prescriptions for a specific development area.

Masterplanning can indeed easily be dismissed as an outdated approach to urban development, forcing the simple ideas of a few on a much more complex reality of a vast territory, its history and population. However, if such a criticism might hold true for many cases – post-war urban renewal projects like New York's Stuyvesant Town figuring as the usual suspects – it still does not answer the question of how to kick-start and implement sustainable change without any kind of central coordination in areas where it is urgently needed, and where there is little existing context to work with. Our selection highlights different degrees of planning control, referring to issues like development initiative, landownership, land subdivision and design management. The interplay of these mainly organisational issues is complicated by the artistic rules governing architectural (and arguably also urban) creation: if order in one sense or the other is considered to be one of their basic principles, it might indeed have to be translated into the mechanics of the development process. Even piecemeal implementation tends therefore to be somehow 'masterminded'. This is where the question of scale becomes a determining factor: some zones might be limited to a minimum planning influence, but, in our understanding, such a logic cannot be endlessly repeated without loss of spatial particularity and sense of place. The optimal efficiency of networks, most

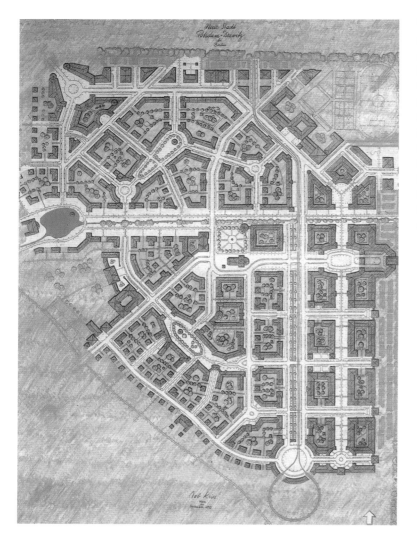

The plan for Kirchsteigfeld is an example of a masterplan in the traditional sense, with one single client and one practice as main designer and coordinator. For the almost 10 times larger La Défense Seine Arche site the situation is far more complex, and it has to be seen as a plan of plans.

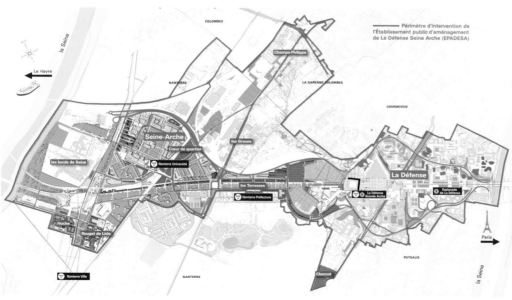

importantly public transport, is another argument that belies a naive vision of perfectly liberal planning.

The difficulty of clearly delimiting between architectural and urban scales and their respective organisational set-ups can be illustrated through the etymological study of the word 'architect' itself. Literally signifying 'master-builder' or 'master-carpenter', it suggests that the construction of buildings has always been considered as the result of teamwork under the supervision of a leading individual. Planning is thus an inherent component of architecture, just as it is of urban design. The boundary between the architect's and the planner's mission is therefore hard to define. Can the 'master-planner' be the same person as the 'master-builder', can he be considered as his superior, or does city-making demand a different approach altogether? While there may be no clear answer to this question, physical size certainly plays an important role. For a single building, the design authority of a single person is meant to assure a positive notion of coherence. For a group of buildings, these rules seem to demand adjustment in order to avoid the point at which coherence turns into monotony.

These considerations raise the question of how much control is desirable and necessary for the practice of urban development. As the case studies we have selected make clear, the answer varies according to the project in question, and must take account of the specific starting position and development culture of each.

THE CASE STUDIES: COMMONALITIES AND CONTRASTS

One of our core aims in preparing this book has been to gain an understanding of how changes in the set-up of a masterplanning project can influence the built result. Within such a broad subject, which covers everything from individual house development on the one hand to regional planning on the other, we have sought to select examples that are suitable for comparison with one another, while offering a useful cross section of approaches and outcomes. We have therefore chosen to focus on medium-scale projects: the creation or major modification of neighbourhoods in central or relatively central locations of an existing agglomeration. They are presented in order of surface area, from Broadgate's mere 11.7 hectares (29 acres) to La Défense Seine Arche's 564 hectares (1,394 acres). Despite this considerable difference in size, most of them have been planned with a focus on the resulting built form, belonging to the domain of urban design as much as that of planning. Most of them are dense mixed-use developments, built as city extensions on usually brownfield and sometimes greenfield land, and all are more or less strictly controlled by a public, private or mixed development entity.

The examples span from the early 19th century, arguably the beginning of modern planning practice, up to today, with some of them not yet fully completed. Their geographical range is equally wide, encompassing Europe, North and South America and Asia. This international focus is key, as explaining the cultural background of each case reveals similarities and disparities between the different local development traditions. Our aim is not to water down these cultural differences in the quest for a generic development model, but to help identify, and potentially abstract, the major questions of planning through the analytic process of comparison.

In view of the diversity in the selected projects, occasional urban, typological and organisational similarities are particularly fascinating, including the simultaneous emergence in the 20th century of public housing agencies across the world, the appearance of mixed development companies as separate legal structures or, on a more formal level, the recent export of Vancouver's tower-on-podium urbanism. It is equally fascinating to examine in what relation these elements stand to parameters like landownership and the size of planning teams. Touching on another frequently debated point, the confrontation of public and private initiative, our findings do not suggest a fundamental difference of development logic according to these two categories. It is actually interesting to analyse how closely a liberal and a public development model can produce similar results. In this respect, the study of projects like Spangen, Stuyvesant Town or even Downtown Dubai is especially elucidating.

Our selection should not be understood as cases of best practice. All examples are considered to be of intellectual and formal interest, but this does not mean that they are all appropriate models for future developments.

THE DESIGNER AND THE PROCESS: HOW TO KEEP THE OVERVIEW?

The considerable complexity of the process and of the structures involved in the construction or regeneration of our built environment leads inevitably to a high degree of professional specialisation. Besides planners, architects, builders, investors, engineers and developers, there is a whole range of related professions, including real-estate agents, bankers, building surveyors, lawyers, facility managers, fire safety officers and cost and traffic consultants, to mention but a few. This selection does not even include the end user or, in most Western countries, the elected authorities which have to give their approval in the form of a building permit, based on a pile of legislation and in many cases months or years of public enquiries. Under these circumstances, it is difficult not to lose the complete picture, and the tendency is then to separate text-oriented from graphically-oriented participants in the development process. This might not necessarily be a problem, but the authors' own professional experience as designing architects and planners suggests that many complications and inefficiencies could often have been avoided if the relation between the development process and the intended built result had been analysed as part of a fundamental consultancy role.

The aim is not to replace other professions with the 'enlightened architect', but to keep an overview of the crucial questions that is, in a more flexible way, comparable to the role that the designer might play in smaller architectural projects. Whether this role should be taken by a trained planner, architect, developer or engineer, is another question, and depends on each project and development culture. Neither Paris's Baron Haussmann nor Berlin's James Hobrecht nor Barcelona's Ildefons Cerdà was a trained architect, but they all had a clear view of what they wanted to achieve in the context of a specific set of socioeconomic and political circumstances, and this view obviously transcended investment targets. Today's increasing lack of planning initiative or use of propositional planners through the public sector is not necessarily a negative feature, but it seems at times not to have been replaced by any other authority with an adequate overview of the whole process and its long-term implications. Our belief is that knowledge is the best way to improve this situation, and it is hoped that, in combining formal and organisational realms, our diagrammatic approach will enable our findings to be understood by the broadest possible spectrum of participating professions.

SUSTAINABILITY AND MASTERPLANNING

Global warming has made sustainability an ever more pressing issue, and this is no less the case for masterplanning than it is in other realms. As some of the case studies testify – notably Vauban in Freiburg and Hammarby Sjöstad in Stockholm – such initiatives can provide an opportunity for re-greening, for the provision of eco-friendly transport infrastructures, and for the installation of low-energy utilities and local recycling facilities. However, in our context, the concept of sustainability extends beyond environmental concerns to encompass a whole set of social, technical, cultural and economic components which are essential for the enduring success of a neighbourhood or whole city. To these are added design issues like connectivity, accessibility and, arguably, aesthetics.

Perhaps the greatest challenge arises from the fact that – in contrast to the limited scale of architecture – urbanism and to a certain extent also urban design are process- and management-driven activities that hardly ever refer to a finished product. From the birth of an idea to the termination of the last construction phase, many project parameters will have changed. Due to this time factor, sustainability in the most literal sense is one of the discipline's natural ingredients. Many failed examples are thus the result of a denial of this notion of change.

The question is how and according to what criteria to measure and potentially rank the degree of sustainability of a set of projects? In this respect our method of historical cross-references raises some enlightening questions, but also considerably complicates the already difficult task of comparison. Should success only be evaluated on the basis of the current situation? Would it financially be possible to repeat Haussmann's Parisian interventions? And if yes, would they be politically enforceable? What level of carbon dioxide emissions does Belgravia produce today, and what would have to be done in order to further reduce them? Could this be achieved with solely technical measures like insulation and optimised recycling networks, or would such changes also affect functional mixture, building envelopes, transport connections and the shape of open spaces?

It quickly becomes apparent that comparing and ranking the sustainability of the featured case studies is not a straightforward task. We have therefore decided to highlight specific sustainability features in each chapter, rather than to rate each project against the others. The development of a complex figure-based rating system would, however, be an exciting undertaking, and could be applied and tested with these case studies. Our comparative tables at the end of the book can be seen as a first step in this direction.

CONCLUSION

It is not an easy task to generalise the outcome of our comparative studies, and it would be foolish to devise a universal step-by-step guide to the process of masterplanning. The uniqueness of each case is often linked to the state's monopoly over the development of its territory, which leads inevitably to a very local development initiative and hence a fairly short list of global players, most of them being engineers or 'starchitects' rather than urban planners.

This does, however, also mean that we are faced with the question of how change and improvement can be achieved. With projects varying so greatly in size, scope, organisation and cultural background, it is difficult or impossible to scientifically identify causalities. Consequently, we believe that the best way to equip professionals for the task is to provide and clarify information about a diverse range of previous schemes, so that the outcomes of different approaches in similar circumstances can be evaluated. It is hoped that this book, with its clear presentation of comparative work and strong visual emphasis, will provide a useful resource for new building and research projects, as well as preparing the ground for more detailed works in this field.

On a less pragmatic level, it can be stated that the intriguing connection between planning type, urban form, ownership and political structure has been the underlying motivation of our study. As Rowe and Koetter argue in *Collage City*, 'the prospects of scientific city planning should, in reality, be regarded as equivalent to the prospects of scientific politics'. Knowledge about the practice of city-making is hence a political virtue in itself, its relation to the potential dangers of utopianism being just one element of a vast discussion which we can only touch upon here, and which merits greater public debate. Who decides upon the future of our built environment, and to what extent does the status quo reflect our democratic principles?

Case Studies

Broadgate

LOCATION: CITY OF LONDON, UNITED KINGDOM
DATE: 1985–91 (EXCEPT 201 BISHOPSGATE AND THE BROADGATE TOWER)
SIZE: 11.7 HECTARES (29 ACRES)

Situated on the fringe of the City of London, the Broadgate development transformed a site comprising a former train station and an adjacent operational station into a major new financial district.

Floor area ratio: 3.61
Residential population: 0
Mix of uses: 98% office,
2% retail and restaurants

Like many other capital cities, the centre of London is served by a ring of terminus stations that connect the busy core with its direct surroundings and the national rail network. Historically, the stations were built by private operators, Euston Station being the first to open in 1837. Because of competition between these operators and the separate use of tracks and real estate, a number of stations were built almost adjacently – one extreme example being King's Cross, St Pancras and Euston Stations, all situated within walking distance of one another. Operation of the railways was nationalised following the 1947 Transport Act, and growing financial pressures, coupled with changes of traffic and transport patterns in the second half of the 20th century, led to a multitude of service alterations and station closures. In the 1990s, the operation of trains was returned to the private sector, while the management of the tracks and stations remained in public hands, latterly under the name Network Rail.

Broad Street Station, a passenger and goods station, was built in 1865 on the northeastern corner of the City of London as terminus of the North London Railway network. After a period of initial success and several expansions, the station began to suffer from a downturn in usage in the early 20th century, a shift due mainly to the growth of bus, tram and tube networks. Damage during the Second World War did not improve the situation and by 1985 – one year before its final closure – only 6,000 passengers were using Broad Street Station every week. The situation for the directly adjacent Liverpool Street Station was very different: opened to the public in 1875 as terminus of the Great Eastern Railways and as a replacement for Bishopsgate Station, its operations were driven by a different set of destinations less challenged by the growth of the local public transport network. Though the station had been in urgent need of renovation and reorganisation since the 1970s, passenger flows were still steadily increasing. Today, Liverpool Street Station remains an important interchange between underground, bus and train services, and after Waterloo and Victoria is the capital's third busiest train station.

The development of the Broadgate project happened in several phases but, in terms of architectural and personal initiative, the construction of 1 Finsbury Avenue – although financially a separate operation – can be considered the starting point. Built between 1983 and 1985 by the developer Rosehaugh Greycoat Estates on the site of Broad Street Station's former goods yards and adjoining buildings, and designed by Peter Foggo of Arup Associates, this elegant and highly successful low-rise office building appeared as a vision of what the market wanted. The design, acclaimed for

LEFT: Axonometric representation of the Broadgate master plan, excluding the ongoing and recent redevelopment works.

BELOW: Aerial view from the north of Broad Street and Liverpool Street Stations before redevelopment.

its large floor plates and generous interior atria, provided an appropriate urban response to the quandary posed by the run-down neighbourhood on the neglected fringe of one of the world's wealthiest financial districts. Although located just outside the traditional City square mile, the building was able to meet the requirements of the financial service occupiers whose businesses were about to change as a result of the 'Big Bang' deregulation of the financial markets.

PROJECT ORGANISATION / TEAM STRUCTURE

In 1975 British Rail had commissioned the well-established architectural practice Fitzroy Robinson & Partners for a major redevelopment study of both Broad Street and Liverpool Street Stations. The outcome, which called for the demolition of all historic buildings on the sites, quickly encountered fierce opposition from politicians and conservationists. A public enquiry was held, resulting in the Grade II listing of several parts of Liverpool Street Station. In 1983 an act of Parliament mandated the redevelopment of the station and British

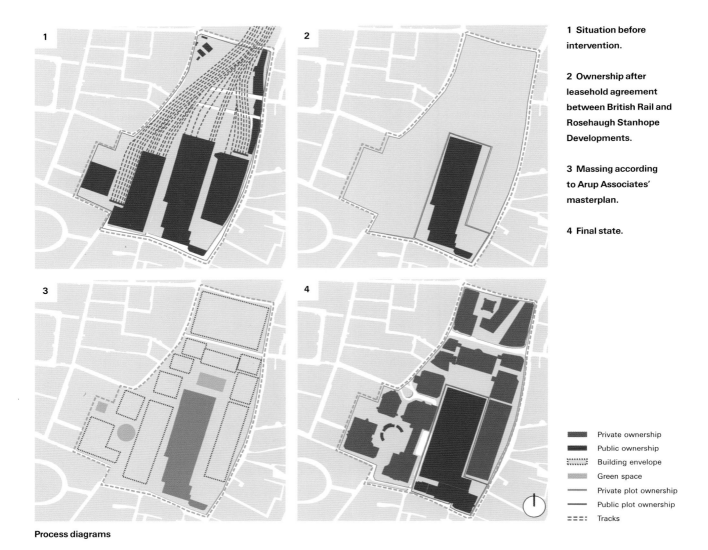

1 **Situation before intervention.**

2 **Ownership after leasehold agreement between British Rail and Rosehaugh Stanhope Developments.**

3 **Massing according to Arup Associates' masterplan.**

4 **Final state.**

■ Private ownership
■ Public ownership
▨ Building envelope
▨ Green space
— Private plot ownership
— Public plot ownership
==== Tracks

Process diagrams

Rail announced a consortium of Taylor Woodrow Property Company and Wimpey Property Holdings as developers of the site. However, the controversy continued, essentially based on the proposal's low viability through the fact that most of the site was still considered backland. British Rail was forced to start afresh, drawing up a shortlist of eight developers to submit new ideas. Due to the success of the brand-new 1 Finsbury Avenue, Rosehaugh Stanhope Developments and their designer Arup Associates were finally appointed in 1985. Their highly profitable proposal transformed the former backland into a first-rate address with significant property values. This enabled the British Rail Property Board to restore parts of the historic Station structure, and to combine it with striking modern features according to the architectural concept of Peter Foggo from Arup Associates.

Unique in the context of this book, but not unusual for infrastructure-related projects, the financial agreement between the public railway company and the private developer secured for British Rail, in addition to a one-off payment, an ongoing financial participation of between 33.3 and 50 per cent in Rosehaugh Stanhope's development profits. Typical for the English development tradition (see Belgravia case study for a more detailed explanation), the developers did not acquire unlimited freehold of land, but only the right of use for a specific amount of time – a leasehold – after which all land including the built properties is returned to the freeholder. In this particular case, however, the granting of a 999-year lease reduces a financial distinction between free- and leasehold to absurdity, the calculation period being far too long compared with leasehold lengths of usually less than one hundred

RIGHT: View down
Liverpool Street with the
new entrance to the train
station to the left.

BELOW: View towards
the north with Liverpool
Street Station to the
right. The new Broadgate
Tower can be seen in the
background of the image.

years (see also Beijing Central Business District case
study for comparison).

The actual buildings of Broadgate were erected in
record time, and in three major phases. After the original
Arup Associates buildings – including 1 Finsbury
Avenue and two later buildings to the east on the same
road (eventually incorporated in the Broadgate Estate) –
followed those around the ice rink on the former Broad
Street Station (also by Arup), and finally those
surrounding and built over Liverpool Street Station (by
Skidmore, Owings & Merrill (SOM)). Unlike the latter,
the Arup constructions were built on terra firma and
therefore on conventional foundations. Standard for
these kinds of developments, each building was held
by a separate legal structure which was owned by
Rosehaugh Stanhope, but with the possibility of being
sold into separate ownership. More unusual is the
fact that all exterior squares are likewise maintained
as separate legal entities, with appropriate legal
mechanisms to secure consistent maintenance for
the whole Broadgate site through contributions from
the directly adjacent buildings. A dedicated company,
Broadgate Estates was established at the outset, in
order to assure the maintenance of these exterior
spaces as well as the individual buildings' envelopes
and the interiors of the multi-tenant buildings, if required.

The role of the public authorities in the construction
of Broadgate is fairly small when compared with other
European projects featured in this book. Since the
abolition of the Greater London Council under Margaret
Thatcher's government in 1986, the planning authority
in London has resided solely with the boroughs, and in

Aerial 1:10,000

the case of Broadgate was essentially limited to the approval or disapproval of the respective building permits for each phase of the development. A masterplan existed from the early stages, but it did not have any legal validity as a long-term development framework. As just one example out of many, the Hilmer & Sattler masterplan for the Potsdamer Platz in Berlin, by contrast, was translated into an official and binding document by the city authority (see separate case study). A particularity in terms of planning background and authority is the unique case of the City of London Corporation, which – together with the Borough of Hackney – was the planning authority in charge of the Broadgate development. It is of medieval origins and

holds a status that situates it somewhere in between a private 'Great Estate' (see Belgravia case study) and another London borough like Westminster, Camden, Kensington and Chelsea or Hackney. The biggest difference compared with these 'normal' boroughs is not a specificity of planning procedure, but its very small population of hardly 10,000 residents. The corporation's main mission is therefore the promotion of the City of London as Europe's major financial centre and, understandably, not the defence of the few voters' and residents' interests in the built environment. This obviously includes and influences the management of building activities, and it can be assumed that it helped align the interests of the landowner, developer and local

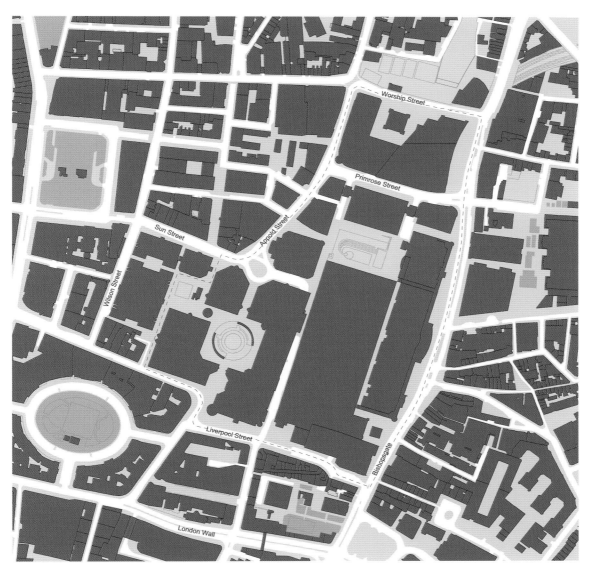

Urban plan 1:5,000

planning authority enabling the delivery of 12 buildings in only six years.

URBAN FORM / CONNECTIVITY

Crucial to the understanding of the urban plan's quality is the fact that its totality, including the three Finsbury Avenue buildings, is situated on land that was formerly mainly inaccessible to the public and predominantly used for the numerous railway tracks of the passenger and goods lines. Historic maps show that, in the 17th and 18th centuries, the area was covered by a dense and presumably dark network of alleys, courts and yards.

Arup Associates ingeniously conceived a masterplan that considered the former rail estate as a publicly accessible and future piece of London, both on terra firma and above the tracks of the renovated Liverpool Street Station. More than just a welcome civic achievement, this strategy of well-designed exterior spaces accessed on foot, enlivened with ground-floor retail, catering and leisure uses, created a new quarter for the City of London and extended the traditional 'Square Mile' to the north. This allowed for the creation of very high real-estate values also in the more remote parts of the development, something that the preceding proposals had not been able to achieve. As much as possible the site's specific limitations were ignored, and the building footprints arranged around pedestrian desire lines – a technique

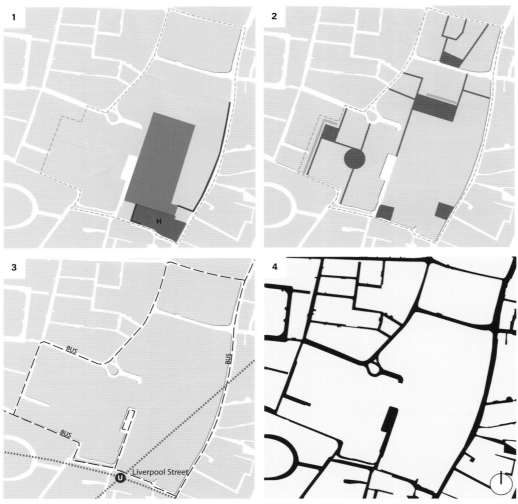

Analysis diagrams

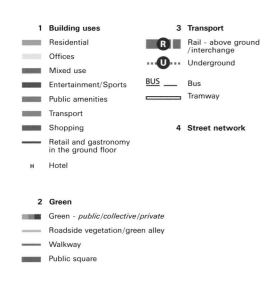

1 Building uses

▬ Residential

▭ Offices

▬ Mixed use

▬ Entertainment/Sports

▬ Public amenities

▭ Transport

▬ Shopping

— Retail and gastronomy
 in the ground floor

H Hotel

2 Green

▬ Green - *public/collective/private*

▭ Roadside vegetation/green alley

— Walkway

▬ Public square

3 Transport

🅁 ▬ Rail - above ground
 /interchange

▪▪🅄▪▪ Underground

BUS ▬ Bus

═══ Tramway

4 Street network

that has been implemented many times since, most
famously by UCL's (University College London) Space
Syntax division. This strategy was not at all easy to
envisage, because the northern section of Broadgate
was at the time of development still part of the
comparably poor Borough of Hackney, an address
that no corporate tenant was especially keen to
highlight. Recognition of the development as a premier
address came in 1994 when Broadgate was in its
entirety incorporated in the political boundary of the
prestigious City of London. Due to the cyclical nature
of property markets and a change of ownership, the
most northern phase of the development south of
Worship Street, including SOM's Broadgate Tower –
London's third-tallest high-rise – has only recently
been finished, in 2008, on structurally complicated
and expensive foundations that had to be inserted
between the underlying tracks.

In terms of functional mixture, it is not the fringe position of Broadgate that explains why the programme does not include any housing, but rather the fact that the City of London's zoning did not allow for such uses on this specific site. This is still the case, even though the ongoing gentrification of East London, including the directly adjacent site of Spitalfields Market, has since deeply transformed the wider area's character, making the potential provision of residential uses appear far more attractive than at the time of development in the mid-1980s. A wide variety of retail and leisure activities, positioned around the lively squares and passages, caters therefore to the needs of the working population, rather than to residents or tourists. It might be added that, in the present context of high densities, the 24-hour servicing of the station

and offices would truly complicate the creation of a desirable residential environment.

However, for a corporate address, the position right next to a major transport interchange with four underground lines and many bus services was not a concern, but rather an inherent advantage of the scheme. In 2010 the extension of the nearby East London Line towards Dalston, partly on tracks that were formerly used by trains which terminated at Broad Street Station, further improved the connectivity of the area and the growing allure of East London and Hackney. The plans for Crossrail, a multi-billion-pound project for a new east–west underground connection through London, include Liverpool Street as one of only six stations in Central London.

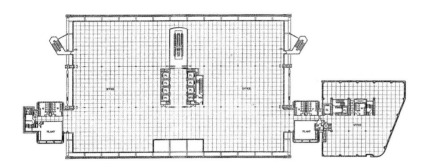

First-floor plan of SOM's Exchange House at the northwestern edge of the development. Situated above train tracks, the building is, from a structural point of view, a bridge.

SOM's Exchange House seen from Exchange Square.

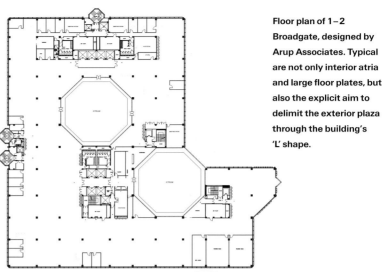

Floor plan of 1–2 Broadgate, designed by Arup Associates. Typical are not only interior atria and large floor plates, but also the explicit aim to delimit the exterior plaza through the building's 'L' shape.

ARCHITECTURAL TYPOLOGIES

In terms of authorship, there has not been any official separation between the design phase for the masterplan and the following architectural design of the office buildings, both undertaken by Arup Associates with Peter Foggo as chief planner. At the time, the office was reluctant to expand too quickly, and this was the reason why Arup Associates did not design the buildings of the third phase – those east and north of the station, along Bishopsgate, Appold Street and Primrose Street. The appointment of the American firm SOM for this task reflects that practice's international track record of hundreds of comparably sized projects.

Broadgate's iconic architectural masterpieces include the Finsbury Avenue buildings by Arup Associates and the Exchange House by SOM. Structurally a bridge, the floors of the latter are suspended from a frame that stretches over the complete width of the tracks behind Liverpool Street Station – some 78 metres (256 feet). The other buildings, though of decent architectural quality, stand back behind the superior landscaping quality of the exterior spaces that they delimit. Their innovation, which started already with the No 1 Finsbury Avenue scheme through the collaboration of the developers with the space planners DEGW, lies primarily in the provision of large and highly efficient floor plates, a new tendency on the European market that reflected a radical change of work techniques for the financial industry in the late 1980s. This is also the reason why Broadgate became an instant success, even during a period of weakening real-estate markets.

ABOVE LEFT: Arup's Finsbury Avenue building, the predecessor of the Broadgate development.

ABOVE: The Great Eastern Hotel and Bishopsgate.

CONCLUSION

Broadgate is now considered to have started a revolution in corporate architecture and urban design. As an extreme example of brownfield redevelopment and densification, it showcases what can be profitably achieved even without public subsidies with the backdrop of very high land values. The promiscuous connection to a railway station has an almost poetic dimension, symbolising the multiple paradoxes of the urban condition and the constant struggle between silence and noise, transport and inertia, remoteness and exchange. It is interesting to compare its development logic with other transit-oriented projects like Masséna Nord (see separate case study), Euralille (see separate case study) or the recent (above-)station developments in Hong Kong (see *The Urban Towers Handbook*, pp 188–95).

Broadgate shows how a private masterplan initiative can incorporate generous open spaces into office developments in order to raise rather than lower land values. An ambitious programme of high-profile public art poignantly illustrates this as a conscious decision, one that explicitly took inspiration from the character of Georgian London and has repeatedly been interpreted as a modern vernacular. This was an unusual concept in the early 1980s when developers were wary of assuming responsibility for publicly accessible spaces. It is worth contemplating whether the success of this arrangement is linked to the fact that all of these squares and walks have a private status, are maintained and supervised by a private company, and are not part of the public street network (see Battery Park City case study for comparison). In order to keep the private status of these spaces, British law requires the landlord to close them off for at least one day during each year. In the case of Broadgate, this happens every year on Christmas Day.

View from Eldon Street into Broadgate Square, with Richard Serra's sculpture *The Fulcrum* (1987) to the right.

OPPOSITE: SOM's
Broadgate Tower,
finished in 2008.

RIGHT: View of the
sunken main concourse of
Liverpool Street Station.

BELOW: Arup's 100
Liverpool Street with
the station entrance
to the right.

Masséna Nord (Paris Rive Gauche)

LOCATION: 13TH ARRONDISSEMENT, PARIS, FRANCE
DATE: 1995–2012
SIZE: 12.6 HECTARES (31 ACRES)

Part of the French capital's largest development zone, the urban plan of Masséna Nord celebrates Christian de Portzamparc's vision of the *îlot ouvert* as a contemporary version of the perimeter block.

Floor area ratio: 2.69
Residential population: 2,430
Mix of uses: 34% office, 31% education, 20% residential, 10% workshops and retail, 5% other

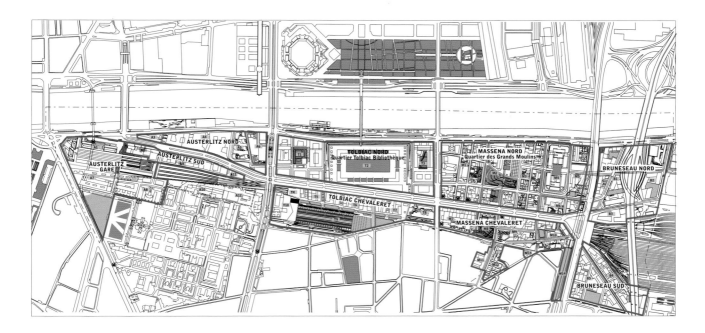

The Masséna Nord project should be seen in the context of the Paris Rive Gauche development zone, a site that extends over approximately 2.5 kilometres (1.5 miles) from Austerlitz Station along the southern bank of the River Seine to the Boulevard Périphérique, the city's major ring road and political boundary. With less than 13 hectares (31 acres), Masséna Nord is just one of nine subdistricts within this 130-hectare (321-acre) brownfield site. Since the construction of Austerlitz Station in 1840, the vast area – owned primarily by the national railway company SNCF – had been used for tracks (almost 30 hectares (74 acres) alone), warehouses, flour mills and related industries. In the wider Parisian planning context, the project should be seen as part of an even larger development site, the Seine Sud-Est zone, which included the adjacent Bercy district on the northern bank of the river. In the early 1980s, several studies examined ways to incorporate both brownfield waterfront sites into a comprehensive plan for the Olympic Games and a Universal Exhibition. However, plans for both events and their subsequent planning proposals were abandoned fairly quickly.

Paris Rive Gauche is by far the French capital's largest and most important urban project since the controversial 1960s and 1970s high-rise developments of the Italie XIII sector and the Front de Seine podium (see page 136 in *The Urban Towers Handbook*). Along with many similar developments of the time, these were characterised by a heroic post-war avant-gardism and the urgent need for living space, modernisation and sanitation. The starting situation for the Paris Rive Gauche development was less dramatic and a good

case study for urban development in the prosperous Western world of the late 20th century. Due to the tight public control of the French planning system and the modest size of the politically independent urban core – the so-called 'Paris intra-muros', which covers just over 100 square kilometres (40 square miles) – the redevelopment of the underutilised brownfield sites in the socially less privileged eastern part of the city was only a question of time. Initially, in the early 1990s, the redevelopment was designed to stop the exodus of employment from central Paris to the outskirts. The area has, consequently, always been seen as a mixed-use development composed of considerably more office than residential space. Due to the real-estate crisis of

TOP: The nine subdistricts of the Paris Rive Gauche development zone. Masséna Nord is situated to the right of the Tolbiac Nord sector with the new National Library as its centrepiece.

ABOVE: An aerial image of the area in the late 1980s.

the early and mid-1990s, and the changing of perceptions over time, the percentages have been slightly modified in favour of apartments, commercial uses and public amenities.

Nationally and internationally, the area gained media attention through the construction of the iconic new National Library (Bibliothèque Nationale) and its four glazed towers. The library was the last of President François Mitterrand's 'Grands Projets' which included, among others, the construction of the Louvre extension, the Opéra Bastille and the Grande Arche de la Défense (all completed in 1989). Designed by Dominique Perrault in the Tolbiac subdistrict just north of Masséna Nord, the new National Library was one of the first buildings on the site to open to the public. When it was unveiled in 1996, it stood as a predominantly freestanding object in an otherwise barren construction site.

PROJECT ORGANISATION / TEAM STRUCTURE

The Paris Rive Gauche project is managed and developed by SEMAPA (Société d'Économie Mixte d'Aménagement de Paris). This semi-public company is presided over by the Mayor of the 13th arrondissement

and composed of the following shareholders: the municipality of Paris (57 per cent), the national railway company SNCF (20 per cent), the Parisian building authority RIVP (10 per cent), the French State (5 per cent) and the Île-de-France Region (5 per cent). Only the remaining 3 per cent is open to private investors. In this context it is useful to mention that the legal status of the 'semi-public' SEM (société d'économie mixte), until recently in many respects responsible for almost all French urban developments of public initiative, was not primarily created in order to open the planning process to private initiative, but rather was designed to allow these legal structures to apply the more liberal rules of private law which offer, among other advantages, less bureaucracy in the tender procedure compared with an entity of public law. Through changes in the European legislation, this situation has recently been challenged, and the semi-public companies, due to the existence of private shareholders, have to be put in competition. Since 2006 the French law therefore allows the use of a new status, the SPLA (société publique locale d'aménagement), which sidesteps this obligation through the return to a solely public shareholding.

The Jardins des Grands-Moulins Abbé Pierre, laid out in 2009 by Ah-Ah Paysagistes, and the flour mill that has been transformed into a university building.

In 1991 the Council of Paris approved the first version of the area development plan (PAZ – *plan d'aménagement de zone*) for the Paris Rive Gauche site. It received the specific status of a ZAC (*zone d'aménagement concerté* – integrated development zone) and was therefore not bound to the planning restrictions, including height limitations and land uses, that are applicable to the rest of the capital. Since 2000, however, this legislation has changed and the ZAC status no longer allows the same freedom of deviations from the city-wide code. The content of the PAZ as planning document of the ZAC had hence to be included in the Parisian PLU (*plan local d'urbanisme*), or would have lost validity. The ZAC status itself goes back to the year 1967, and superseded the priority development zones (ZUPs – *zones à urbaniser en priorité*) which had previously provided the legal framework for large-scale developments. At that time,

the ZUP had been identified as one of the reasons for the proliferation of monofunctional public housing projects known as *grands ensembles* which were increasingly mutating into hotspots of social tension. The ZAC status was intended to foster more diverse developments with a greater mixture of functions and social classes. Most importantly, the designation also facilitated the investment of private capital in publicly controlled developments. Today the semi-public development companies like the SEMAPA only finance the construction of infrastructures and some public amenities. The majority of the actual buildings are developed by private investors. The complex details of the development procedures have changed over time and adapt to the specific circumstances of each project. An interesting example in the case of Paris Rive Gauche is the fact that the SEMAPA legally owns the land only for a very short time, acting as a middleman between

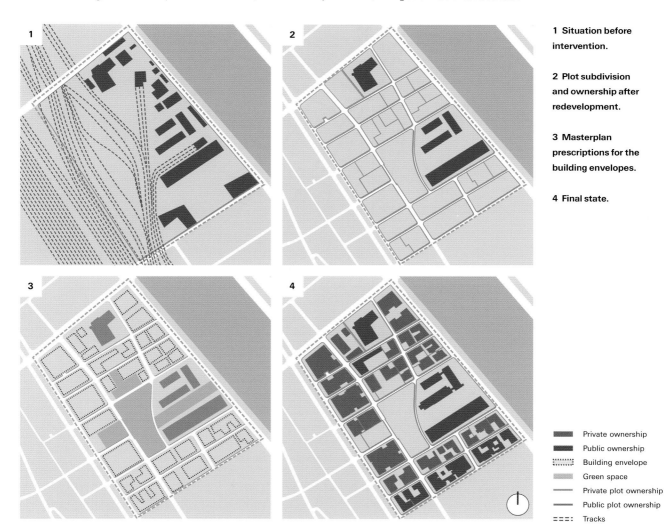

1 Situation before intervention.

2 Plot subdivision and ownership after redevelopment.

3 Masterplan prescriptions for the building envelopes.

4 Final state.

▬ Private ownership
▬ Public ownership
⣿ Building envelope
▬ Green space
— Private plot ownership
— Public plot ownership
=== Tracks

Process diagrams

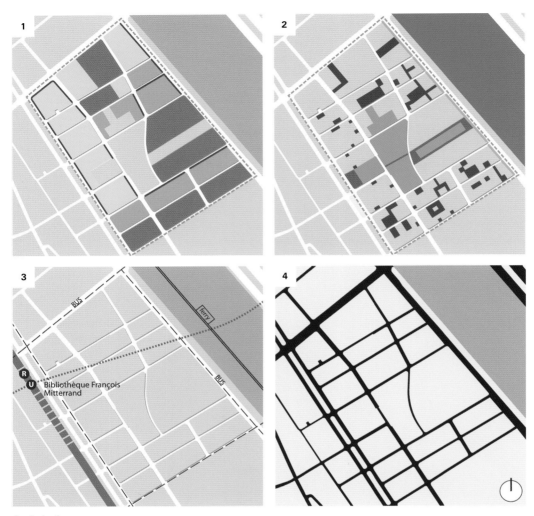

Analysis diagrams

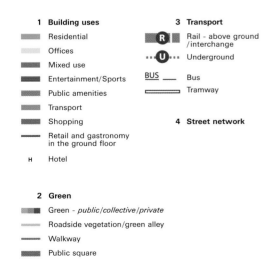

1	**Building uses**		**3**	**Transport**
	Residential		R	Rail - above ground / interchange
	Offices		U	Underground
	Mixed use			
	Entertainment/Sports		BUS —	Bus
	Public amenities			Tramway
	Transport			
	Shopping		**4**	**Street network**
	Retail and gastronomy in the ground floor			
H	Hotel			

2 Green

Green - *public/collective/private*

Roadside vegetation/green alley

Walkway

Public square

the railway company SNCF, which owns the majority of the plots, and interested outside investors. The construction of infrastructure for the site is hence financed through the difference in acquisition and sales price between both parties. This system, arguably facilitated through the railway company's public status, stands in stark contrast to projects like the aforementioned Front de Seine: for that project the local semi-public development company had to acquire all land at the project's start and hence immobilised its capital for a very long period of time, until the sale of the last development rights over 20 years later (see *The Urban Towers Handbook*, pp 136–41 for more details).

URBAN FORM / CONNECTIVITY

In terms of design, not all of the subdistricts of Paris Rive Gauche have been treated in the same manner and they did not follow the same planning procedure. The overall

OPPOSITE: View from the promenade along the River Seine into the new district.

concept has been elaborated in many small steps since the early 1980s by the Parisian Atelier of Urbanism (APUR) which commissioned a series of external design consultations in order to constantly update its own vision. After much deliberation, a plan was eventually completed and approved in 1991. Interestingly, the approved plan did not yet bridge the tracks of Austerlitz Station or provide any major physical connection between the eastern and western parts of the 13th arrondissement. This principle, perhaps now the driving force behind the entire undertaking, developed slowly over time. The most radical intermediate vision originated from a privately financed counterproposal that moved the train station to the border of Paris in order to allow for a complete redevelopment of the liberated surfaces on terra firma. Eventually, this proposal was abandoned based on

SNCF's concerns about relocating a heavily utilised train station.

Under considerable time pressure, detailed studies for the project began as soon as the general plan was approved in 1991. Two architects, Paul Andreu and Roland Schweitzer, were directly commissioned and split the development site in separate sectors, with Andreu taking the Avenue de France and Schweitzer masterplanning the mainly residential Tolbiac sector. It was the first one to be developed, and its horizontal volumes deliberately frame the four towers of the new National Library. In order to make quick progress and to formally exemplify a design model, the SEMAPA organised not only the urban study, but also the following binding architectural competitions. As an inversion of the usual development process, the acquirers of the development rights had to accept

View from the new pedestrian bridge, Passerelle Simone-de-Beauvoir, towards the two southern towers of the new National Library. The beginning of the Masséna Nord district can be perceived on the far left of the image.

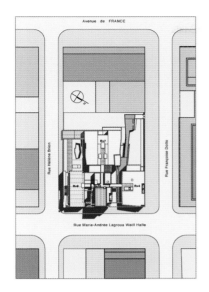

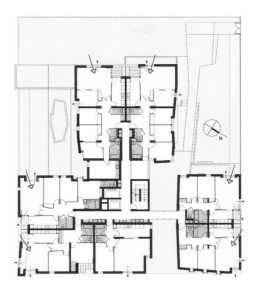

Location, fourth-floor plan and photograph of an apartment building by Frédéric Borel (2009). Built for the mixed development company of the City of Paris, SIEMP, it accommodates ground-floor retail, underground parking and 47 affordable residential units. It is situated opposite the southwestern corner of the Jardins des Grands-Moulins Abbé Pierre.

Aerial 1:10,000

the design prescriptions of the competition, even though the buildings did not yet exist.

In order to assure the sustainable development of the area it was important to improve the existing public transport links. This was accomplished with the opening of the new underground line 14, known as METEOR, which has connected the National Library with Saint-Lazare Station in the northwest of Paris since 1998. The new station also replaced a former stop of the Regional Express train RER C and has since then become an important interchange in eastern Paris. In addition to these trains and several bus lines, the Voguéo boats have been offering a 15-minute ferry service across the river since 2008.

ARCHITECTURAL TYPOLOGIES

The office of Christian de Portzamparc won the international design competition for the Masséna Nord district in 1995. The proposal was based on his ideas for the *îlot ouvert* (open block), which had been developed over many years but were applied here at a large scale for the first time. The open-block concept is essentially a composite of a traditional urban form with closed perimeter block developments, and a more Modernist vision of freestanding and well-ventilated mini-towers. Portzamparc hence combined a clearly defined street space, one of the key qualities of Parisian urbanism, with the freedom of a looser arrangement of buildings and a greater amount of green and communal open spaces.

Urban plan 1:5,000

Such a concept stands in contrast to the clear-cut separation of courtyard and street space which is inherent in the traditional local typology in the form of the *fin-de siècle* Parisian apartment building. Portzamparc first defined a network of streets and relatively small blocks, and then spent a long period of time analysing the best ways in which future building volumes could be arranged to preserve high levels of light and air. In order to allow enough room for the individual creativity of each plot's privately commissioned architect, the prescribed building envelopes of the masterplan are larger than the permitted amount of buildable surface in each case. Sheets defining allowable building masses and the rules of development are provided for the

bidders of each plot. In this system, the relationship between urbanism and architecture becomes especially complex: despite a set of fairly prescriptive rules, the arrangement allows a higher degree of variation than most other block-oriented planning concepts, in which the architect can often be perceived as little more than a facade designer.

As a feature that is valid for the whole Paris Rive Gauche development zone, the maximum building heights grow from the river towards Avenue de France. The main reason for this rule, unprecedented in Parisian planning history, was the desire to avoid a level difference in the connection between the new avenue, built above the tracks, and the surrounding areas at

LEFT: Rue Françoise Dolto.

BELOW: View down Rue des Frigos.

LEFT: View down Avenue de France, built above the tracks leading towards Austerlitz Station. The white building in front of one of the National Library's four towers is a cinema designed by Wilmotte & Associés SA.

Offices

Garden

Offices

Garden

Atrium

Garden

Offices

Garden

Offices

Typical floor plan of the office building on Avenue de France, designed by Foster + Partners with Rolinet & Associés and completed in 2004. It is the headquarters of the Accor hotel group.

ground level. The buildings of Masséna Nord are therefore all situated on an artificial slope, leading smoothly up to Avenue de France, a costly undertaking that was motivated by the wish to optimise ground-level connections and to avoid the unsustainable tabula-rasa urbanism of podium developments like Front de Seine, Italie XIII or Montparnasse that would have extended the upper datum towards the river. Along Avenue de France the allowable building height has been further increased for the plots that are directly positioned above the tracks. The resulting higher financial value of these commercial developments stands in direct relation to the substantial cost of covering the tracks. In order to avoid homogeneously sloping building heights throughout the site, Portzamparc succeeded in slightly altering the urban rules and accentuated the height of some building envelopes according to their position and importance in the masterplan (see also *The Urban Towers Handbook*, pp 80–85 for more details).

CONCLUSION

If the analysis of the relationship between development structure and its resulting urban form is one of the precepts of this book, the question of the relation between the high level of sophistication of the French

planning system and the equally high level of sophistication of Portzamparc's concept for the open block becomes crucial. Could the same scheme have evolved with less public control and in a strictly liberal development culture? Compared with other examples in this book, but also compared with other variations of the urban block found in the Paris Rive Gauche development, the variety of spaces and the delicacy of their intersections and delimitations bear an element of surgical intervention. Highly flexible, though potentially not applicable to every kind of programme, it represents an important contribution to contemporary urbanism. If the last three decades have witnessed the denial of many of the Modernists' most radical urban principles, the question of an alternative still remains acute. The initial reorientation towards the 'traditional block' has been revealed to be more problematic than expected. Recent years have highlighted a certain monotony of block proposals, partly due to practices such as avoiding party walls and creating superblocks of single ownership which contradict the actual development logic of the traditional city. In the Parisian case, the frequently cited works carried out by Baron Haussmann in the 1850s and 1860s are an especially complicated example of block urbanism, as his most famous and

Apartment building by Epstein & Glaiman.

OPPOSITE: Office buildings in the northern section of Avenue de France, part of the historic Nord subdistrict.

successful interventions like Rue de Rivoli or Avenue de l'Opéra (see separate chapter) tend to be those that have been cut through the pre-19th-century fabric, creating an overly complex, if not random result of historic layers. They are arguably not an appropriate base of comparison for contemporary masterplan projects that often evolve on cleared brownfield sites. The following development of peripheral quarters in the late 19th century, like the Plaine Monceau in the 17th arrondissement, that were built from scratch on predominantly empty land according to formal principles theoretically similar to those of the earlier

Haussmann interventions, are more convincing precedents, but they initially earned the same criticism as many of today's new developments. Namely, they were often condemned for being too antiseptic and homogeneous, lacking diversity and life. The question of time and the complexity that it engenders is therefore crucially important, and Portzamparc's design proposal and his way of organising the relation between all intervening parties seems to be able to simulate the complexity of an imaginary aging process for an impatient market.

Stuyvesant Town

LOCATION: MANHATTAN, NEW YORK CITY, USA
DATE: 1943–49
SIZE: 24.7 HECTARES (61 ACRES)

With an urban form easily mistaken for a built example of Le Corbusier's Plan Voisin of 1925, Stuyvesant Town leaves a particularly complex and ambiguous heritage. On the one hand it figures as a prominent and radical case of tabula-rasa urbanism; on the other it clearly highlights the advantages of a tower-in-park configuration, especially when compared with the cramped living conditions in large parts of the surrounding Lower East Side.

Floor area ratio: 2.86
Residential population: 18,000
Mix of uses: almost entirely residential, with a small share of retail and restaurants

Beginning at the turn of the century and increasing rapidly after the First World War, the flight of the middle classes from the city centres to the suburbs became a major social and financial problem. The phenomenon began in Europe, with London as the earliest and most prominent example, and was quickly exported to the New World. This growing sprawl followed the intense rhythm of construction of new train lines and motorways.

With dwindling populations, the tax incomes of major cities dramatically dropped during the 1930s and 1940s, paradoxically endangering the existence of the urban entities that were economically considered to be the birthplaces of progress. In this context of inner-city decay, urban renewal programmes and slum clearance gained major importance for the city administrations. New York City, with its chronic overpopulation and

Aerial view of Stuyvesant
Town (left) and Peter
Cooper Village soon after
completion of the latter
in 1951.

social tensions, became an especially interesting case. Robert Moses, who had famously changed the geography of New York since the 1920s through a construction programme of motorways and bridges of unprecedented scale, quickly became the driving force behind these equally ambitious undertakings. Never holding elected office, he became New York's powerbroker as the director of multiple public agencies and commissions, presiding through an increasingly opaque network over a budget of several billion dollars. From 1948 to 1960 Moses, who has frequently and understandably been likened to Paris's Baron Haussmann, was also Chairman of the Slum Clearance Committee.

Stuyvesant Town was the first of a new generation of large-scale developments and public–private partnerships, and was meant to become the model and proof of the vision that mass housing needs could be satisfied through the private sector. Unlike earlier schemes like Parkchester or even the upmarket Forest Hills Gardens which were built on the outskirts of the city, it had to show that privately funded mass housing developments could also be accomplished in a very complicated and dense setting. Stuyvesant Town was announced in April 1943 and subsidised through aids from the State of New York (see details below). The project should be considered against the background of controversial discussions that were occurring at the federal level during this time regarding urban redevelopment and public housing.

The chosen site covered 18 blocks of the so-called Gashouse District, infamous for unhygienic living conditions, gang crime and a very high percentage of poor immigrants. The alleged slum's population had reached 27,000 by the end of the 19th century and, although it had significantly diminished since then, some 11,000 remaining residents had to be displaced at the time of site clearance in 1945. Density was to remain the focus of discussion, as the Metropolitan Life Insurance Company's proposed scheme included a planned population of 24,000 which almost re-established the historic figure. Ambitiously, this was to be achieved with a site coverage of only 25 per cent – down from the almost 70 per cent of the Gashouse District – and a forest of 35 12- and 13-storey-tall buildings. Conceived as affordable housing for the middle classes, the scheme's new population would only include about 3 per cent of the former 'slum' inhabitants, leaving the others to be forced into neighbouring districts with hardly better living conditions. Only one in five of the original residents met the conditions to claim accommodation in modern affordable housing blocks, a precarious figure that reflects the social challenges of the whole urban renewal programme. It became clear that the economic stimulus of such vast building activity and the purely quantitative provision of housing units was considered more important than the improvement of the local residents' living conditions.

ABOVE LEFT: View from Avenue A towards one of Stuyvesant Town's entrances on East 14th Street. These entrances were formerly closed to the public.

LEFT: Due to the abundance of trees, Stuyvesant Town's radical urbanism can more easily be perceived during the winter months.

ABOVE: The fountain in the central space – the Oval. It is a popular spot for the development's residents.

ABOVE RIGHT: A pavement on East 14th Street: except for some retail spaces, Stuyvesant Town turns its back towards the exterior. Large parts of the estate are actually elevated in order to accommodate underground parking. The wall to the left is therefore also a sustaining wall.

RIGHT: In order to allow for a more functional mixture, the ground floors of the buildings next to the Oval have been transformed recently into communal spaces, including study rooms, cafés and a crèche.

1 Situation before
intervention.

2 Plot subdivision and
ownership after
redevelopment.

3 Masterplan
prescriptions for the
building envelopes.

4 Final state.

Private ownership
Public ownership
Building envelope
Green space
Private plot ownership
Public plot ownership
Tracks

Process diagrams

PROJECT ORGANISATION /
TEAM STRUCTURE

In this particular case the legal framework of the project
is of more interest than the planning method as such.
As was typical for many large-scale housing projects
of the post-war period, it seems that there was no
organisational separation between urban, landscape
and architectural design. Being, from this point of view,
one of the most extreme of the 20 featured examples
in this book, it invites the reader to appreciate the
relation between the simplicity of the organisational
arrangement and the alleged simplicity, if not
uniformity, of the built result. As a fairly rare case, a
single private owner was able to develop a vast site
in a short time and without any cadastral restrictions.
In Europe this type of set-up was usually reserved for
the public sector as direct client of social housing

projects. Declared a (model) project of public interest,
Stuyvesant Town's financial success was assured by
the shortage of housing and the return of a large
veteran population. As rental concessions were part
of MetLife's deal with the city, the risks of unrented
apartments and financial loss were practically excluded.
There was simply no better offer on the market, and
soon after announcement of the project thousands of
rental applications invaded the developer's offices.

The highly advantageous development
circumstances were the result of the Hampton-Mitchell
Redevelopment Companies Law of 1943, tailored
specifically to the needs of Stuyvesant Town in view of
urban redevelopment undertaken through an insurance
company (unofficially already known as being MetLife,
at that time the world's largest private company). As a
major improvement of the Urban Redevelopment Law

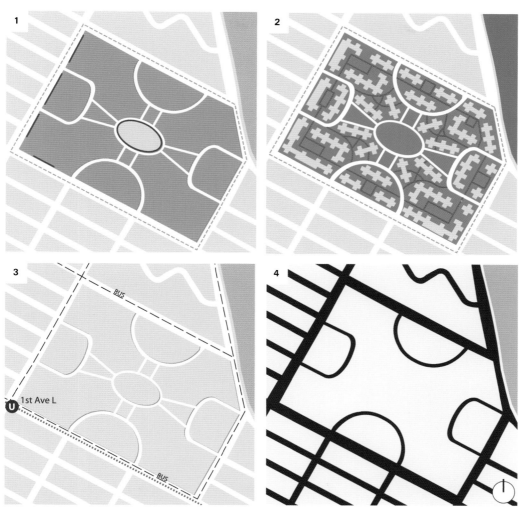

Analysis diagrams

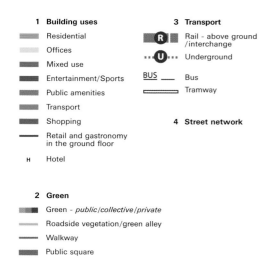

1 Building uses
- ▬ Residential
- ▬ Offices
- ▬ Mixed use
- ▬ Entertainment/Sports
- ▬ Public amenities
- ▬ Transport
- ▬ Shopping
- — Retail and gastronomy in the ground floor
- H Hotel

2 Green
- ▬ Green - *public/collective/private*
- ▬ Roadside vegetation/green alley
- — Walkway
- ▬ Public square

3 Transport
- 🅡 Rail - above ground /interchange
- 🅤 Underground
- BUS ___ Bus
- ▭▭▭ Tramway

4 Street network

of 1942, which had not managed to attract enough interest from private investors, the new law enabled the city to sell the site at cost after use of eminent domain and to offer tax exemptions over 25 years, based on real-estate values before and not after redevelopment of the site in question. For the same amount of time and in exchange for these extremely favourable conditions, the city asked to limit the insurance company's return on capital investment to 6 per cent. As shown by the rise of rent from the announced 14 dollars per room to 17 dollars for the moving-in of the first tenants – explained through unexpectedly rising construction costs – the 6-per-cent profit limitation was a flexible notion and could be perceived as a 6-per-cent profit guarantee. MetLife also received en passant over 6.5 hectares (16 acres) of public land, the site of the streets that previously ran through the Gashouse District.

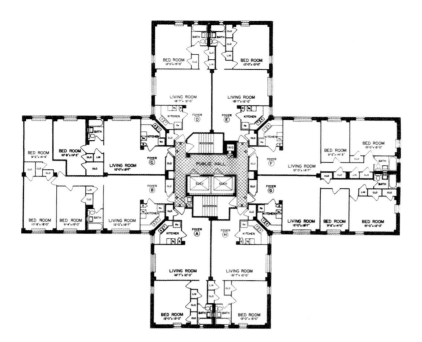

Typical floor plan of a
building in Stuyvesant
Town. The apartment
layouts are very simple
and repetitive, and
variations mainly depend
on the number of
bedrooms.

URBAN FORM / CONNECTIVITY

It is difficult to contemplate a bird's-eye view of
Stuyvesant Town and not to be reminded of Le
Corbusier's 1925 Plan Voisin proposal for the tabula-
rasa redevelopment of central Paris. Neither the height
of the buildings (13 compared with 60 storeys) nor their
use (residential compared with office) actually coincide,
but the general urban strategy of exchanging a whole
quarter of overcrowded tenement buildings through a
strictly repetitive and park-like layout of cruciform-plan
units does indeed bear similarities. Of central importance
for this comparison is the high density of both proposals,
equalling or – in the case of the Plan Voisin – even
increasing the population in respect to the previous
situation. Among many other differences, the built
reality of the private American model eventually
produced an issue of enclosure towards its environment
that the completely theoretical French proposal never
had to address. The MetLife design was essentially
marketed as a green and safe 'suburb in the city', and
underlines this status through its quasi-closure and
clear demarcation towards 1st Avenue and 14th Street,
where blank walls, raised ground floors, setbacks and
ill-positioned commercial units are read as hurdles
rather than ways to address and enhance street life.
It became known as a 'walled city', and access to the
interior of the 24.7-hectare (61-acre) estate through just
one entrance on each side was therefore initially limited
to residents. The lack of public amenities and through-
traffic was an explicit component of the programme.

Internally, the estate is indeed experienced as a complete
though pleasant reversal of Manhattan's spatial logic,
and generous green features manage to enliven the
architecturally austere character. A central space, the
Oval, underlines the communitarian claim of the new
district and its exceptional status in the city's otherwise
utilitarian urban grid. Critics have interpreted the
centralised and airy disposition as an urban panopticon,
claiming that it enabled supervision of the majority of
the estate from a single viewing point on the Oval.

Situated on Manhattan Island and in the direct vicinity
of the L Underground Line's First Avenue Station,
connectivity has not been a major issue for the project.
Similar to other radical tabula-rasa projects like the
tower-on-podium developments of the Front de Seine
in Paris (1967–90; see *The Urban Towers Handbook*,
pp 136–41) or the Barbican in London (1963–76), it
might be argued that the relative success of Stuyvesant
Town largely depends on this substantial advantage of
location, rather than on its urban and architectural
merits. The scheme includes four underground car
parks, but many cars are also parked along the internal
streets and on small exterior parking lots.

ARCHITECTURAL TYPOLOGIES

It is one of the central issues of modern urbanism
that the architectural and the urban realms can hardly
be separated: the (mostly repetitive) buildings as
constituent parts of the masterplan are therefore often
designed by the same authors as the masterplan itself.

**OPPOSITE: Extensive
green features act as
balancing counterpoints
to the austerity of the
scheme's architecture.**

Aerial 1:10,000

It is indeed difficult to imagine how the actual buildings of Stuyvesant Town could be designed differently without fundamentally altering the logic of the urban plan. This is crucially different from most development and planning practices of the late 19th century (see Avenue de l'Opéra and Sarphatipark case studies), but also from more recent ones (see Masséna Nord and Kirchsteigfeld case studies), which are trying to promote architectural diversity despite an increasingly large-scale financial background. In the case of Stuyvesant Town it was a design board of several architects, led by one of the designers of the Empire State Building, Richmond Shreve of Shreve, Lamb & Harmon, and his chief architect Irwin Clavan, who had been

commissioned by MetLife to conceive a modern and efficient answer to the demands of middle-class housing. A similarly constituted team had already worked for the same company on the earlier development of Parkchester. The result was a modular approach, in which cruciform-plan units with eight apartments per floor can be assembled into slabs of different lengths and shapes. The layouts of the floor plans are fairly conventional, with the majority having only one or two bedrooms, and are linearly organised along one facade. Only the larger ones with three or five bedrooms are genuinely double-oriented and cross-ventilated. In order to allow for more privacy, the ground floor of all buildings is slightly elevated. The pragmatism

Urban plan 1:5,000

of the urban design translates into architectural terms through the fact that the living units' sun orientation is essentially aleatory: this is a consequence of the cruciform modules as much as of the disposition of the buildings on site. The planners apparently considered the spatial generosity of the tower-in-park configuration to be hygienically sufficient, and preferred to avoid the urban austerity of the *Zeilenbau* logic – the juxtaposition of perfectly east–west-oriented slabs – in favour of a centralised arrangement. This decision can be considered to be somehow consistent with Manhattan's urban history, as one of the downsides of the local grid and its rectangular plots can be seen in the imbalance of purely north- and purely south-oriented apartments.

In order to be light efficient, the orientation of the whole grid would have had to be rotated by 90 degrees.

CONCLUSION

Stuyvesant Town, the largest of the inner-city renewal projects of its time, acquired special notoriety not only due to its tabula-rasa approach and prominent location in Manhattan's Lower East Side, but also and predominantly through the developer's discriminatory rental practices. These issues were first raised when Frederick H Ecker, the mighty CEO of MetLife, casually remarked during a press conference that 'negroes' would not be allowed to apply for apartments, as 'black and white did not mix well'. Over the years and after

many lawsuits and legal setbacks, this rather dark aspect of the development's history can be regarded as a turning point in the fight for abolition of racist housing practices. Initially, the legal argument was not even based on racial discrimination as such, but limited to the fact that the construction of Stuyvesant Town had been the result of massive public aids and could not be considered to be a truly private investment. Its owner, and receiver of public funds, should in consequence not be allowed to exclude black tenants who were taxpayers as anybody else. Only in the long run did the legal battles around Stuyvesant Town and similar developments lead to the ban of all discriminatory practices being undertaken in the private or public sector, a ban that alone could not solve the still-existing and highly socially complex problem of racial segregation.

Another interesting political feature of this project is linked to the critique of the American urban renewal programme through authors such as Lewis Mumford and Jane Jacobs. In the introduction of her book *Death and Life of Great American Cities* (1961), Jacobs hints at the fact that civil servants who were appealing to the great American virtues of liberalism and individualism were at the same time organising and defending publicly funded large-scale urban interventions in which existing communities were destroyed and taxpayers' money wasted through inefficiency. This discussion points

out the fact that urban policies are often seen as an instrument for the promotion of political principles rather than an application of these principles in real life. Are construction activities that make up for a considerable percentage of the nation's GDP just a means to an end, and at what stage does the relationship between means and ends lose any coherence? In the case of highway construction, the expropriation of land from local landowners and the destruction of local communities might be considered justified in order to sustain the freedom of car owners on a far larger regional or national scale, making the 'sacrifice' of some individuals arguably worthwhile. In the case of slum clearance the issue is at least statistically more dubious, since the alleged qualitative plus-value of the new developments stands almost one-to-one against the loss of the former population. The stimulation of building activity becomes in this context, and not only from a moral point of view, an argument of secondary importance.

The comparisons with Le Corbusier's Plan Voisin and the German *Zeilenbau* urbanism of the 1920s can therefore be seen in a different light, highlighting how the ideologies and utopian visions of the early Modernists have – all over the world – been adjusted, modified, falsified or sometimes even perverted in order to serve, justly or not, the urgent demands of the post-war era.

Battery Park City

LOCATION: MANHATTAN, NEW YORK CITY, USA
DATE: 1979–2012
SIZE: 37.6 HECTARES (93 ACRES)

A vestige of a comprehensive plan for all of Lower Manhattan, Battery Park City appears today as a unique case and urban paradox. Built in its entirety on reclaimed land, it nevertheless symbolises the 1980s rejection of Modernist planning principles and the return to a more contextual urbanism.

Floor area ratio: 5.17
Residential population: 13,314
Mix of uses: 47% office, 46% residential, 4% hotel, 3% other

The development of Battery Park City in the southwestern part of Manhattan Island should be viewed against the background of a multitude of ambitious regeneration initiatives which were designed to avoid further urban decay due to the exodus of business and building activity from Down- to Midtown. The Downtown Lower Manhattan Association (DLMA) had been founded in 1958 by the financier David Rockefeller, who was equally responsible for Chase Manhattan's symbolically important decision to build its new headquarters just off Wall Street with a 60-storey tower designed by Skidmore, Owings & Merrill (SOM).

1958 was also the year of David's brother Nelson Rockefeller's election as Governor of the State of New York. Nelson was personally involved in the creation of several new proposals, including the 1966 plan for Battery Park City which had been designed by the family's house architects and one of the country's best-known design companies, Harrison & Abramovitz. In the same year the City of New York published its 'Vision for Downtown' plan, elaborated for the entire zone and not only Battery Park City by Wallace, Mc-Harg, Roberts & Todd and Whittlesey, Conklin & Rossant. Both proposals and others envisaged the construction

of a housing belt of massive dimensions on reclaimed land around Downtown's strengthened financial core and a new Civic Center. Due to changing water transport patterns and the construction of the Sea-Port Container Terminal in Newark, the large piers along Manhattan's waterfront had become obsolete, and the infill of these zones appeared as an appropriate solution in order to promote a new functional mixture of uses for the southern part of the island. Of decisive importance for Battery Park City's survival as an implemented project was the adjacent construction on terra firma of the gigantic World Trade Center Complex from 1966 onwards: the use of the excavation's gravel for Battery Park City's land infill proved to be an efficient arrangement and represented considerable savings. The comprehensive plans for Lower Manhattan have never been implemented, primarily because of the 1970s downturn of the real-estate markets, environmental concerns, and the plan's apparent inability to inspire sufficient enthusiasm in the population and development community. With 'only' 37.6 hectares (93 acres), Battery Park City can be seen

as a relatively modest leftover of these plans. A much smaller residential project, Waterside Plaza, had been inaugurated in 1974 on reclaimed land on the eastern banks of the island, close to Stuyvesant Town (see separate case study), but was situated above the northern boundary of the 1966 plan for Lower Manhattan.

During infill works and for several years after their completion in 1976, the empty site of Battery Park City suffered from a considerable lack of development interest. This was due not only to the situation of the real-estate markets, but also to the impracticality of the official 1969 masterplan. Elaborated by a team made up of Rockefeller's architects Harrison & Abramovitz and the city's favourites Conklin & Rossant, with Philip Johnson as a binding element, this had been conceived on the basis of a futuristic podium- and spine-based urbanism. Developers were deterred by the difficulty of subdividing the project and did not know how to envisage a phased construction which would limit their financial risks. In 1979 it was hence decided to start afresh, a task for which the office of Cooper, Eckstut

BELOW LEFT: Masterplan by Cooper, Eckstut Associates from 1979. The following years brought several modifications, but the plan's urban principles have been implemented.

BELOW RIGHT: The World Financial Center as the commercial centrepiece of the development. Until the terrorist attacks of 11 September 2001, it was directly linked through a pedestrian bridge with the World Trade Center on the opposite side of West Avenue. This also explains why the complex's major circulation level was the first floor.

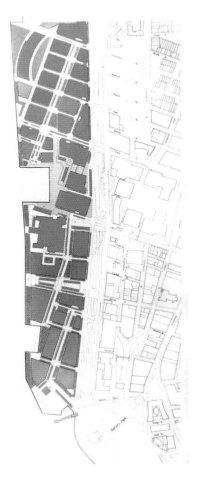

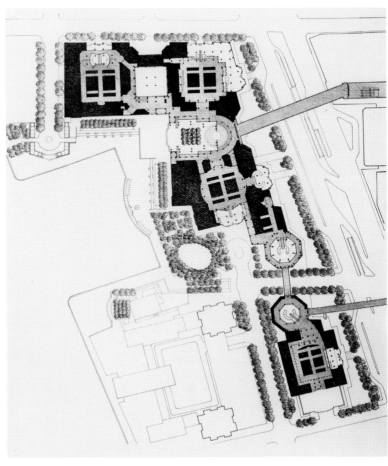

Associates was directly commissioned. Their plan has guided the development without major modifications until today.

PROJECT ORGANISATION / TEAM STRUCTURE

The Hugh L Carey Battery Park City Authority was created by the State of New York in 1968. As a legally separate entity, it manages its own finances and does not fall within the remit of the state budget. This independence had been made possible through ownership of land until eventual retrocession to the city, and the special issue in 1972 of a 200-million-dollar bond, backed though not guaranteed by the State. The sum was invested in the works for the infill and the construction of the first infrastructures. More recently, the budget has been balanced through the sale of ground rents to private developers and PILOT payments (Payments In Lieu Of Taxes) from building and apartment owners. The maintenance of the parks and streets is ensured by a dedicated structure which receives fees from the local users. The plots' developers are chosen through requests for proposals (RFPs), and the authority's final choice is based on the public benefit of the programme and the amount of the financial offer. Unusually for the American development tradition, the plot sales do not refer to freeholds. Instead, they establish leaseholds which remain valid until 2069, with no guarantee of being extended thereafter. However, in line with common practice – a well-known example being given by the British leasehold system (see Belgravia case study) – the lease is likely to be extended after negotiation of an additional sum. The yearly profits of the Battery Park City Authority are given over to the City of New York which is meant to employ most of these to fund the construction of affordable housing. Despite the public control of the operation, it was decided that Battery Park City itself was not an appropriate location for lower-market housing, and that it would be more efficient to maximise the operation's profits for later reinvestment in less privileged areas.

Crucial for the project's success in difficult economic circumstances was the offer made in 1980 by the Canadian developer Olympia & York to buy several of the development's central plots just west of the World Trade Center Towers for the construction of the World Financial Center. As a response to an official RFP for initially only one sub-site, this offer for four linked towers not only assured the first major income of the Authority over 10 years after its foundation – desperately needed in order to service the bond's debt – but also included a bold vision of a Grade A office location that matched the Authority's own ambitions. Battery Park City was now in

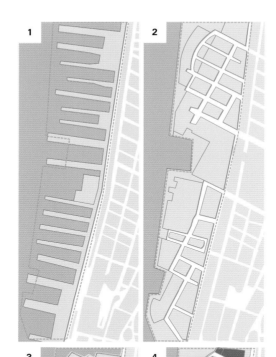

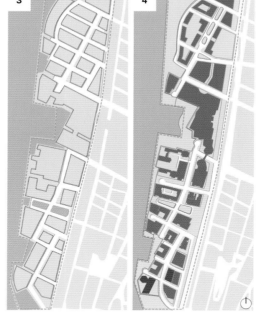

Process diagrams

1 **Situation before intervention.**

2 **Plot subdivision and public freehold ownership after infill.**

3 **Masterplan prescriptions for the building envelopes.**

4 **Final state.**

▨	Private ownership
▨	Public ownership
⠿	Building envelope
▧	Green space
—	Private plot ownership
—	Public plot ownership
≡≡≡	Tracks

BELOW: View up West Street at the height of 3rd Place. Considerable efforts have been undertaken in order to transform one of the island's major transport links into an appreciable environment. The masterplan's strategy of perpendicular cross-connections depends on the success of these measures.

RIGHT: Pedestrian connection bridging the heavy traffic of West Street in the northern limit of Battery Park City. It is the closest link to Chambers Street Underground Station.

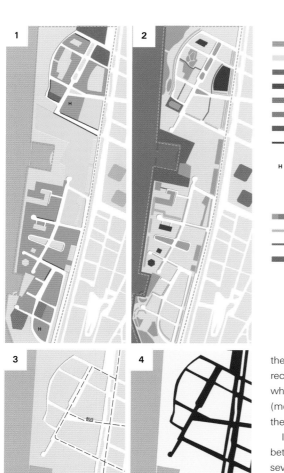

1 Building uses

- Residential
- Offices
- Mixed use
- Entertainment/Sports
- Public amenities
- Transport
- Shopping
- ─── Retail and gastronomy in the ground floor
- H Hotel

2 Green

- Green - *public/collective/private*
- Roadside vegetation/green alley
- ─── Walkway
- Public square

3 Transport

- **R** Rail - above ground /interchange
- **U** Underground
- <u>BUS</u> ─── Bus
- ═══ Tramway

4 Street network

Analysis diagrams

the focus of international real-estate markets and had received the confidence of one of its biggest players, who were contemporaneously also involved in the (more problematic) development of Canary Wharf in the London Docklands.

In terms of design process, the collaboration between the state and the city had the advantage that several elements of the Authority's fairly strict coding guidelines were incorporated into the city's zoning plan, namely building uses, floor area ratios and massing prescriptions. Hence, the developers still have to apply to the city's building department for each building permit, but the process is simpler than usual, and a project that has received the support of the authority is likely to be endorsed by the city services. The high floor area ratios (FARs) of the masterplan prescriptions meet the demands of the developers and avoid the usual lengthy negotiations and legal battles for the maximal utilisation of every square centimetre of Manhattan ground. In contrast, for larger investments in other neighbourhoods it has become common practice to apply for an increase in development rights in return for the provision of public space on parts of the site's perimeter – a long-drawn-out process that is part of the ULURP (Uniform Land Use Review Procedure) regulations.

URBAN FORM / CONNECTIVITY

One of the major changes of the 1979 masterplan by Cooper, Eckstut Associates compared with its predecessors was the move of the project's commercial core from the southern tip to the centre. An advantage

OPPOSITE: Three of the four towers of the World Financial Center (1981–5). The area's highlight of corporate architecture, it was developed by the Canadian company Olympia & York and designed by Cesar Pelli – the same team responsible for Canary Wharf in the London Docklands.

of this decision was that the phasing could start in the middle of the linear estate, where the neighbouring marina served as an attractive focus, thereby avoiding the possible loss of development interest for an overly long plot of empty infill to the north. The construction of the World Financial Center, begun in 1981 and completed in 1985, was followed by the development of residential areas to the south, around Rector Place, and later on to the north around North End Avenue. The southernmost tip, east of the remaining walls of the historic Battery, has only recently been released and is partly still in construction.

The masterplan's basic design principles, notably the extension of the existing street grid and the respect of a locally inspired urban and architectural character, may sound obvious from today's point of view, but stood in stark contrast to the podium proposals and most urban visions of the late 1960s and 1970s. In order to avoid the isolation of the infill through the nuisance of West Avenue, one of the island's major traffic arteries, it had been decided to extend the grid structure of the

neighbouring districts of Lower Manhattan to the west. Despite the still-problematic noise hazard of West Avenue, the urban plan clearly reveals the success of this strategy and the fact that it grounds the new piece of land in the memory of the city. Another important urban aspect is the very generous provision of open space – 14 hectares (35 acres) in total (including 15 per cent of streets) – in the form of several squares and a park on the northern part of the infill. Together with the spectacular and highly successful waterfront promenade, these spaces manage to balance the high density of the built plots.

It is easy to underestimate the advantage offered to the planners by the impeccable public transport connections and the comparatively modest provision of parking spaces. Less than 10 per cent of the built surfaces are hence used for cars, a figure that can be up to four times higher in other American cities like Houston or Los Angeles. Despite the site's infill nature, these spaces are usually positioned below ground. As had been one of the explicit objectives for the Lower

OPPOSITE: The interior of a beautifully landscaped courtyard in the northern part of Battery Park City.

BELOW: The facade of one of the buildings on Rector Place, explicitly inspired by the great tradition of New York's residential blocks.

Aerial 1:10,000

Manhattan plan of 1966, many residents can indeed walk to their workplace. Others can use the underground or the replacement of the PATH train station which is currently under construction as part of the World Trade Center redevelopment. North of the marina, a small ferry terminal provides additional connections to New Jersey and several stops around Manhattan Island.

ARCHITECTURAL TYPOLOGIES

The Cooper, Eckstut Associates masterplan for Battery Park City is often mentioned as an early example of New Urbanism, an influential, predominantly American urban design movement that is dedicated to pedestrian-friendly place making. In planning terms this translates

through the establishment of fairly strict design and coding guidelines, which are meant to facilitate the emergence of an aesthetically coherent environment. The idea is to separate the design work of the masterplanner from that of the respective architects of each plot while still avoiding a completely uncoordinated design. In addition to land-use prescriptions, a clear set of rules defines the footprint and height of each architectural element, and gives – among other points – indications regarding the vertical tripartition of the facades, their materials and colours. It was an explicit aim of Cooper, Eckstut Associates to imagine architectural variations of the New York apartment building, combining a local tradition and

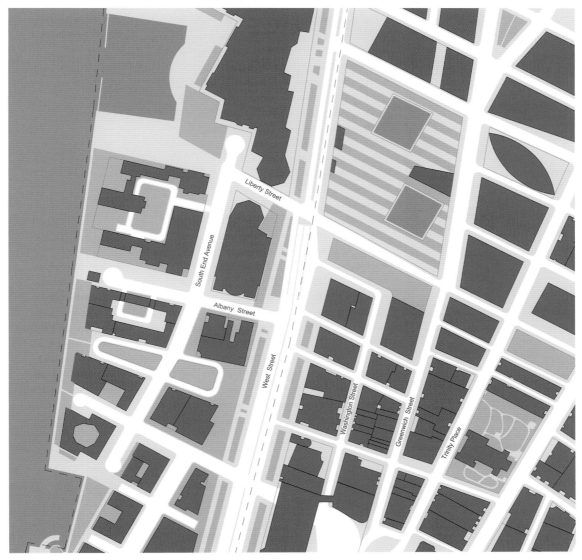

Urban plan 1:5,000

atmosphere with the provision of contemporary
housing comfort. The treatment of open spaces plays
an important role in this strategy, and appears in the
plan as a balancing element. These landscape schemes
have usually been chosen through an RFP process
organised by the Battery Park City Authority.

One exceptional feature of the 1979 plan was the
incorporation of the residential Gateway building, a
vestige of the 1969 plan, and the first building to be
erected on site. Probably the district's least appreciated
construction, it stands in stark and somehow unfortunate
contrast to its direct neighbour: Cesar Pelli's elegant
World Financial Center which is one of the city's most
successful pieces of corporate architecture.

CONCLUSION

The interesting point about Battery Park City is not only
its highly prominent location, but also and foremost the
fact that its status and set-up do not fit the stereotype of
an American, and therefore allegedly ultra-liberal,
development pattern. Rather French in terms of public
control, the project essentially follows, with a different
set of architectural ideas, the same development
procedure as, for example, the new district of Masséna
Nord in Paris (see separate case study).

This divergence from what may be considered the
'norm' of American planning might be explained
through viewing it in conjunction with the other USA
case study in this book, Stuyvesant Town. Both projects

suggest that public intervention in urban affairs is more difficult to prevent in very large and dense urban fabrics than in less dense ones. This might be triggered by a greater urge to balance public and private interests, due to the higher number of local stakeholders, but also by the sheer complexity and cost to intervene on a large scale in an inner-city environment. For Stuyvesant Town, the latter case seems to prevail, and massive public subsidies and the use of eminent domain had been provided by the State of New York in order to guide private companies into the slum-clearance programme. In Battery Park City, due to the specificity of the infill and the lack of ownership or cadastral restrictions, public intervention has rather to do with the problematic financial kick-start and the project's considerable development length which surpassed the mid-term investment horizon of most private developers.

The land reclamation effort, far from unique in New York's history, draws a parallel to another very prominent case, which is the creation in Victoria Bay of the new waterfront between Hong Kong Island and Kowloon (see *The Urban Towers Handbook*, pp 188–95). Here, the differences of design and planning concepts become very apparent, highlighting the fact that the improvement of transport links and the accompanying impact on land values stand at the very forefront of Hong Kong planning. The actual

LEFT: Streetscape up North End Avenue.

BELOW: View across South End Avenue towards the eastern half of Rector Place. Aside from the Gateway building, which is a residue of the 1969 masterplan, this area was the first residential development of Battery Park City.

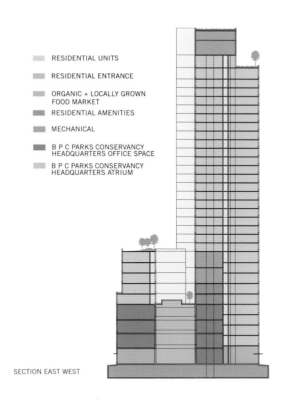

RESIDENTIAL UNITS

RESIDENTIAL ENTRANCE

ORGANIC + LOCALLY GROWN
FOOD MARKET

RESIDENTIAL AMENITIES

MECHANICAL

B P C PARKS CONSERVANCY
HEADQUARTERS OFFICE SPACE

B P C PARKS CONSERVANCY
HEADQUARTERS ATRIUM

SECTION EAST WEST

**East–west section of
The Visionaire.**

THIRD PLACE

BATTERY PLACE

LITTLE WEST STREET

SECOND PLACE

**Sixth-floor plan of
The Visionaire (2008),
a residential building
forming a whole block
on its own. Designed
by the New York City
office of Pelli Clarke Pelli
Architects, it is one of
the last developments
in the southern tip of
the area.**

BELOW: View down the highly successful river promenade from the development's northwestern tip.

masterplanning is undertaken in a second step, if at all, following the privatised construction of the stations and their massive commercial developments. Kowloon Station (2010) or the International Finance Centre (IFC) (2005) would be the largest examples of this type. Just like the 1969 masterplan for Battery Park City, these contemporary Chinese developments are podium-driven megastructures, underlining the link between the emergence of such constructions and topics like land reclamation, large-scale landownership and cadastral autonomy.

ABOVE: Detail of the promenade's landscaping next to the marina in front of the World Financial Center. The towers in the background are in New Jersey, across the Hudson River.

Avenue de l'Opéra

LOCATION: 9TH ARRONDISSEMENT, PARIS, FRANCE
DATE: 1854–79
SIZE: 40 HECTARES (99 ACRES)

The radical transformations around Charles Garnier's opera house are a typical example of the development logic during the Second Empire in Paris. Today mainly known for its aesthetic qualities through the provision of a perhaps overly homogeneous streetscape, the modernisation programme's actual motivations were far more complex and strategic.

Floor area ratio: 3.04
Residential population: 3,480
Mix of uses: mostly offices and apartments in the upper floors, and retail or restaurants in the ground floors

By the mid-19th century it was evident that the French capital was in need of major renovation works. Similar to the situation of many American cities in the pre-war period, Paris had suffered from significant population losses in its central core, with the upper and upper-middle classes being drawn to new fashionable suburbs like Neuilly, Passy or Batignolles. The centre's streets were too cramped, air and traffic circulation limited, and crime on the rise. As was at times also the case during the 20th century, some of these points may have been artificially exaggerated and could be dismissed as anti-urban propaganda. Nonetheless the truth remains that most of the real estate offered for the new bourgeoisie was to be found outside the central core, where private developers took advantage of cheap and essentially vacant land.

Surprisingly, in view of the French system's reputation for state control, public intervention in the city's urban renewal and controlled development was historically limited. While the state led the construction of some famous squares such as Place Royale or Place Vendôme, and some scattered linear interventions like Rue Dauphine or Rue du Roule, it repeatedly failed to accomplish more ambitious undertakings. In order to minimise expenses, the city's strategy at the beginning of the 19th century focused on gradual changes through the application of building regulations, rather than direct interventions. Since 1807, an alignment law had obliged all municipalities to draw up a comprehensive plan which designated existing streets for widening. In reality, the redevelopment process was far slower than anticipated, as the city authorities could not afford to use eminent domain on a sufficiently large scale, the necessary compensations being considered too high. The theoretically more cost-efficient alternative was the provision of subsidies for piecemeal redevelopment through the existing landowners, who were meant to be motivated by the prospect of higher real-estate values resulting from the widening of the public street in front

BELOW: Alternative and unbuilt proposal of 1856 by the architect Hippolyte Barnout for the construction of a new theatre and a new connection between the Tuileries Palace and Boulevard des Italiens. Avenue de l'Opéra would have been positioned in parallel to the Palais Royal and Rue de Richelieu.

BOTTOM: One of many expropriation plans for the breakthrough of Avenue de l'Opéra.

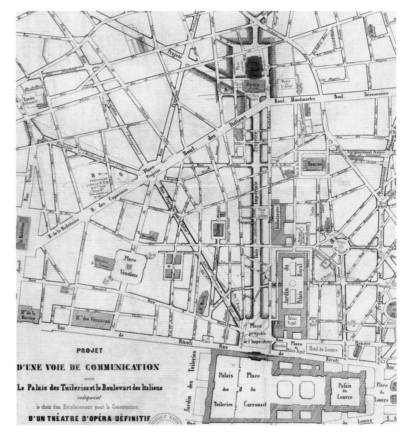

LEFT: Photograph taken during construction in the early 1870s, on the corner of today's Avenue de l'Opéra and Rue Saint-Augustin.

BELOW: Map by Adolphe Alphand showing the interventions of the Second Empire according to their date of completion. Though dating from 1889, the plan only shows projects finished between 1854 and 1871. Avenue de l'Opéra is hence only represented by a dotted line.

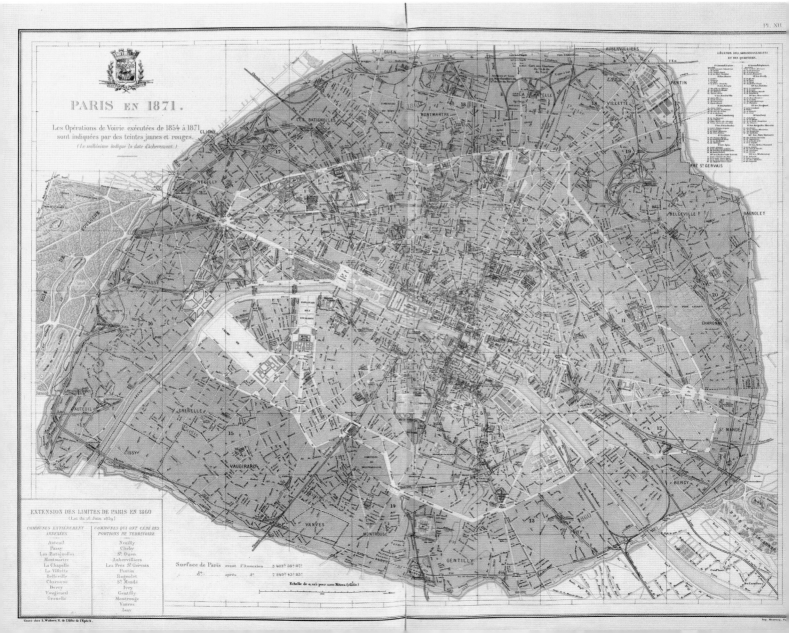

of their properties. Although essentially justified, this concept overestimated the profits from such interventions, and underestimated the difficulty of harmonising the setback in a piecemeal manner. For taller and older constructions, the legal and economic situation could be especially complicated, as their redevelopment could, according to a law of 1783, be restricted to a lower height than the pre-existing buildings.

It is essentially the failure of this 'soft' masterplanning attempt that paved the way for the city's radical redesign, which in the end encompassed far more than street widening. As increased public intervention appeared to be inevitable, it became clear that comprehensive expropriation could be used not only to widen existing streets, but to create new ones altogether.

PROJECT ORGANISATION / TEAM STRUCTURE

Partly prepared by his predecessors, these new openings and many other improvements were the works that Baron Haussmann, prefect of the Seine from 1853 to 1870, famously, brilliantly and – some might say – ruthlessly implemented following the prescriptions of Napoleon III, President of the second French Republic from 1848 to 1852, and French Emperor from 1852 to 1870. Inspired by recent local examples like Rue de Rivoli, Rue Rambuteau, Rue des Ecoles and Boulevard de Strasbourg, as well as John Nash's bold plans for Regent Street in London (1814–25), Napoleon Bonaparte's nephew certainly did not invent the technique of cutting new streets through an existing urban fabric. He did, however, apply it at a heretofore unheard-of scale which would eventually change the face of the whole city.

From a legal standpoint, the creation of this new network of traffic arteries, squares and monuments had been facilitated through the expansion of the city's expropriation powers in 1852. Though usually aiming for an amicable acquisition, the city was now in a position to directly and quickly gain control of all land not only on but around the planned breakthroughs. This included the at times unfortunately shaped residues of truncated plots, and also the neighbouring plots if these were needed in order to close newly created urban blocks. Expensive as these measures may have been, they enabled the city to take an active role on the real-estate markets, and to profit from speculation gains. As much as possible, Haussmann's administration tried to involve private development companies at an early stage, through (often subsidised) concessions, but the substantial cost of expropriations, demolitions and public infrastructure works did usually

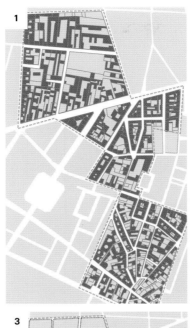

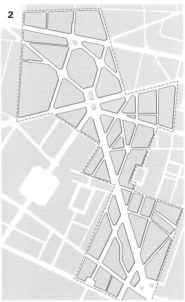

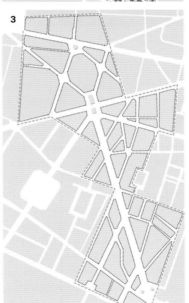

Process diagrams

- ▪ Private ownership
- ▪ Public ownership
- ░ Building envelope
- ▒ Green space
- — Private plot ownership
- — Public plot ownership
- ▪▪▪ Tracks

1 Situation before intervention.

2 Plot subdivision and public ownership after expropriation and before auction to private investors.

3 City prescriptions for the creation of new perimeter blocks.

4 Final state.

require a strong public investment until the sale by auction of the empty plots. This was also the case of Avenue de l'Opéra, and the final costs for the acquisition, expropriation and destruction of 168 buildings amounted to 66 million francs. Only 24.5 million francs of this sum could be made up through the sale of plots to 36 individuals and development companies; the remaining land had to be given over to the owners of the previous buildings. Increasingly affronted by the press, the administration defended its abysmal debt as an economic driver for the whole nation, strongly influenced by Saint-Simonian theories of 'productive expenditures'.

The case of the Opéra district is especially complex, and took almost 25 years for completion, because it combined two initially separate interventions: the link of the Louvre and Rue de Rivoli with the area around Saint-Lazare Station, on the one hand, and the construction of a new opera house on the other. Strictly speaking, they are not Haussmann works, as they were both completed after his resignation in 1870. The reason they did not feature at the top of the administration's agenda was linked to the special complexity of the project and the impossibility of creating a more direct connection with Saint-Lazare Station.

URBAN FORM / CONNECTIVITY
Most important for the appreciation of Haussmann's breakthroughs, Avenue de l'Opéra included, is the understanding that urban embellishment was a side

effect rather than a driving force. The first reason for the undertaking of such pharaonic works was the improvement of connectivity and traffic flows. As the trains had become the most efficient means of transport, the links between the capital's major stations had superseded the former core–gate relation as determinant force of spatial organisation. Saint-Lazare Station had opened in 1837, Montparnasse and Austerlitz Stations in 1840, Gare du Nord in 1846 and Gare de l'Est in 1849. Among other cross and radial connections, it seemed appropriate to link these modern exploits in the best possible way. Underlining the capital's undisputed position as the nation's political, economic and cultural leader, these connections also symbolised the political solidification of the French state's very diverse provinces. Typical of the pragmatism of these urban principles is the fact that the alignment plan, elaborated by Eugène Deschamps as one of Haussmann's most important colleagues, does not establish any geometric order or urban symmetries. The aim is to extend, widen and connect, and only a few of the new openings – especially those around Place de l'Etoile and Place du Trône, both of which originate in the 17th and not the 19th century – relate to the Baroque aesthetics of a grand urban form. The triangular, quasi-symmetrical developments surrounding Charles Garnier's opera house are from this point of view unusual, and specific design guidelines had been established in order to mirror the new building's civic grandeur. They were designed

ABOVE LEFT: View down Rue Daunou towards Avenue de l'Opéra: the buildings in the background and to the immediate right predate Haussmann's works, while the others are a result of the avenue's opening.

ABOVE: View of the eastern facades of Avenue de l'Opéra, with typical apartment buildings wrapping the corners of the connections with the pre-existing street network.

OPPOSITE: Junction of Avenue de l'Opéra and Rue d'Antin: in order to save costs and to avoid the destruction of Hôtel Gabriel, seat of an important bank, the new building on the avenue adopts the sharp edge of a leftover plot instead of wrapping around the corner.

1 **Building uses**
- Residential
- Offices
- Mixed use
- Entertainment/Sports
- Public amenities
- Transport
- Shopping
- Retail and gastronomy in the ground floor
- H Hotel

2 **Green**
- Green - *public/collective/private*
- Roadside vegetation/green alley
- Walkway
- Public square

3 **Transport**
- R Rail - above ground /interchange
- U Underground
- BUS Bus
- Tramway

4 **Street network**

Havre - Caumartin
Chaussée d'Antin - La Fayette
Auber
Opéra
Quatre-Septembre
Pyramides

Analysis diagrams

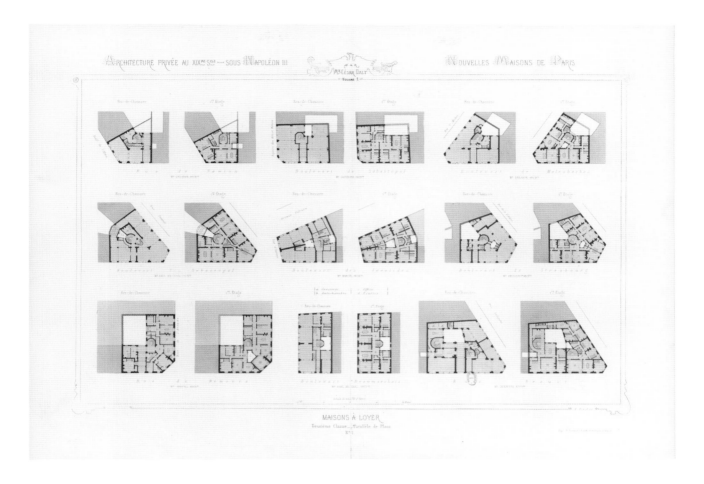

in 1860 by the architect Charles Rohault de Fleury as a frame for his own (failed) opera-house proposal. After several public objections to his design, they became the fittingly mediocre context of Garnier's winning competition scheme of 1861. Due to complications with the swampy ground and the Franco-Prussian war, the opening of Garnier's masterpiece occurred years later in 1875.

The emphasis on traffic flows should not overshadow the existence of many other motivations for Haussmann's urban surgery, including the provision of modern residential accommodation, the installation of an efficient sewer system and the improvement of the military's operational readiness in formerly inaccessible quarters. Avenue de l'Opéra itself, initially planned as Avenue Napoléon, not only improved the connectivity with Saint-Lazare Station, but also offered the advantage of destroying large parts of an alleged slum. As previously mentioned, the city was interested in attracting the wealthier layers of the population back to the centre, and could most easily do so in pushing the working and lower-middle classes towards the periphery, as a mid-19th-century example of planned

gentrification. The high social status of the new avenue, and its only recently established symmetry towards the opera house, was emphasised through the decision in 1876 to abandon the initial – and usual – plan of tree planting on the pavements: the rare occasion to offer a majestic and unobstructed view from the new opening to a new monument was not to be missed. The last buildings on Avenue de l'Opéra were finished in 1879.

ARCHITECTURAL TYPOLOGIES

The above-described 'city planning NOT according to artistic principles', as an allusion to Camillo Sitte's critique of the technical pragmatism of late 19th-century urbanism, has some fairly straightforward formal consequences for the position of the architectural elements in its midst. The paradox of one of the 19th century's most famous and influential housing types, the Haussmannian apartment building, is the fact that it theoretically does not have any repetitive footprint or prescribed form. It is born as a space filler that has to adapt as much as possible to the random shapes of building plots left over from the breakthrough technique. Strict facade prescriptions assured the urban continuity

A plate of César Daly's book *L'Architecture privée au xixe siècle sous Napoléon III (Domestic Architecture in the 19th Century under Napoleon III)* published in 1864. It shows a summary of apartment buildings that were developed as a consequence of Haussmann's renovation works and breakthroughs. The examples precede the construction of Avenue de l'Opéra, built in the 1870s.

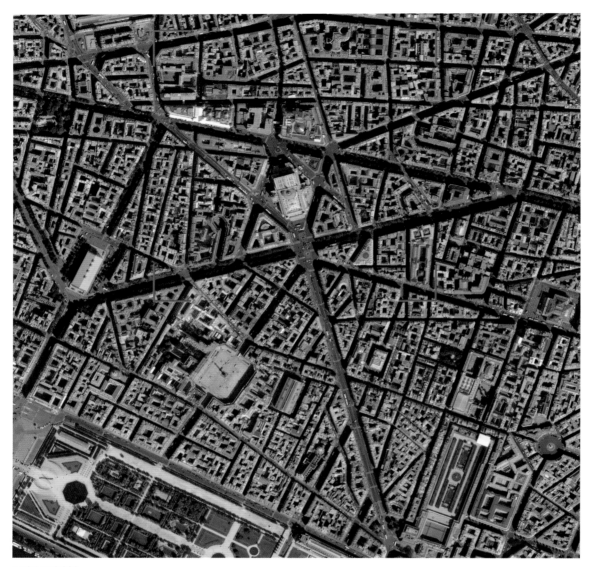

Aerial 1:10,000

of the new openings. However, this might not necessarily be in contradiction with the notion of type, and it is indeed fascinating to observe how the buildings' respective architects managed to adapt the formal spatial programme for the new bourgeoisie to the often sparse and highly diverse reality of available land.

The most rigid element of this formal programme was the so-called 'enfilade' of reception rooms along the street facade, necessitating approximately 15 metres (49 feet) of street frontage. Of aristocratic origin, it had since the end of the 18th century become a must, first for the upper and then also for the middle bourgeoisie. All other elements of the apartment – bedrooms, bath- and service rooms – could more freely be laid out according to the realities of the building plots, and

tended to be arranged around the internal courtyards. With the exception of very large or deep cadastral subdivisions, these courtyards had essentially become generous light- and air-wells, and no longer accommodated carriages or servants. The latter could now be found in the attic, with direct access to the master kitchens through a dedicated servants staircase.

The best examples of the period's typical floor plans can be observed wherever the urban interventions were built on vacant (or vacated) land, such as in the 17th arrondissement's Plaine-Monceau district, rather than as a breakthrough through existing blocks. These were also the areas which could most easily be sold at a profit to development companies. Less limited through an existing cadastral pattern, the relationship between the

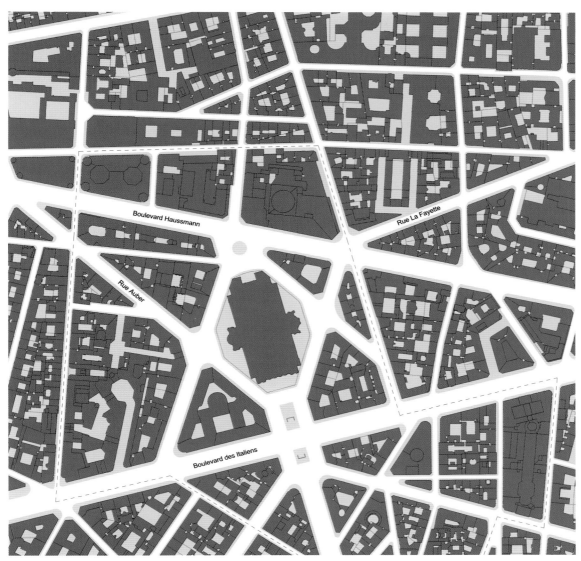

Urban plan 1:5,000

architectural element and the urban block could be studied and optimised. In the case of the Opéra quarter, it was the Pereire brothers' Compagnie Immobilière de Paris that began the construction of apartment buildings in the southern surroundings of the future Opéra. In total, over 15 urban blocks were eventually built around the new avenue and opera house. At least half of them, however, were too small or elongated to establish a truly repetitive type.

Bird's-eye views, more than street images, document how the above-mentioned facade prescriptions as part of the sales agreements led to an illusion of homogeneity, namely through the wrapping with superficial stone shells of the highly complex and diverse interiors of the blocks. The initial plan of 1854 for Avenue Napoléon

(later renamed Avenue de l'Opéra) was more radical yet, and intended to treat the facades in perfect repetition, just like those of Rue de Rivoli. This regulation was abandoned in 1876, when the project was resumed after several years of deadlock following the downfall of the Emperor.

CONCLUSION

The inclusion of a Haussmann project in the selection of this book is a result of its considerable historic relevance. Being predominantly linear, Haussmann's interventions do not really fit the scope of most other chosen case studies. This fact provokes many questions, because the renovation of Paris under the Second Empire tends to be considered highly successful. Why is it, then, that

LEFT: Unlike many other avenues in Paris, Avenue de l'Opéra is not tree-lined, in order to emphasise the view towards one of the city's most spectacular monuments.

BELOW LEFT: Ground floor of two buildings on Rue d'Antin, just east of the junction with Avenue de l'Opéra. The right-hand building is older than the one on the left that has been redeveloped in order to frame the new avenue.

LEFT: A little square on Rue Saint-Augustin, just one block east of Avenue de l'Opéra. It was not modified by the urban renovation works.

we frequently refer back to these interventions, but apparently never apply genuinely comparable means for ongoing urban renewal? Several of the answers to this question have already been touched upon, and are linked to the fact that the Baron's name is today, at least for the wider public, mainly associated with aesthetic questions and pure facadism. The urban component and its background tend to be overlooked, because – at least in the rich Western world – urban sanitation is no longer a significant problem and traffic issues are no longer considered to be efficiently solvable through the construction of new roads. Another reason, however, for today's tendency to use brownfield sites for urban renewal, rather than to cut into the existing fabric, is simply linked to the cost of such interventions. Diminishing public investment, and the almost total reliance on private capital, amplify this situation. Expenses have not only grown through the improved protection of private property and the subsequent rise

in expropriation costs, but were already considerable in the mid-19th century, when the city often did not succeed in selling the concessions and was forced to undertake all works on its own account.

Most importantly, increasing sprawl and the dislocation of major urban functions have altered the status of the city centre. Often reduced to an essentially touristic area, its partial destruction and costly reorganisation would seem to make little sense. Even the fairly recent revival of the train stations through high-speed connections, and the return of wealthier residents to the urban core, cannot hide the fact that the regional logic of most cities is incomparable to the mid-19th century. New York's High Line and the recent tunnelling and landscaping of Madrid's inner-city freeways are examples that document the treatment of traffic networks at the beginning of the 21st century, through reconversion rather than extension.

ABOVE: This triangular block is the one of the smallest of seven blocks created in direct proximity to the new opera house. Its facade design followed particularly strict rules that had to be applied for all buildings facing the opera.

RIGHT: Charles Garnier's opera house (1875) and its eastern surroundings.

FAR RIGHT: View down Rue de la Chaussée d'Antin. The street itself predates the works for the opera house and the avenue, but the church, l'Eglise de la Sainte-Trinité, was part of Haussmann's renovation works and built between 1861 and 1867.

Vauban

LOCATION: FREIBURG, GERMANY
DATE: 1994–2010
SIZE: 41 HECTARES (101 ACRES)

One of the world's most famous examples of sustainable urbanism, the lesson of Vauban goes much further than the display of advanced building technologies. Its success is based on extensive community work, a large functional and social diversity of the programme and the piecemeal approach of the planning process.

Floor area ratio: **1.40**
Residential population: **5,300**
Mix of uses: **86% of the marketable plots are zoned for residential uses, 14% are mixed use**

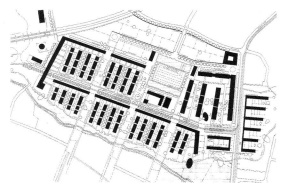

LEFT: Aerial view of the site in the early 1990s, just before the French forces left Germany and the Vauban estate became available for redevelopment.

RIGHT: The Kohlhoff & Kohlhoff masterplan from 1994, winner of an open competition with 60 entries. Over the following three years it was considerably modified, but the main principles were respected.

The name 'Vauban' can be misleading, as the famous eponymous 17th-century French military engineer was indeed active in Freiburg, but only in a central location, approximately 3 kilometres (2 miles) to the northeast of the new suburban district which is the topic of this case study. He was in charge of building the fortifications for the town that had been conquered in 1677 by the armies of Louis XIV. The site of the current development received its honorific name after the Second World War with the transformation of German barracks into French barracks, as part of the Allies' imposed military presence on German ground. After the end of the Cold War and the political changes that came with the reunification, the French forces left the site in 1992.

With its beautiful and convenient location, the area's development potential was quickly appreciated, and the city bought the land from the federal state in 1994. In the same year, a regional masterplan competition was organised and won by the Stuttgart office Kohlhoff & Kohlhoff together with the landscape architects Luz & Partner and the traffic engineer Hans Billinger. Chosen out of 60 entries, the proposal should be understood as a spatial framework, rather than a blueprint, and has been considerably modified over time.

The city authority's central position in the development process is highlighted by the fact that it handled the piecemeal sale of plots to interested investors itself, and undertook the construction of the infrastructures through the gain made from these sales: having bought the land from the state at a low as-is value, it sold it on at prices that had been fixed by an expert in view of the future development. Due to the decision to sell the plots at fixed prices and not by auction, the city was able to pick the best architectural and social concepts. Some of the former barracks buildings were retained for use as student dormitories, but the vast majority of the site was cleared of its existing structures. This excludes the natural features, and the competition's brief called for the retention of at least 80 per cent of the original tree stock. Additionally,

the plan had to accommodate approximately 2,000 dwellings and a business and manufacturing area of 6 hectares (15 acres) intended to create 600 jobs. Situated towards the north, this part of the development also had to function as a buffer between the residential areas on the one hand, and the train tracks and a major street on the other. Too expensive and less well connected compared with alternative locations in the Freiburg region, these plots received little interest and were subsequently transformed into additional residential space. Vital to the district's sustainability claim is the connection of Vauban to the city centre via a purpose-built tram line which opened in 2006. Financially, the city's calculations seem to have been accurate, and the sale of plots covered the expenses for the construction of infrastructures, including the section of the tram line that is situated on the project perimeter.

PROJECT ORGANISATION / TEAM STRUCTURE

Crucial next to the city's direct and controlling involvement was the decision to follow a small-scale approach in terms of cadastral subdivision and not to hand over the whole site to a single private or public developer. Historically, the land had been under single ownership since 1936. Under the current scheme, many plots were bought by so-called *Baugemeinschaften* (building communities) or *Baugruppen* (building groups), associations of private individuals that were created for the construction of a single project, generally for the stakeholders' own housing needs. Legally flexible and adjustable to the future occupier's competence and desired degree of involvement, they now represent an increasingly important part of the residential market throughout Germany. In the beginning, these projects were often initiated and organised by motivated non-professionals who commissioned an architect after having found like-minded future neighbours. Today, the process has reached a certain degree of professional maturity, and

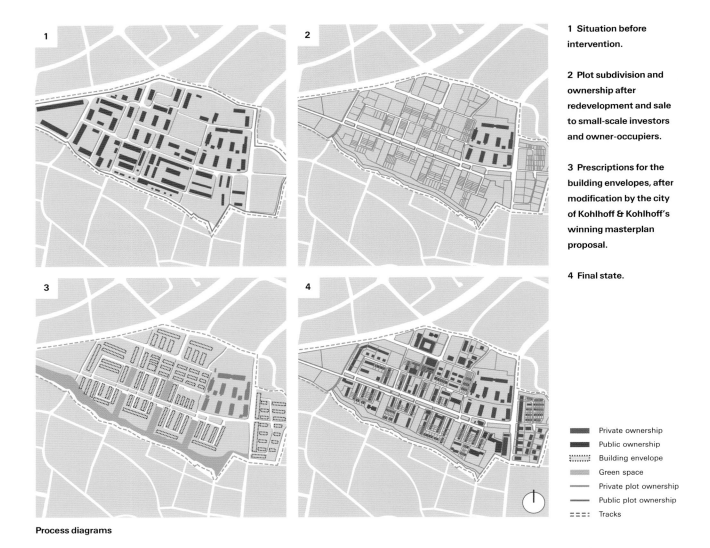

1 Situation before intervention.

2 Plot subdivision and ownership after redevelopment and sale to small-scale investors and owner-occupiers.

3 Prescriptions for the building envelopes, after modification by the city of Kohlhoff & Kohlhoff's winning masterplan proposal.

4 Final state.

Private ownership
Public ownership
Building envelope
Green space
Private plot ownership
Public plot ownership
Tracks

Process diagrams

many projects are launched and masterplanned by architects as a new building venture. The clients' motivation for such a time-consuming undertaking is not only financial gain compared with the acquisition of an apartment or townhouse from a developer, but the opportunity to define the shape of one's future home, a rarity in an urban environment that is not constituted of freestanding houses. This method and process also enables the establishment of a community of like-minded people in an urban setting that is usually rather defined by its anonymity. Taken to the extreme, such a development system, which is also often applied for renovation works, can have a major impact on the social and physical fabric of the built environment.

Vauban's reputation as an 'alternative' urban project is a consequence of not only its built reality as a sustainable development, but also the variety of political groups that – directly or indirectly – contributed to its implementation. Early after the French forces left, some of the barracks were used by the city and the Salvation Army for the temporary accommodation of socially underprivileged groups, Bosnian refugees, homeless people and asylum seekers. This legal population was eventually complemented by squatters, political activists and party ravers, forming an unusual mixture of marginal groups. Parts of this nonconformist spirit have been retained through the detailed planning and public consultation process, in which the 1994 masterplan was modified and eventually a legally binding development plan approved in July 1997. This process was greatly assisted by not only the consultation work of the 'Forum Vauban' – founded by former student activists – and the existence of Genova and SUSI ('self-organised independent settlement

initiative') as alternative housing associations, but also the fact that the whole project attracted people who seemed motivated rather than disturbed by such a background. In conjunction with the above-mentioned specificity of the legal structure, and the architectural influence that it confers to the clients, it might be assumed that the ecological success of the scheme is closely linked to a relative coherence of the population's lifestyle. The alternative approach is understood as a political engagement for change, and not only an eco-friendly attitude. It is not by chance that over 60 per cent of Vauban's population vote for the German Green Party, which has until recently remained a minority force at national level with less than 20 per cent of overall support.

URBAN FORM / CONNECTIVITY

The (updated) masterplan's general prescriptions are simple: through the quasi-abandonment of manufacturing and business activities in Vauban's northern sector, the remaining functional separation on site consists in the concentration of retail around a central east–west corridor. This corridor clearly represents the district's major spine, and accommodates the new tram line and the centrally located Alfred Döblin Platz. A closed longitudinal building with mixed uses

LEFT: View from the south side of Vaubanallee to the west. On this side of the street, most buildings accommodate retail and restaurant uses on the ground floor. The arcades provide an urban feeling that is not an obvious feature of the scheme's *Zeilenbau* logic. The VIVA 2000 development, designed by Böwer Eith Murken and completed in 2003, can be identified as the next building to the left.

BELOW: A long structure delimits the area to the east along Merzhauser Strasse as major connection to the city centre. It is a hybrid building, and accommodates housing above office and retail uses.

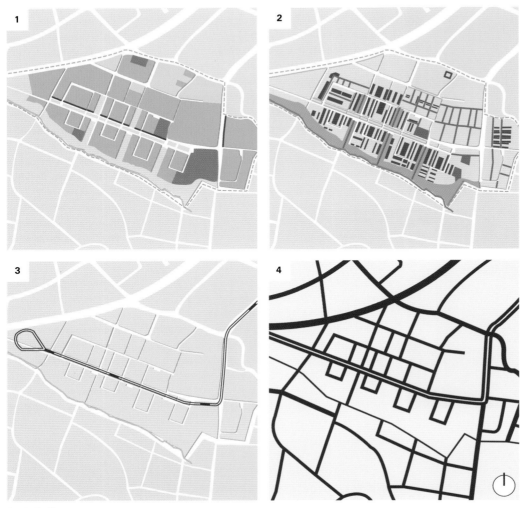

1

2

3

4

Analysis diagrams

1	**Building uses**		**3**	**Transport**
	Residential		**R**	Rail - above ground /interchange
	Offices		**U**	Underground
	Mixed use		BUS	Bus
	Entertainment/Sports			Tramway
	Public amenities			
	Transport		**4**	**Street network**
	Shopping			
	Retail and gastronomy in the ground floor			
H	Hotel			

2	**Green**
	Green - *public/collective/private*
	Roadside vegetation/green alley
	Walkway
	Public square

shields the site's eastern districts and its solar village from the noise of Merzhauser Strasse. A stream forms the southern boundary of the site. This, along with three green corridors that lead perpendicularly from the stream's protected biotope northwards through the settlement, provides the backbone of the area's landscape design. In addition to their aesthetic and ecological benefits, these elements allow the southern mountain winds to sweep through the urbanised zone.

In terms of urban form, a quick glance at the built plan and its repetition of narrow linear buildings, even more legible in the initial competition entry, evokes the historic notion of 1920s and 1930s German *Zeilenbau*. This might be linked to the appropriateness of such an arrangement for the construction of terraced houses, but also provides a contextual link to the fairly geometric disposition of the barracks prior to destruction. Even

ABOVE: View of Georg-Elser-Strasse and its rainwater trench. Car traffic is restricted.

LEFT: This solar-energy development is situated behind the linear structure on Merzhauser Strasse. It was designed by the architect Rolf Disch.

Aerial 1:10,000

more so than in the former military scheme, the new development relies on east–west-oriented slabs which allow the majority of dwellings to have the optimum exposure to natural light. Given this rigidly functional and somehow neutral urbanism, the area's living quality heavily depends on the aesthetic quality of the landscaping concept. It seems difficult to imagine how further densification, which would lower the visual impact of green elements, could be achieved without considerable loss of urban appeal. More imposing building masses and the loss of the beautifully landscaped setbacks would have to be counterbalanced by a stronger and more evocative urban form.

The subtlety of Vauban's traffic and parking concept plays a central role in its overall green character. Though not literally car-free, Vauban manages in a remarkable way to present private transport as a background element. This has been achieved through a well-conceived hierarchy of publicly or privately accessible streets, pedestrian walkways and a mixture of on- and off-street parking and – most importantly – two above-ground parking garages that accommodate the large majority of the district's car stock. Indeed, a stroll through the area confronts the visitor more often with originally designed bicycle shelters than with the usually omnipresent signs of Germany's most important industrial product. It is worthwhile mentioning that the

Urban plan 1:5,000

existence of the area's highly ecological constructions is closely linked to the project's car-reduction claim. An essential part of Kohlhoff & Kohlhoff's initial masterplan submission, it attracted a special and fairly homogeneous group of ecologically minded individuals. These, due to the reluctance of professional developers to participate in a scheme with such a minimal amount of private parking spaces, hence became under the aforementioned legal status Vauban's principal small-scale investors. In view of federal planning legislation, the provision of less than one parking space per residential unit was not easy to implement, and a reservation for the construction of a third parking garage had to be provided. This will

have to be built if demand for parking spaces returns to 'normal standards'.

ARCHITECTURAL TYPOLOGIES

Architecturally, the multitude of participating interests has led to a multitude of built solutions. The residential part alone – mainly four and occasionally five storeys tall, with usually four to 20 units per construction – offers a large variety of designs and densities. Most original, next to more conventional apartment blocks and one-family terraced houses, is the provision of small-scale apartment buildings, whose two or three separate units – often stacked duplex apartments – are partly accessible from exterior staircases. As explained

One of the few taller buildings with five storeys. Most developments are only three to four storeys tall. The building is situated in the very west of the area, between the tram loop and the train tracks. It acts as a buffer for the rest of the development.

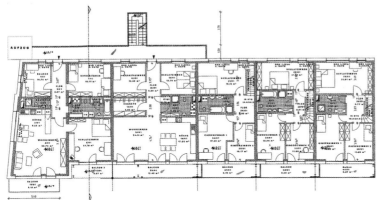

Second floor of the ISIS passive house (2001), designed by the architect Meinhard Hansen. Most units are duplex apartments, and the external staircase leads directly up to the second floor. The very low energy consumption is based on extreme insulation, triple windows and the efficient use of air flows. Typical for this first generation of passive houses is the south–north orientation of the building.

above, most constructions have double-exposure, and often privatised exterior spaces. Stylistically, almost all types are represented, though a preference is given to timber architecture. The above-mentioned *Zeilenbau* analogy seems to have inspired several architects in their design of neo-Modern purist facades and horizontal openings.

Surpassing the German legal norms, all buildings in Vauban are low-energy constructions and must consume less than 65 kilowatt hours per square metre per annum (6 kilowatt hours per square foot per annum). This is made possible through particularly

efficient insulation and a communal heating station that is situated in the northern part of the site. Some projects have voluntarily further reduced energy consumption to less than 15 kilowatt hours per square metre per annum (close to 1 kilowatt hour per square foot per annum). Even more efficient than these so-called passive houses are structures like the solar houses that create energy and share it. The entire production is fed into the public network and the owners are compensated by an above-market sale price. Due to these generous subsidies, the constructions are currently profitable. A sign of Vauban's success and pioneering role is the

ABOVE: A communal pizza and bread oven is situated in one of the green zones which cross the development from the river to the north.

ABOVE RIGHT: Two mixed-use buildings in the north of Vauban: the Villaban (2002) to the left, and the Amöbe ('amoeba'; 2006) to the right, both designed by Architekten Broß, Pulling, Kurzberger.

RIGHT: Conversion of former barracks buildings into student dormitories. Most of the site has, however, been cleared of the military residues.

fact that all new constructions in Freiburg now have to follow passive house standards, if they are situated on a plot that was owned by the city. Remarkable from a morphological point of view was the need to allow exceptions to the aforementioned east–west orientation of the masterplan's building volumes, as the first generation of passive houses usually had to be north–south oriented. Also interesting in terms of new building techniques is the recent shift away from central heating systems back to individual heat production. This can be explained through the extremely efficient insulation and a consequently low consumption that does not necessitate the installation of a dedicated underground network.

The sustainability concept, however, is not limited to the question of individual energy consumption. Walking through the streets, one of Vauban's most visible features are the well-designed trenches which support the creation of a healthy rain- and groundwater cycle. On the private lots, cisterns collect the rainwater and allow for local reuse. Green roofs filter the water and avoid inundations in the case of heavy showers.

CONCLUSION

It is not easy to evaluate the importance of Vauban in the frame of this work, as it is the least dense project and one of the few to incorporate a fairly large percentage of one-family units. It therefore defines the lower boundary of our analytic spectrum and can arguably be considered suburban rather than urban, and this in the context of a city with just over 220,000 inhabitants. With its international reputation as a brilliant example of sustainable planning, and the way it addresses the topic of family living in a green urban environment, Vauban is nevertheless relevant to this study. Despite its own model value as a densified suburb, Vauban can also be seen as a placeholder for smaller and more central developments, like the Berlin-Townhouse project near Hausvogteiplatz in the core of the German capital. Taking a cue from Freiburg, Berlin tested a programme in which it sold land directly to private owner-occupiers for the construction of individually designed one-family (row) houses, rather than solely engaging professional developers. This method, seen in conjunction with the larger *Baugruppen* schemes, represents an internationally still underestimated shift away from a consistently top-down planning process, in which the customer has to choose from a conventional, often very limited offer, and towards a far more complex market. This market has always existed, but it was marginal and reserved for the luxury or informal sector. Major planning changes are often the result of economic pressures; in the aforementioned Berlin case, the city had to find solutions for the fact that, for many years after the reunification, even the most prominent sites could not find a professional purchaser. Projects like the Townhouses were a successful attempt to test alternative development methods, and to find solutions for a shrinking rather than growing urban core. These strategies are not only valuable experiences in the fairly exceptional East German context of stagnating or even

decreasing urban populations, but can also be applied in specific sectors of overall growing agglomerations. Densification might be one of the major issues for the future of our cities, but it cannot be the only available strategy for a highly diverse and complicated urban reality. Vauban can hence be appreciated as a dense and architecturally diverse suburb, but also as a development model for the attraction of the middle classes to often still struggling urban centres.

Ground-floor plan of the VIVA 2000 development, designed by Böwer Eith Murken. It accommodates, in addition to two stacked rows of duplex apartments, retail surfaces along Vaubanallee, the new district's central axis.

Section through one of the two rows of the VIVA 2000 development. The top units are accessed through an exterior gallery that is connected to a staircase in the front building.

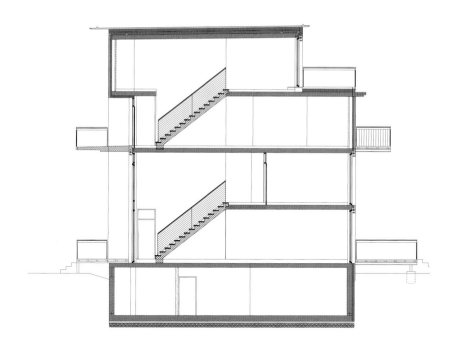

BELOW: The VIVA 2000 development and its ground-floor retail, seen from Vaubanallee (see also plans).

Antigone

LOCATION: MONTPELLIER, FRANCE
DATE: 1979–2000
SIZE: 50 HECTARES (124 ACRES)

One of the rare and largest examples of Post-Modern neoclassicist urbanism, Antigone is also an early case of contemporary urban marketing, using the eastward extension of the city as an opportunity to advance Montpellier's ambitions as a regional leader.

Floor area ratio: 1.04
Residential population: 8,000
Mix of uses: 64% residential, 16% office, 10% public amenities, 6% hotel, 4% retail and restaurants

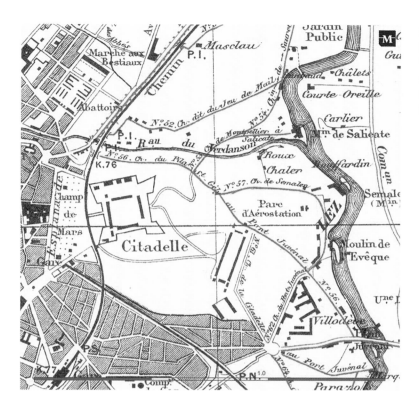

Map of the area east of Montpellier's centre in 1896. Today's Antigone district lies directly to the south and southeast of the citadel.

The history and challenges of Antigone should be viewed in the light of three major aspects: the population's explosive growth during the 1960s and 1970s; the increasing criticism of post-war urbanism in France; and the decision to kick-start the eastward extension of the urban area, historically hindered by the citadel, army barracks, shooting grounds and the floodplains of the River Lez. Due to Montpellier's election as regional capital in 1956, the opening of a large IBM factory and, perhaps most significantly, the decolonisation of French North Africa, the city's population doubled from 80,000 to over 160,000 between 1958 and 1975. This demographic trend still continues, and the thriving city – famous not only for its beautiful old town, but also for its university, hospitals and several high-tech industries – has since exceeded the quarter-million mark, making it the eighth most populous agglomeration in France.

When the socialist Georges Frêche became mayor in 1977, he decided to challenge the liberal laissez-faire way in which urban development had been handled by his conservative predecessor, the most recent and controversial project at that time being the construction of the Polygone shopping mall right next to Place de la Comédie. Built in a central location, on parts of former military grounds that had been retroceded to the city, this large commercial building symbolised not only

the challenges of a new type of urbanism, but also the development issues in this specific zone which was liable to flooding and therefore chronically underutilised. As a private piecemeal intervention, the Polygone mall, which took its name from the army shooting grounds, did not help to solve these issues, and essentially acted as a cul-de-sac to Montpellier's east. It served the city centre with its extensive retail offerings, but did not allow for new connections to the outskirts.

When directly commissioned in 1979, the Catalan architect Ricardo Bofill and his office Taller de Arquitectura had not yet achieved the international recognition that he would receive a decade later. Bofill was, however, already working on major urban and social housing projects in the French *Villes Nouvelles* (new cities) of Marne-La-Vallée and St Quentin-en-Yvelines. The name of Antigone is a double entendre, relating to the scheme's Greek-inspired neoclassicism as much as to the failed urbanism of the mall ('Anti-Polygone') which is situated between the project's perimeter and Montpellier's historic core. The relationship between these two important developments was to remain problematic for the next 20 years, experiencing periods in which the owner of the mall was menaced with expropriation in order to allow for the channelling of pedestrian flows through his development. While it is not obvious in a large-scale plan view, the height difference of approximately 6 metres (20 feet) between Place de la Comédie and the plains of the River Lez makes it difficult to access the Antigone site from the city centre any other way than through the mall.

PROJECT ORGANISATION / TEAM STRUCTURE

The project's implementation has been steered by the SERM (Société d'Equipement de la Région Montpelliéraine), a structure established in 1961. Officially a public-private partnership, the vast majority is owned by public entities like the city of Montpellier and the structure that steers the development of the wider urban region, Montpellier Agglomération. A minor number of shares are held by a group of specialised private banks including the Caisse des Dépôts et

Consignations and Dexia. This set-up is typical for the French development culture, and had the advantage of vastly simplifying the administrative procedures compared with a project that would have been directly undertaken by the city as a public client. Just like in the cases of Euralille and Masséna Nord (see separate case studies), some of the legal advantages have since been lost, including the ability to directly designate a masterplanner without any design competition.

After retrocession to the city, the SERM became the owner of the Polygone army ground which counted for approximately 40 per cent of the site. The rest was acquired in a piecemeal manner. The largest pieces of land were, however, covered by vast industrial estates, the most notable being a soap factory, that could be dislocated or were already at the end of their life cycle. Consequently, a 50-hectare (124-acre) site was

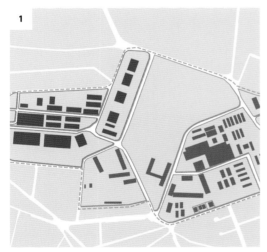

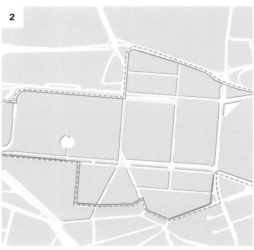

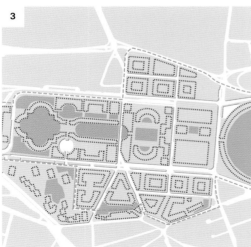

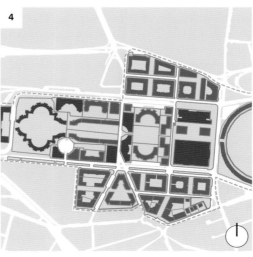

1 Situation before intervention. Almost half of the site, former army grounds, was in public ownership, and the rest covered by private industries.

2 Single public ownership before sale of properties to public and private entities.

3 Masterplan prescriptions for the building envelopes.

4 Final state.

▬▬ Private ownership
▬▬ Public ownership
⋮⋮⋮⋮ Building envelope
▬▬ Green space
— Private plot ownership
— Public plot ownership
≡≡≡≡ Tracks

Process diagrams

1 Building uses

    Residential

    Offices

    Mixed use

    Entertainment/Sports

    Public amenities

    Transport

    Shopping

    Retail and gastronomy
    in the ground floor

H   Hotel

2 Green

    Green - *public/collective/private*

    Roadside vegetation/green alley

    Walkway

    Public square

3 Transport

    R   Rail - above ground
        /interchange

    U   Underground

  BUS   Bus

    Tramway

4 Street network

gathered under single ownership, allowing for the implementation of a large-scale planning vision that was different in ambition from the fragmentary development logic of the 1960s and 1970s. As is usually the case in the French planning system, the site was declared a ZAC (*zone d'aménagement concerté*) at the beginning of the development process, and was therefore excluded from the city's usual planning restrictions. The zone's perimeter was repeatedly extended in order to cover the entire surface of the SERM's gradual land acquisitions. After the establishment of Bofill's masterplan, which went through many different design phases, the plots were sold to public or private developers. On certain exceptional occasions, the SERM itself acted also as a client, retaining ownership of the land and organising architectural works for several public office buildings

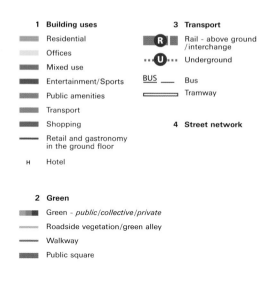

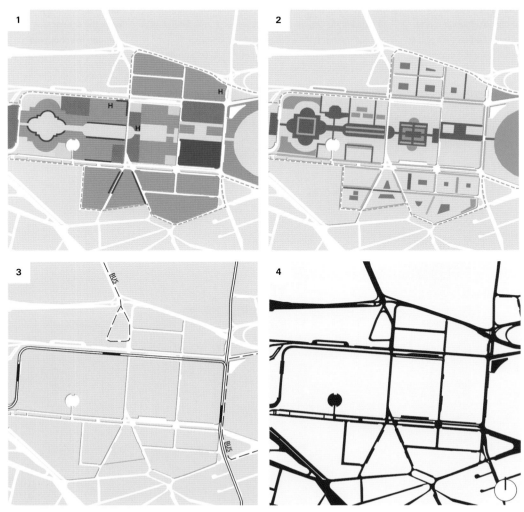

Analysis diagrams

and amenities such as the Médiathèque (by Chemetov & Huidobro) and the Olympic Pool (by Ricardo Bofill). Social rental housing makes up about 25 per cent of the residential area. The remainder of the residential programme was built by private house builders, but many of these units received state support (through low interest rates, resale guarantees, etc) making them accessible to lower-middle-class buyers. It is one of the successes of the scheme that the real-estate values have since been confirmed on the private market, and that Antigone has socially progressed upwards. A downside of the scheme's eccentric architecture is the fairly small number of balconies and terraces, making the apartments less attractive for a certain type of customer. In order to keep the architectural coherence of austere neoclassical facades, the majority of the few private exterior spaces have hence been designed as recessed loggias.

Excluding long-term gains and taxpayer income, the overall operation was not financially profitable for either the SERM or the city. Due to the construction of many public amenities and the subsidised sale price for social housing, the sale of plots could not cover the enormous

acquisition, management and infrastructural costs. The development of Antigone did, however, indirectly pay for the heavy infrastructural works that the city would have had to undertake in order to allow for its eastward extension towards the sea. Such projects include the construction of a tunnel and the dislocation and levelling of the River Lez. As an interesting natural feature, Bofill decided to keep the central part of the river bank prone to flooding, therefore allowing a more intimate and direct relationship with the water than along the more protected zones of the river.

URBAN FORM / CONNECTIVITY

On the scale of the whole city, the monumental axis at the centre of Antigone directly relates to the Esplanade du Peyrou and its aqueduct, built in several stages since the end of the 17th century on the western and opposite border of the old town. Both are approximately one kilometre (two thirds of a mile) long and represent the city's boldest urban gestures that have been imagined as structuring design elements for its planned extension outside the historic nucleus. In terms of regional planning, Antigone can be perceived as a preparation

OPPOSITE: View into Place du Nombre d'Or and its sumptuous neoclassical architecture. The buildings are residential and accommodate restaurant and retail uses in the ground floors.

View from the top of Ricardo Bofill's Echelles de la Ville building (2000) into Place du Nombre d'Or and the monumental axis to the east. The large opening was only created once the connection through the shopping mall had been ensured.

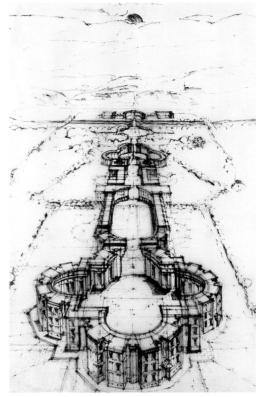

LEFT: View westwards from the replica of the *Victory of Samothrace* into the monumental axis.

Sketch of the monumental axis, drawn by Ricardo Bofill.

for and the first development phase of a far larger zone called Port Marianne. This area, situated to Antigone's south and east, reaches down to the Mediterranean Sea. Initially, the office of Bofill was also working on this scheme, but then withdrew in 1989, when the city realised that such a large area should not be conceived by a single office. Port Marianne has since been subdivided into eight subdistricts, accommodating masterplans and building designs by well-known architects such as Christian de Portzamparc, Jean Nouvel, Claude Vasconi, Architecture Studio and Michel Desvigne. The two designs in this development zone that are usually attributed to Post-Modernism – Antigone itself and Consuls de Mer by Krier & Kohl (see Kirchsteigfeld case study) – are both situated on the western river bank while the projects on the eastern bank follow a different set of urban principles. Consuls de Mer was the first sector of Port Marianne

to be planned and built, and the city chose the masterplanners on the advice of Ricardo Bofill. The district's broad urban principles therefore refer back to Antigone and the Catalan architect's initial work on the whole sector. The connection with this heritage was lost for the newer districts of Port Marianne, partly due to the real-estate crisis of the mid-1990s and the delays that it provoked.

Antigone's own urban principles are simple, relying on the strength of the central axis and its prominent open spaces. The surrounding buildings, essentially organised as single blocks in an orthogonal grid, appear as background buildings with internal courtyards. They provide a calm frame for the spectacular spatial experience at the centre.

As previously mentioned, the opening of a pedestrian connection with the city centre through the Polygone mall was of major importance for the success of the project. The connection was not created until 2000 with the completion of Bofill's Les Echelles de la Ville (the stairs of the city), a commercial building that was directly attached to the blind eastern wall of the mall. The building's major functions are the channelling of pedestrian flows between the historic centre and Antigone, and the compensation of the level difference through a network of exterior staircases and terraces. The legal status of the right of way through the mall was troublesome, and it still has to shut each day after midnight. Previously, the spectacular Place du Nombre d'Or as western limit of the monumental axis was closed off towards the mall and could only be entered through comparatively small gates, for which the inspiration as a monumental but secluded space was taken from Plaça Reial in Barcelona. The current generous opening had to be cut out of the finished building, which had opened as Antigone's first segment in 1983 and consists essentially of social housing above commercial ground floors, with restaurants and retail outlets bringing life to the street.

The area's public transport strategy is based on the construction of a new tram line which was opened in 2000, and features three stops on the Antigone site perimeter before continuing through the different districts of Port Marianne. A second line will open in 2012, linking the city centre with Antigone and neighbourhoods to the north along the River Lez. More than in most other countries, the reintroduction of the tram has been a tremendous marketing success of French urban renewal. Famous examples can be seen in Strasbourg, Nantes, Bordeaux and Nice. As a result of the above-mentioned difficult access of the site, a winding ramp had to be built which links the southwestern edge of Antigone with Saint-Roch Station. Before the opening of the tram line, the ramp was used by a bus service.

ARCHITECTURAL TYPOLOGIES

Antigone can be seen as an example of so-called *architecture urbaine*, the French version of an architectural style that emerged in the late 1970s as a reaction to the failings of the post-war tower-in-park or slab-in-park urbanism. The interesting outcome of this discussion about the principles that dictate the change of our built environment was the concentration on design and open space principles, more than the review of the implementation process. This is an important point in the rationale of this book which, among other considerations, focuses on how the project set-up influences the built result. Unlike more recent examples, Antigone was conceived in a holistic spirit that is similar to earlier post-war developments, including the

notorious *grands ensembles* (see explanation in Masséna Nord case study), in which a single architect is commissioned by a single client to provide the combined services of masterplanning, landscaping and architecture. Bofill's office may not have designed all the buildings, but it did create all the key structures and hence approximately 40 per cent of the whole project. The other participating architects had to follow his strict design guidelines in terms of massing, height, choice of materials, window details and vertical layering. Except for the then unusual insistence on social and functional mix, the planners and designers of Antigone focused more on what to build than on how to plan. This is crucially different from those examples in this book that can be attributed to the movement of New Urbanism (see Kirchsteigfeld and Battery Park City case studies) – often equally likened to the notion of

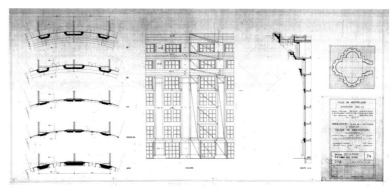

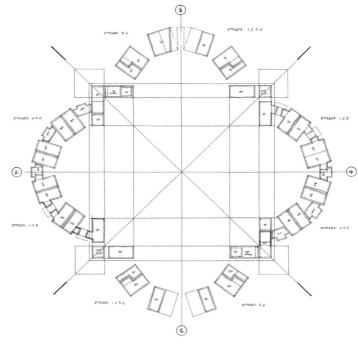

TOP: Facade detail with indication of the prefabricated concrete panels, for the buildings situated on Place du Nombre d'Or.

ABOVE: Diagrammatic plan with apartment subdivision of the buildings situated around Place du Nombre d'Or, designed by Ricardo Bofill's office, Taller de Arquitectura. Most units have two or three bedrooms.

Aerial 1:10,000

Post-Modernism – that tries to restore some past urban qualities through the separation of the architect's and masterplanner's role and the establishment of a small-scale urban fabric.

Despite its neoclassicist architectural language, Bofill's explicitly monumental approach shares many similarities with the heroism of the Modernists, with the difference that Bofill restores precisely defined public squares as the central element of his urbanism. His work expresses the belief that a harmonious society cannot emerge and thrive in the context of the fleeing spaces of Modernism, where freestanding buildings are essentially cut off from their neighbours. These Modernist spaces are typified by Le Corbusier's vision

of the Ville Radieuse or Berlin's Hansaviertel as well as the numerous and far less elaborate housing developments of the post-war era. Despite this radical break with Modernism, some similarities can be perceived in the vision of architecture and urbanism as an object: Bofill's exuberant monumentalism does not ultimately allow any differentiation between these two realms, and presents an entire sector of the city as a single entity. In addition to the spatial experience of the squares as negatives of the built form, Antigone is therefore a huge object on its own, for which the expression 'urban fabric' seems almost inappropriate. As a monument to the people, it is more reminiscent of philosopher Charles Fourier's early-19th-century

Urban plan 1:5,000

utopian and autarkic vision of the phalanstère as a Versailles-style residential community than of the quoted Plaça Reial, where the generosity and strict geometry of the internal square stands in stark contrast to the high density of its cramped urban setting.

CONCLUSION

Bofill's version of Post-Modernism is challenging and at times paradoxical. It is arguably this paradoxical character and the apparently incoherent use of signs, rather than the employment of neoclassical design elements, that establishes him as a Post-Modernist in a literal sense. Similar to the work of other well-known Post-Modern architects like Michael Graves or Robert Venturi, though less based on intellectual games which are difficult to carry from the architectural to the urban scale, Bofill's evocation of the antique world cannot be taken literally, as neither the scheme's urban nor its architectural features have anything in common with the genuine Greek city. Modern in spirit, Bofill believes in progress and in the 'honest' use of the most advanced materials. The building facades are constituted out of prefabricated concrete panels, and are explicitly not meant to appear as stone walls, as the historical analogy could suggest. Bofill's work is unique, and can be considered as the only large-scale example of Post-Modern urbanism. Possible historic references intriguingly not only relate to the Antique, but more

Accommodating a media library, the Echelles de la Ville building's main purpose is the connection of the monumental axis to the city centre through the Polygone mall (1977).

BELOW: The western entrance of the Polygone mall, situated approximately 6 metres (20 feet) above the ground of the Antigone district which is located behind it.

recently also to the 1950s development of Stalinallee (now Karl-Marx-Allee) in former East Berlin, where oversized housing blocks define a fragmentary monumental axis to the honour of a new socialist society and the working man.

While the theoretical discussion of Post-Modernism cannot be the aim of this book, it is nevertheless interesting to compare the traditionalist branch, to which Bofill's work belongs, with the Deconstructivist one, exemplified by projects like Bernard Tschumi's Parc de la Villette and OMA's Euralille (see separate case study). The former branch supposedly expresses doubts on the self-sufficiency of the Enlightenment project and attempts to restore lost meaning through the re-appreciation of traditional values, stylistic symbolism and spatial knowledge. The latter branch, strongly inspired by the Post-Structuralist thinker Jacques Derrida, rejects this option and attempts to materialise the conviction of 'non-sense' and the human impossibility to approach final truth, through – among other features – the abolition of the right angle in architecture, and the invention of a new type of exterior space in urbanism. The interest of Antigone lies in the fact that, as a built artefact, it obviously belongs to the first group, but it nevertheless incorporates through its unorthodox iconography elements of the second group which was born out of Derrida's insistence on the primary role of language as a bearer of (non-)sense. Bofill's fake analogy of the Greek society and its alleged values appears eventually as a deliberate incoherence, and his deconstructed communication cannot be understood on a purely rational basis.

TOP LEFT: Interior courtyard of a residential building. In contrast to the public squares along the monumental axis, these spaces are owned by the development companies.

TOP: Rue de l'Acropole, one of the perpendicular streets on the south side of the major axis.

View south from the Regional Council building towards the Consuls de Mer district, masterplanned by Rob Krier.

View of the River Lez, with the Regional Council of Languedoc-Roussillon (1988) to the right and the crescent of Esplanade de l'Europe (1989) to the left. Both structures were designed by Ricardo Bofill.

Potsdamer Platz (including Leipziger Platz)

LOCATION: MITTE, BERLIN, GERMANY
DATE: 1989–2015
SIZE: 51 HECTARES (126 ACRES)

As Germany's most prestigious construction project after 1989's fall of the Wall, the Potsdamer Platz development had the difficult task of reunifying the two parts of Berlin on an essentially vacant site.

Floor area ratio: **2.16**
Residential population: **4,500**
Mix of uses: manifold (mainly offices with abundant retail, cinemas, restaurants, museum, musical theatre, hotels), **20% residential uses**

The redevelopment of Potsdamer Platz and Leipziger Platz is inextricably linked to the fall of the Berlin Wall and the subsequent German reunification in 1990. However, the involvement of Daimler-Benz, one of Germany's largest companies and the main driver behind the whole project, reaches further back to 1987, when it started discussions with the city of Berlin for the construction of a service centre in close proximity to the Wall. At that time nobody expected its fall, and one of Daimler-Benz's reasons for considering development in this fairly remote location in West Berlin was politically driven, as a symbolic statement of protest against the East. Such a motivation brings to mind the provocative action of publisher Axel Springer who, in 1959, two days prior to the elapse of Moscow's ultimatum to withdraw armed forces from West Berlin and before

the Wall's construction had begun, laid the foundation stone of his headquarters building right next to the border. Once completed, the tower's roof was topped with a giant news ticker oriented towards the east.

For Daimler-Benz, the story would be very different. Beginning in 1989 with the Wall's destruction, Germany experienced a period of turbulence and rapid change. A series of major events, including the government's decision to relocate the capital back from Bonn to Berlin, made it clear that Daimler-Benz's former plans for the site were inadequate. The company, through its service subsidiary Debis AG as official client, found itself involved in Germany's most important and symbolic construction project in decades. The planning conditions for such an ambitious undertaking, meant to physically reunite the two Germanies in the capital's historical centre, were relatively advantageous because large chunks of land on the western side were already owned by the city. After the reunification, the city also inherited the land that had been nationalised by the Eastern communist state. In many cases the previous owners were identified and had to be compensated. Despite this lengthy legal process, the absence of any surrounding urban structure made developing this site less problematic and expensive than expropriation in an intact urban environment would have been.

PROJECT ORGANISATION / TEAM STRUCTURE

In June 1991, the city organised a competition to develop a vision for the site. The 16 invited teams were asked to plan an area that covered 51 hectares (126 acres), including the prominent urban centres of Potsdamer Platz and Leipziger Platz. Worth mentioning

is the fact that the selection comprised only companies which also had comprehensive experience in architectural work, pure planners being apparently not considered to provide the right answers for the site's scale and specific demands. One year earlier, Daimler-Benz had purchased 61,000 square metres (657,000 square feet) of land. Other investors such as Sony, ABB, Roland Berger and Hertie soon purchased similarly sized parcels and joined the project. This left only Leipziger Platz for small-scale development applications. With a thin majority of one vote, the Berlin branch of the Bavarian office Hilmer & Sattler won the competition with a high-density mixed-use scheme inspired by an image of the traditional European city, its closed perimeter blocks and limited building heights. The proposal, however, also included some high-rise buildings as urban icons and expressions of Berlin's re-emerging claim as a world city.

The high-profile project soon became the centre of fierce public debate and many architects, politicians and planners questioned the need to force through a large-scale development at such an unreasonably swift pace. They argued that a piecemeal process of land purchase and individual building development could potentially provide better results. The investors in turn did not question the large-scale approach, but they considered the city's intention to transform the scheme literally and with an advanced degree of detail into a legally binding planning framework as an intrusion into their rights as landowners and risk-taking developers.

According to German planning law, a building permit can only be delivered on the basis of an existing *Bebauungsplan* (zoning plan), developed or at least approved by the city's planning department. In the case

ABOVE LEFT: Aerial view eastwards of Potsdamer Platz and Leipziger Platz in 1969. The Berlin Wall can be perceived as a white line at the top of the image, and the large buildings in the foreground are Hans Scharoun's State Library (1977) and Philharmonic Concert Hall (1963), both part of the Kulturforum.

ABOVE RIGHT: Hilmer & Sattler's winning competition scheme of 1991.

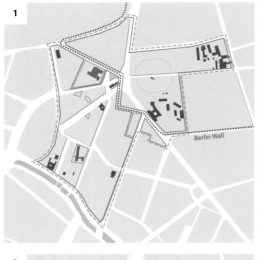

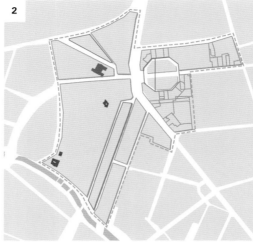

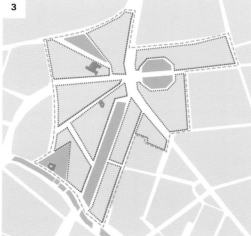

Process diagrams

1 **Situation before intervention.**

2 **Plot distribution after the sale to private developers.**

3 **The city's zoning plan as a result of Hilmer & Sattler's winning masterplan scheme.**

4 **Final state.**

▬	Private ownership
▬	Public ownership
⫶⫶⫶	Building envelope
▬	Green space
—	Private plot ownership
—	Public plot ownership
====	Tracks

of Potsdamer Platz, because of the recent changes in ownership as a result of the reunification, no such plan yet existed. The usual development process of creating a masterplan based on an existing zoning plan was consequently inverted. The city intended to use the ideas of the masterplan competition for the definition of its future *Bebauungsplan*. Anxious to maintain control of the project, the investors commissioned Richard Rogers to develop an alternative scheme even before the official competition entries had been submitted. In a theatrical and provocative act, a detailed model of this counter-proposal was presented to the press, putting considerable pressure on the planning authorities.

URBAN FORM / CONNECTIONS
Eventually, the investors and the city came to an agreement, and the final zoning plan was in several points slightly less prescriptive and more flexible than Hilmer & Sattler's competition scheme. The city also complied with investor demands for more parking space by raising the number of places from 2,500 to 4,000. As a result of these successful negotiations, the investors agreed to withdraw Rogers' counter-proposal and to proceed with the official one in order to respect the ambitious goal of starting construction in 1994. Due to this considerable time pressure, some of the investors and the city planning services worked simultaneously on the design development of the same sites, and the official zoning plan – approved in 1994 – already included elements of Renzo Piano's masterplan for the Debis (Daimler-Benz) estate. Two years before the approval, a jury including representatives of the city and the masterplan-winners Hilmer & Sattler had chosen the Italian starchitect's proposal out of an invited

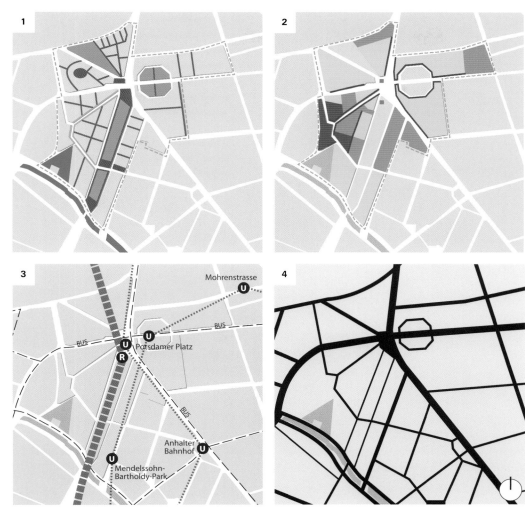

Analysis diagrams

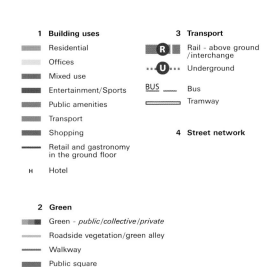

1	**Building uses**
	Residential
	Offices
	Mixed use
	Entertainment/Sports
	Public amenities
	Transport
	Shopping
	Retail and gastronomy in the ground floor
H	Hotel

2	**Green**
	Green - *public/collective/private*
	Roadside vegetation/green alley
	Walkway
	Public square

3	**Transport**
R	Rail - above ground /interchange
U	Underground
BUS	Bus
	Tramway

| 4 | **Street network** |

group of 14 national and international teams. It had been seduced by the multitude of Mediterranean analogies and use of warm materials. In the end, Piano's office not only conceived the masterplan of the Debis estate, but also designed several of the actual buildings together with the five other prizewinners from the 1991 competition. The other investors proceeded in a similar way for their own plots, and the office of Murphy/Jahn was chosen for the planning of the Sony estate while Giorgio Grassi received the commission for the ABB estate. All these designs, developed between 1992 and 1993, should be understood as sub-plans and not counter-proposals of the 1991 masterplan.

Piano showed particular sensibility in his handling of the project's western perimeter which borders Hans Scharoun's State Library (completed 1977), part of the Kulturforum complex and one of Berlin's architectural masterpieces. Piano deliberately extended the

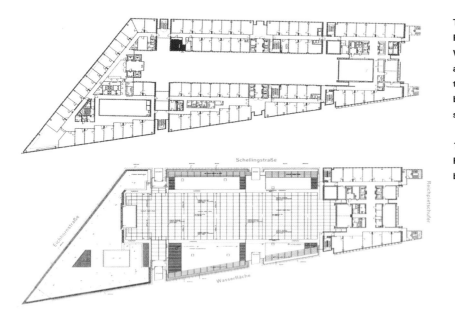

Third-floor plan of Renzo Piano's Debis building. What may at first glance appear from the exterior to be a row of separate buildings, is in reality a single megablock.

13th-level floor plan of Renzo Piano's Debis building.

Renzo Piano's Debis Tower, seen from the southern edge of the site.

competition's official planning perimeter and mirrored the Library's organic shape in the form of his Casino building, effectively resolving one of the site's most problematic features. In terms of traffic organisation, he decided to create a predominantly pedestrianised interior around Marlene Dietrich Platz by constructing a tunnel whose western entrance is partly hidden by an artificial lake. These measures represent a considerable transformation for Potsdamer Platz which, prior to the Second World War, was one of Europe's busiest crossings. A return to its former state would not have been possible, as Scharoun's post-war and post-Wall Library had been built right on Potsdamer Strasse, blocking the historically major connection between the square and its western surroundings.

A major factor in the scheme's final form and in the quality of its green spaces was a law that imposes an ecological impact study on every new development, and demands compensation for potential nuisances through measures taken inside the project's own

perimeter. In the case of Potsdamer Platz, this would have meant the economically dubious creation of over 30 hectares (74 acres) of green areas on a project site of 51 hectares (126 acres). This impressive figure was based on the particularly high ground-sealing level of the high-density development, and the fact that the comparative analysis had to be made in regards to the area's previous essentially vacant state. In addition to influencing the local airflows and microclimate, it was feared that the massive development could have detrimental consequences for the ground water level of the adjacent Tiergarten Park. In the final scheme, after a series of legal and technical studies and battles, 19 hectares (47 acres) of new green spaces were created in and around the site.

Though pressure from investors had increased the parking provision, the still relatively low number of spaces was justified through the connection of Potsdamer Platz Station to the city's highly efficient metro and (underground) city train networks.

Old and new: Hans Scharoun's State Library (1977) to the left, and Renzo Piano's Casino (1999) and Debis headquarters (1997) to the right.

Aerial 1:10,000

Designed by Hilmer & Sattler, the two monumental and Minimalist station entrances – in material, colour and structure reminiscent of Mies van der Rohe's nearby New National Gallery (1962–8) – are regularly praised as the development's secret architectural highlight. Indeed, the extent to which the whole underground development acted as a design driver should not be underestimated: the accommodation of a car tunnel, a high-speed train tunnel, the metro system and extensive underground parking was technically more demanding than the construction of the actual buildings, and the masterplan as such was strongly informed by these conditions, including the reservation of large non-constructible zones in its southern part.

ARCHITECTURAL TYPOLOGIES

The project's considerable size, subdivision into separately planned subdistricts and varied combination of uses inevitably leads to a great mixture of architectural typologies. As in many comparable projects, a certain tension can be felt between the need to accommodate large building programmes and the wish to create a traditionally inspired urban fabric. Except for the northern Lenné Triangle and Leipziger Platz, the scheme is based on an accumulation of super-blocks. While these have kept comparatively modest dimensions and might superficially be reminiscent of Berlin's historic blocks, they lack any cadastral subdivision or party walls and follow, intentionally, a very different internal logic.

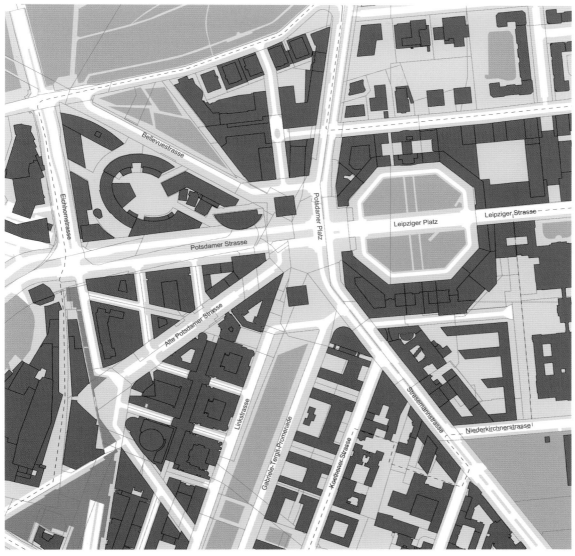

Urban plan 1:5,000

Extreme examples are the Sony Centre (2000), a unique megablock with an open and covered courtyard as a contemporary version of a market square, on the one hand, and the collection of plots around the Potsdamer Platz Arkaden mall (1998) on the other. Conceived as a covered street with several lateral entrances, the existence of this building element was the main reason for Oswald Mathias Ungers' deliberate withdrawal from further involvement in the Potsdamer Platz project. For one of Germany's best-known architects it symbolised the application of an inappropriately Americanised and commercialised development model, and deeply contradicted his ideas of how to rebuild the capital's new unified centre.

The tension between programme and urban form translates also into the architects' choice of facade design. While the majority of them implemented the guidelines of relatively stony and closed surfaces, most rigorously contemplated in the neoclassicism of Giorgio Grassi and Hans Kollhoff, others such as Richard Rogers and Helmut Jahn provocatively discounted the notion of 'critical reconstruction', as propagated by Berlin's planning director Hans Stimmann, and attempted to circumvent them through high-tech elements and a more abundant use of glass and metal. This stylistic discussion went on for many years, and can also be perceived in the nearby reconstruction of the Pariser Platz. Here, the pastiche re-creation of the famous

LEFT: The two buildings of the Beisheim Center (completed 2010) and the entrance to the railway and underground station.

BELOW: Rendered view of Leipziger Platz 12. Due to legal issues and the over-provision of floor space through the earlier developments of Potsdamer Platz, the sale of plots on Leipziger Platz took much longer than initially anticipated by the city.

BOTTOM: Ground-floor plan of the Leipziger Platz 12 building, designed by Architekturbüro Pechtold and NPS Tchoban Voss. Situated on the former site of the prestigious Wertheim department store, this retail, office and apartment complex is the masterplan's last key development, scheduled to open in 2013.

Adlon Hotel (1997) by Patzschke, Klotz & Partner and the Post-Modern design of the new US Embassy (competition won 1995; opened 2008) by Moore Ruble Yudell clash even more vehemently with Frank Gehry's DG Bank (2001; now DZ Bank) and Günter Behnisch's mostly glazed Academy of Arts (2005).

CONCLUSION

The large-scale approach used for this prestigious development stands in stark contradiction to the then state of Berlin's real-estate market. Interestingly, the western part of the perimeter has become the site of a marketing showdown between a handful of corporate heavyweights, especially Daimler-Benz and Sony; while the internationally publicised call for tender of smaller plots on Leipziger Platz did not lead to any financially acceptable offer, even over a time span of several years. The fact that the investors were, in terms of core business, not even real-estate professionals, and that they have actually sold their participations over the last few years, may not be unrelated to this. The marketing opportunities and political statement were potentially as valuable to them as the rather meagre return on their physical investment. The marketing phenomenon was, and still is, an unexpected and important boon for the city of Berlin, which over the last two decades has experienced spectacular growth in tourism. For several years, a visit to the red Info-Box

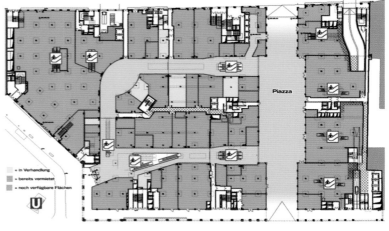

ABOVE: Richard Rogers'
contribution of three
futuristic urban blocks as
part of the Debis estate
(1999).

LEFT: The interior of Renzo
Piano's Potsdamer Platz
Arkaden mall (1998),
designed as a covered
street.

View from the Gabriele-Tergit-Promenade towards the Park Kolonnaden development, masterplanned by Giorgio Grassi.

BELOW LEFT: The Lenné Triangle, with the Tiergarten Park to the left and Helmut Jahn's Sony Centre (2000) to the right.

BELOW: The interior of Helmut Jahn's Sony Centre.

on Leipziger Platz, a temporary display of the area's future changes, was a must for every visitor to the city.

With an average floor area ratio (FAR) of over 5, Potsdamer Platz cannot currently be used as a model for other ongoing developments in the economically still frail German capital. This fact is highlighted by the chronic and continuing problems encountered by Hans Kollhoff's high-rise masterplan for Alexanderplatz. The project is based on ambitious densities comparable to those of Potsdamer Platz, relying even more on a tower typology that German building codes and their high demands for natural light do not make easy to construct cost-effectively. With large development companies until recently reluctant to make investments, planning authorities have begun inventing new development strategies in which private individuals

play an ever-growing role. A high-profile example of this phenomenon is the Townhouse scheme next to Hausvogteiplatz where, barely 300 metres (330 yards) from the elegant Gendarmenmarkt, several former urban blocks have been subdivided into small strips of land. The plots, sold by auction, provide individual families with the opportunity to realise their one-family terraced-house dream according to the rules of a pattern book. These and similar projects suggest that, in a weak market, the residential sector might offer more flexibility than the business sector. While the 20-per-cent residential use at Potsdamer Platz was initially considered too high a proportion by several of the investors, it is these very elements that have now become the financially most successful of the whole scheme.

OPPOSITE: The three main towers of Potsdamer Platz, seen from Leipziger Platz.

Kirchsteigfeld

LOCATION: DREWITZ, POTSDAM, GERMANY
DATE: 1989–97
SIZE: 58.7 HECTARES (145 ACRES)

As the largest housing project in East Germany at the time of the reunification, the Kirchsteigfeld development holds an important and symbolic position. Designed with an explicit respect for traditional urbanism, it is one of the most comprehensive and successful examples of how to work with a mid-density apartment building typology.

Floor area ratio: 0.73
Residential population: 5,000
Mix of uses: 46% residential, 30% business park (to be developed), 22% public amenities, 2% retail and restaurants

After the fall of the Berlin Wall in 1989, the city of Potsdam, capital of the federal state of Brandenburg, calculated a need for over 10,000 new housing units. Even before the reunification of Germany, Kirchsteigfeld in the southeastern subdistrict of Drewitz had been envisaged as an appropriate site for housing, and was initially meant to be used for the second phase of the *Plattenbausiedlung* that abuts it to the north. The word *Plattenbau*, literally meaning 'panel building', describes the most frequently applied housing typology in East Germany, based on multistorey slab blocks that were assembled with a system of prefabricated panels. On a national level, as a consequence of the ideologically grounded neglect of the inner-city cores, these buildings had a higher social status than similar developments in Western countries. They often were the only available option that offered modern living comfort, and therefore housed a wide spectrum of the population. This situation was instantly challenged when reunification allowed the influx of a quick supply of housing design alternatives; thereafter, the extension of the Drewitz 1 *Siedlung* (settlement) with its slab urbanism was hardly considered to be an appropriate symbol for the bright future of a new Germany.

The development company Groth + Graalfs (now Groth Gruppe) from West Berlin quickly understood the opportunity offered by the turmoil, and bought the former agricultural land from about 80 small-scale landowners with the help of the city's pre-emption right. The city itself already owned approximately 10 per cent of the site. At the end of the process, Groth + Graalfs was the sole landlord of a 58.7-hectare (145-acre) estate, and signed a contract in which it agreed to build 2,800 apartment units for approximately 10,000 new inhabitants by 1997. Most importantly, the city pledged in return major subsidies for the construction of affordable and social housing, only 450 units being destined for the private market. The financial means for these subsidies did not originate from the local budget, but were based on a federal law that had been passed after the reunification in order to quickly provide housing and support the construction sector in the economically fragile new *Länder* (states) of former East Germany. In addition to these substantial housing subsidies, which were the crux of the project, the city paid for the public transport connections through a new tram line and committed to the construction of the new district's amenities.

It might be worthwhile to mention that the City of Potsdam holds an exceptional position compared with other East German municipalities after the reunification, and this especially as a state capital of 150,000 inhabitants. This status is not only linked to its important

Aerial view of the Kirchsteigfeld before development. The Drewitz I Siedlung is to the right, and the historic village of Drewitz to the left.

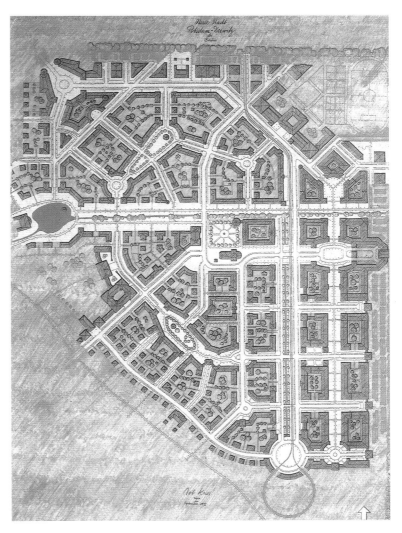

Hand-rendered masterplan of the Kirchsteigfeld. The commercial sector to the east has not yet been implemented.

historic heritage as former seat of the Prussian kings, with the palace and gardens of Sanssouci as just one highlight among many others, but also to the proximity of Berlin as the country's former and new capital. Potsdam can therefore be seen as both an independent place with its own economy, increasingly specialised in sciences, and also, at a distance of only 20 kilometres (12 miles), as a noble suburb of the capital city, comparable to Versailles in France or Richmond in England. The latter situation, however, applies primarily to the wealthy northern parts of the city, the south being relatively underprivileged.

PROJECT ORGANISATION / TEAM STRUCTURE

According to German law, a building permit can only be delivered based on its accordance with a development plan that has been elaborated and adopted by the local authorities (see also Potsdamer Platz case study). Due to the special circumstances of the post-reunification period, notably the urgent need to provide housing and the absence of such a development plan, the usual planning process had to be artificially accelerated. Soon after acquiring the site, the private developer Groth + Graalfs organised a charrette with six invited architects and members of Potsdam's planning services. The idea was to make swift progress, to formulate an urban vision and to avoid a confrontational atmosphere between the interest groups that could have led into a political bottleneck. After three months and several sessions, the office of Rob Krier and Christoph Kohl (KK Architects) was asked to continue with the detailed processing of the urban plan. As initially promised by the developer, all other charrette members were subsequently asked to participate in the architectural design of the plots of the future masterplan.

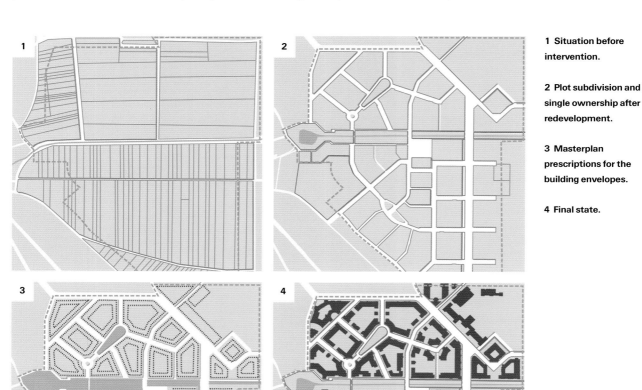

1 Situation before intervention.

2 Plot subdivision and single ownership after redevelopment.

3 Masterplan prescriptions for the building envelopes.

4 Final state.

Private ownership
Public ownership
Building envelope
Green space
Private plot ownership
Public plot ownership
Tracks

Process diagrams

Similar to the Potsdamer Platz case, and as an inversion of the historically intended planning logic, the city's official development plan was based on this privately commissioned study, defining the heights, densities and uses of buildings as well as their approximate position in relation to the streets. As is now common practice, this work was not done internally by the city's planning services, but by a specialised third party – the Freie Planungsgruppe Berlin GmbH (FPB) – that was, like the masterplanners, paid by Groth + Graalfs. The simultaneous processing of the development plan and the masterplan resulted in a closer correlation of these two elements than would usually be the case.

With the client's approval, several other architectural practices were added to the participants of the workshop, each of them receiving for every single building plot a sheet with design guidelines established by the practice of Krier & Kohl. In total, 24 parties participated in this lengthy process, representing a wide range of architectural styles. Of major importance for the project's urban coherence, and crucial to Krier & Kohl's design concept, was the decision to subdivide blocks into plots that were treated by separate practices. The only exceptions to this rule can be observed in two centrally positioned blocks built by the offices of Skidmore, Owings and Merrill (SOM) and Kohn Pedersen Fox (KPF) – two of the world's largest design companies, neither of which is known for small-scale residential work. They convinced the client to allow them to apply their design ideas on a less modest level, more comparable in size to the urban logic of the Potsdamer Platz development.

URBAN FORM / CONNECTIVITY

Krier, deeply attached to the values of traditional urbanism and sometimes (mis)understood as a Post-Modernist, had already acquired international renown through the design of the Rauchstrasse scheme for the 1984–7 IBA (Internationale Bauausstellung) in Berlin. For the same developer, he had masterplanned an area in the Tiergarten Park with nine large apartment villas which were implemented by well-known architects such as Hans Hollein, Giorgio Grassi, Aldo Rossi and Rob Krier himself.

An analysis of Kirchsteigfeld's design development from the earliest sketches of the charrette to the official masterplan reveals major adjustments from an initial fairly dense fabric of arguably medieval inspiration to a much lighter and airier network of relatively wide streets and open courtyards. The previous spatial tension between open squares, and narrow lanes and compact building blocks, has been eased and slightly diluted in order to improve livability. A quick glance at an aerial

BELOW: View of the main square, with Augusto Romano Burelli's Church of Reconciliation (1997) to the left. The building in front was designed by the office of Krier & Kohl. Usually used as a car park, the square can also be transformed into a marketplace.

BOTTOM: View up Clara-Schumann-Strasse, with SOM's residential tower (1997) as focal point. It is attached to a larger residential block to its right and accommodates retail in the ground floor.

The buildings of the Rondell (1995) were all designed by Krier & Kohl in order to emphasise the architectural effect and symmetry.

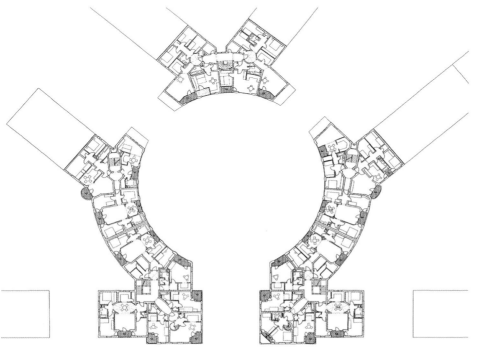

Plans of the buildings around the Rondell, designed by Krier & Kohl.

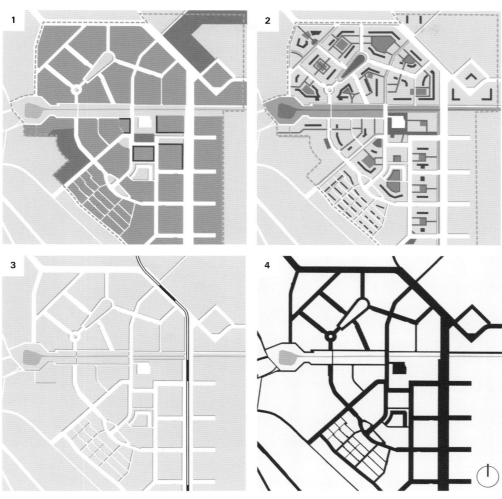

Analysis diagrams

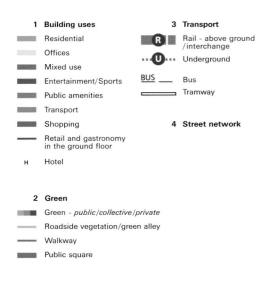

1 Building uses

- Residential
- Offices
- Mixed use
- Entertainment/Sports
- Public amenities
- Transport
- Shopping
- Retail and gastronomy in the ground floor
- H Hotel

2 Green

- Green - *public/collective/private*
- Roadside vegetation/green alley
- Walkway
- Public square

3 Transport

- R Rail - above ground /interchange
- U Underground
- BUS Bus
- Tramway

4 Street network

image and the comparison with the neighbouring historic village or the historic centre of Potsdam makes clear that the physical result of the new district is essentially a new kind of urbanism, a densified version of the modern garden city more than a modification or adaptation of the traditional town. Particularly intriguing is the opportunity to experience the district in two different ways: the urban promenade along the streets, and the almost rural hike which leads through the impeccably landscaped courtyards. Architecturally fairly unusual, but typical for the practice's work, is the introduction of curved elements in an otherwise very geometric and Cartesian ensemble. Looking at the plans it is difficult not to be reminded of the work of Camillo Sitte, author of *City Planning According to Artistic Principles* (1889), who pioneered the method of applying the shape of traditional urban spaces – grown over a long period of time – to the establishment of modern city plans.

Part of the programme for the new district was a rich mix of uses, including not only housing, but also two schools, three kindergartens and retail and commercial activities. Similar to Vauban in Freiburg (see separate case study), the latter were meant to be positioned along the motorway and to act as a buffer between the new town centre and the traffic nuisance of the highway. As the only major modification of the plan, sign also of a still relatively weak economic situation, this area has not yet been developed. Plans to build a dedicated motorway exit for Kirchsteigfeld have recently resuscitated some interest in these activities. Not helpful for the commercial development of the area was the nearby construction of a shopping mall, the Stern Center, that has driven away investment not only from Kirchsteigfeld, but also from Potsdam's city centre.

ARCHITECTURAL TYPOLOGIES

Examining Kirchsteigfeld raises questions about the attractiveness of suburban multi-family housing, particularly for the middle classes and the private sector. It is no secret that this project would never have been initiated without the existence of generous public

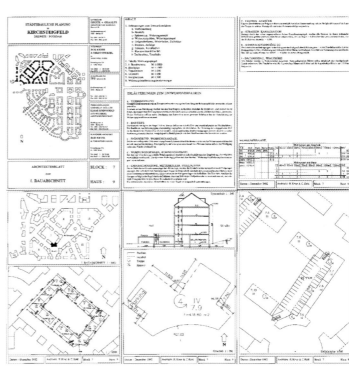

RIGHT: View down the development's main east–west axis, Am Hirtengraben.

OPPOSITE ABOVE: The tram station is positioned in proximity to the town square and its church. The area behind was intended to be developed as a business park, but currently remains empty.

OPPOSITE: Example of a data sheet that the masterplanners provided to the implementing architects. It defines the design guidelines for each sector, block and plot.

Aerial 1:10,000

subsidies. It is hence revealing and somehow disappointing that a piece of the estate, sold by the developer after it failed to generate a profitable scheme before the expiry of these federal subsidies, has eventually been built up with standard family and terraced houses as symbols of the 'real' suburban market. This sudden change of architectural and urban paradigm suggests that, outside a city's central core, only a private house seems to be attractive enough to achieve an economically viable price. This might be the reason why several comparable private projects, especially in the United States and in the Netherlands, have been architecturally themed and more aggressively marketed in order to produce the

additional value that is needed to compensate for the lack of public subsidies. The provision of walkable environments, first-class landscaping and local retail facilities, all of which are viable only through densification in the form of apartment buildings, still does not seem to convince the largest part of the target group. The majority of the market – those who do not have to rely on the cheapest offer, but cannot afford the luxury market – will often prefer a freestanding house, with its modest but private garden. Apartment living may have considerably gained in acceptance during the inner-city revival of the last 25 years, but this only applies to centrally located cases. The single-family house option should not be blindly condemned, but

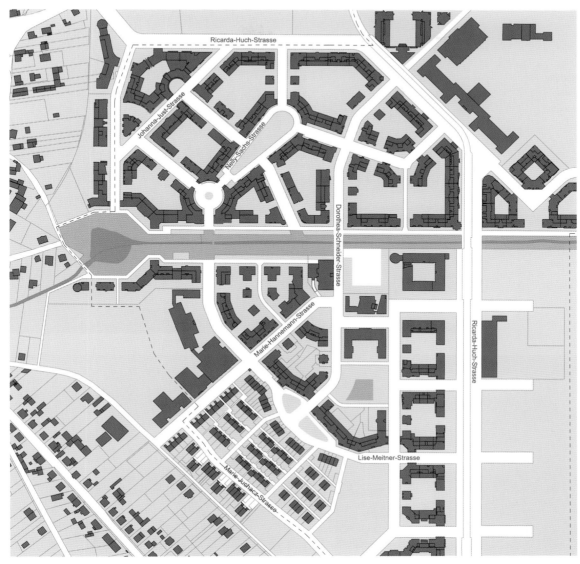

Urban plan 1:5,000

growing ecological concerns and the aim to minimise car dependency have raised the question about the environmental impact of such low densities. The point can be made that one-family suburban housing is indirectly subsidised through the publicly funded construction of the street network that it necessitates.

CONCLUSION

Within the scope of this study, it is somehow ironic to realise that the most comparable project in terms of organisational set-up and funding background is also urbanistically the most contrary: Stuyvesant Town. Both schemes were built by a single private company with the massive help of public subsidies, both promote affordable rental housing, and both are under long-term single ownership; yet the one represents European New Urbanism, while the other exemplifies American tabula-rasa Modernism. This comparison, admittedly diluted through a considerable difference in densities and urban setting, clearly shows that design can be influenced and informed by the development process, but that it cannot be seen as its direct result. In the case of Kirchsteigfeld, there are two major reasons for such a massive shift in planning principles since the early post-war era. The first has simply to do with a different set of urban objectives, rediscovering the well-defined space of the street and the tension between public street and communal courtyard as major constituents of a thriving

RIGHT: One of the largest courtyards in the northwestern part of Kirchsteigfeld. The courtyards are beautifully landscaped and publicly accessible. The residents' car parks have been skilfully integrated in the house design.

BELOW: View from the interior of the same courtyard to the northwest. Several paths connect the surrounding streets, offering an alternative way to cross the area.

LEFT: View into the elevated courtyard of SOM's residential block. It is the area's largest building and, unlike most other blocks, has not been subdivided into separate architectural lots.

ABOVE: Curved surfaces are used to link architectural element and urban form: this building marks the end of a view axis, and can be crossed at ground-floor level.

BELOW: The western fringe between the Kirchsteigfeld and the village of Drewitz.

and attractive urban life. The second refers back to organisational issues, and to the above-mentioned strict separation between masterplanner and architect. It is intriguing to imagine how Stuyvesant Town could have been developed with 24 separate architectural teams, and how this would have challenged and questioned the masterplan's strict uniformity. Often considered together with the contemporaneous Neu-Karow development by Moore Ruble Yudell, in Berlin, as a German example of New Urbanism (see also Battery Park City case study), Kirchsteigfeld and its complex cooperation of numerous architects show how a piecemeal design process can artificially be created in order to aesthetically counterbalance the consequences of a consistently large-scale approach.

Spangen

LOCATION: DELFSHAVEN, ROTTERDAM, THE NETHERLANDS
DATE: 1913–22
SIZE: 64 HECTARES (158 ACRES)

Primarily known for architect Michiel Brinkman's Justus van Effen Complex and its galleries, the Spangen district is also an intriguing piece of urban design. Conceived as one of the Netherlands' first social housing developments, it witnesses the tension that persists between a large-scale programme and a traditionally inspired urban form.

Floor area ratio: 0.86
Residential population: 9,800
Mix of uses: predominantly residential, with a football stadium, some retail and schools

Like many other cities in the Netherlands, Rotterdam experienced a demographic explosion at the end of the 19th century, the population growing from 90,000 to over 320,000 between 1850 and 1900. A severe housing shortage had been identified as early as the 1840s, when a cholera epidemic brought to light the harsh reality of the conditions in which many people were living; but the country's developer-friendly laissez-faire attitude limited the emergence of appropriate solutions, and it was not until the turn of the century that the municipalities and government

were finally ready to act. As shown in the example of De Pijp in Amsterdam (see Sarphatipark case study), it had been hoped that the private sector alone would be able to provide the right answers, but this turned out not to be the case. In De Pijp and many other districts, dwellings were eventually let by the room – including the basements – resulting in gross overcrowding. Back-to-back housing without cross-ventilation was common, and tenements were frequently constructed in formerly empty block interiors. Housing associations, like the Benevolent Society, had existed in the

Netherlands since 1818, but their impact on the market remained negligible for at least another 50 years.

An official and scientific investigation into the problem was finally commissioned in 1887, and reports prescribing crucial improvements followed in 1894 and 1896. Among other measures, they recommended the lending of money to building associations at low interest rates, the provision of cheap land, the establishment of general building ordinances and the use of eminent domain for slum clearance. Just like the early housing associations, these proposals were strongly inspired by English models and by Britain's Housing of the Working Classes Act of 1890. The Dutch Housing Act was finally accepted in 1901 and received approval from the Crown in 1902. It included not only building regulations regarding sanitation, fire safety and sewerage, but also encouraged the foundation of building associations and cooperatives in order to increase the number of potential agents of production. These associations could then apply through the municipalities for advantageous state mortgages, and were thus able to offer more comfort at a lower price than the private market could provide. Despite the increasing initiative and pressure being exerted on the national level, it is important to understand that the final decisions for new regulations and policies still remained with the municipalities. In Rotterdam, for example, despite the national guidelines, protests from influential developers delayed the prohibition of the construction of alcoves until as late as 1937.

Another crucial component of the Housing Act related to city planning, requiring all municipalities above 10,000 inhabitants, or those with a growth rate of more than 20 per cent over the last five years, to draw up expansion plans which had to be updated every 10 years. These, unlike for example Jacobus van Niftrik's 1866 proposal for Amsterdam (see Sarphatipark case study), had to be comprehensive and cover the municipalities' entire territory. This latter point is particularly notable in the history of city planning as it marks the point at which the Netherlands became one of the leaders in the field. While the Netherlands were rather late to the game in terms of building regulations and social housing, they were in advance of many of their neighbours in terms of regional planning, even though the Housing Act was not immediately put into action and most interventions in the above-mentioned sectors had to wait for the end of the First World War.

PROJECT ORGANISATION / TEAM STRUCTURE

Five locations were proposed for the construction of Rotterdam's first public housing project, Spangen.

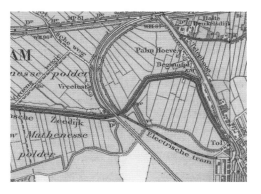

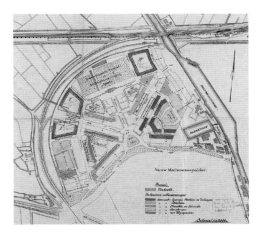

LEFT: Historic map of the area in 1901.

BELOW: Pieter Verhagen's masterplan of 1915.

BOTTOM: Plan of 1918, showing the distribution of lots to different architectural firms.

The final site was chosen by the department of public works for very pragmatic reasons: it already belonged to the city, and hence did not require additional time and money for wasteful expropriation procedures. It is situated in the district of Delfshaven which was the port of the city of Delft until 1811, when it became an independent municipality. It was not until 1886 that it was incorporated by the city of Rotterdam. Except for its relative proximity to the port, Rotterdam's major employer, the site was not considered to be well located. Featuring no constructions at all in its direct vicinity, the area was not even connected to the city's core, east of the canal, until 1924: before the construction of a bridge, the first inhabitants of Spangen had to take a ferry to cross the water. Spangen's nickname 'de Put' (the pit) can be attributed to the polder nature of the site: it is below sea level and surrounded by dykes. One of these, built in the first years of the 20th century, carries a train line which connects the regional railway network with the port. Its curved shape eventually became the project's main geometric driver. When the city decided to build the new housing district, it chose not to raise the ground before construction, as would usually be the case when former agricultural estates were transformed into buildable land. This decision not only saved money, but also considerably sped up the construction timetable. Despite the need to constantly pump out water, the low

ground, however, also meant that the new district displayed its underprivileged social status even more openly, like a sunken rather than elevated fortress. In this context it is worthwhile mentioning that Spangen was not built for the very poor, but rather for lower civil servants and qualified workers.

The young architect Pieter Verhagen, employed as an urban designer by the director of the department of public works, Abraham Cornelius Burgdorffer, had drawn up several proposals for the area since his arrival in office in 1913. These were not the first schemes, as Burgdorffer's predecessor Gerrit de Jongh had already sketched a fairly unspecific block structure for the same site when he worked on the city's first comprehensive extension plan of 1903. Verhagen's final scheme, subdivided into four segments of a circle, should be understood as a framework for further intervention

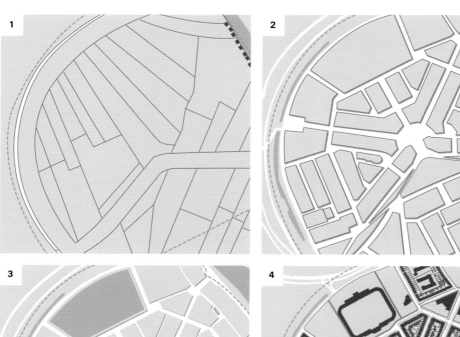
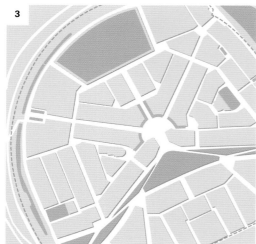
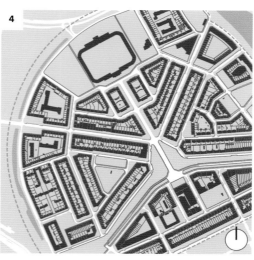

1 Situation before intervention.

2 Plot subdivision and ownership after redevelopment.

3 Masterplan prescriptions for the building envelopes.

4 Final state.

Private ownership
Public ownership
Building envelope
Green space
Private plot ownership
Public plot ownership
Tracks

Process diagrams

by a group of selected architects, including Michiel Brinkman, van Wijngaarden, Meischke & Schmidt, Piet Buskens and the office of Verhagen himself, founded in 1916 together with his partner Marinus Jan Granpré Molière. On these plans, JJP Oud and DB Logemann are listed separately, because they worked directly for the municipal housing department under the director August Plate and not for one of the newly founded independent housing associations. As the municipality's chief architect from 1918 to 1933, Oud holds an especially influential role in the city's architectural history. Verhagen's urban plan prescribed the street network and an approximate building envelope, but still left considerable space for each designer's creativity in terms of interior layout and facade details. In order to avoid burdensome monotony, he subdivided the blocks usually into at least two

segments, each of them attributed to a different architect.

As a matter of fact, Spangen's structure of housing production was slightly more complex than the district's international reputation as one of the first 'social housing schemes' might suggest. Everything had indeed been initiated by the public sector, but the actual building activity was not only given over to housing associations, but also to private investors. The housing associations themselves had an independent not-for-profit status, and only some of them were directly owned by the municipality.

URBAN FORM / CONNECTIVITY
The fact that Spangen is almost exclusively known for Oud's and Brinkman's buildings, rather than for Verhagen's urban plan, is indicative of how little urban

View from the waterfront on the eastern border of Spangen towards the centre.

design is appreciated in the history of Modernism.
Between 1916 and 1950, Verhagen, along with his
partner Granpré Molière and later an additional
collaborator named Kok, designed over 120 plans for
the extension of Dutch villages and cities. His work had
a strong impact on defining the relationship between
the built environment and nature. Due to the country's
high density and the imminent danger of flooding, this
relation is a central preoccupation in the history of the
Netherlands and includes a notion of artifice that many
less dense and less threatened countries have focused
on only recently. 'Untouched nature' is, in the Dutch
context, an almost meaningless concept. Verhagen
was highly influenced by the American philosopher HD
Thoreau, and saw it as his duty to pursue harmony and
continuity between civilisation and nature, rather than
rupture. His projects always started with an analysis
of the landscape, trying to guide development around
and along remarkable topographic features. In the case
of Spangen, it is the Spaanse bend of the train line that
takes this role. In contrast to the Sarphatipark district in
Amsterdam (see separate case study), the cadastral
logic of the drainage channels was overridden. This
crucial fact, a fundamental principle of 'modern
planning', results as much from the large-scale
approach and initiative of public housing as from the
fact that the whole site was already owned by the city.
In contrast to de Jongh's earlier draft of 1903, Verhagen
grounded his scheme through the curved and
concentric design in the memory of the site and its
surroundings. The noble intention of public housing is

TOP LEFT: Untypical for
such projects at that time,
for reasons of money and
time, the ground of
Spangen was not elevated
before the beginning of
construction works.

TOP: The buildings on
Mathenesserweg to the
south of Spangen's
boundaries, slightly taller
and consistently mixed-
use, were not built
according to Pieter
Verhagen's initial plans.

ABOVE: The Sparta
football stadium seen
from the southern corner.
Built in 1916, its eastern
front and main entrance
are covered by a brick
facade in order to fit the
urban ensemble.

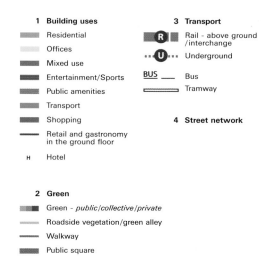

1 Building uses

▬▬ Residential
     Offices
▬▬ Mixed use
▬▬ Entertainment/Sports
▬▬ Public amenities
▬▬ Transport
▬▬ Shopping
▬▬ Retail and gastronomy
     in the ground floor
 H   Hotel

2 Green

▬▬ Green - *public/collective/private*
     Roadside vegetation/green alley
▬▬ Walkway
▬▬ Public square

3 Transport

🅡▬ Rail - above ground
     /interchange
••🅤•• Underground
BUS ▬ Bus
══ Tramway

4 Street network

expressed through the symmetry of the layout and a multitude of viewpoints, both features that were unusual in the context of the Dutch historical city and especially the port city Rotterdam.

The strong influence of Hendrik Petrus Berlage, himself deeply inspired by Camillo Sitte, can be felt through the use of closed building blocks and clearly delimited open spaces. A comparison with Berlage's 1897–1917 plans for Amsterdam Zuid (see *The Urban Housing Handbook*, pp 244–9) makes this analogy clear. Interestingly, the district's amenities are hidden behind residential facades, avoiding the emphasis on any monument other than housing as such. Two schools are hence positioned in the courtyards of the residential blocks co-designed by Oud. If this was at that time common practice based on cost issues, the case of the Sparta football stadium is less obvious, its main entrance mimicking the brick facade of a civic

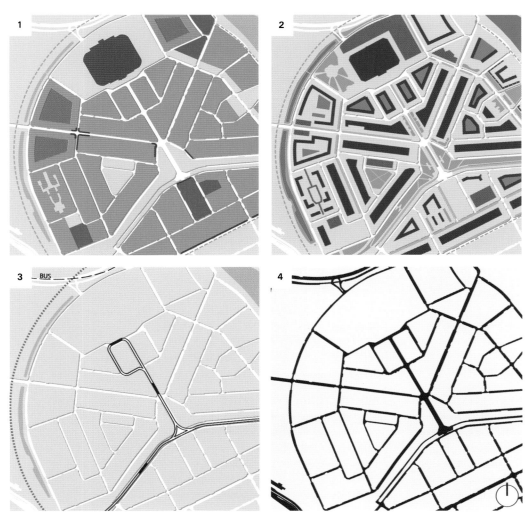

Analysis diagrams

Aerial 1:10,000

building. The latter point suggests that the project's
social importance and dignity was meant to be
expressed through the use of a symbolism that was
based in history, rather than through architectural
avant-gardism. Verhagen's plan for Spangen can
therefore be analysed in the same context as Berlage's
more famous work and the discussions that took place
between 1910 and 1930 around the Amsterdam School
and De Stijl, the former group being frequently criticised
as being too traditionalist by the members of the latter.
Due to its round shape and the existence of a central
space, the scheme is indeed more reminiscent of ideal
Renaissance cities or of Barry Parker and Raymond
Unwin's Hampstead Garden Suburb in north London

(begun 1906) than of the German *Zeilenbau* or the
Bos en Lommer district in Amsterdam (Merkelbach
& Karsten, 1936), one of the first Dutch schemes of
this type.

ARCHITECTURAL TYPOLOGIES
The district's by far most important architectural
masterpiece is Brinkman's Justus van Effen Complex
(1922). A good deal of the project's fame is directly
linked to the aforementioned discussion about
traditionalism, and the fact that Brinkman introduced a
building typology that played in an admirable way with
the notion of the block enclosure. In deciding to build
one large block instead of two or even three narrow

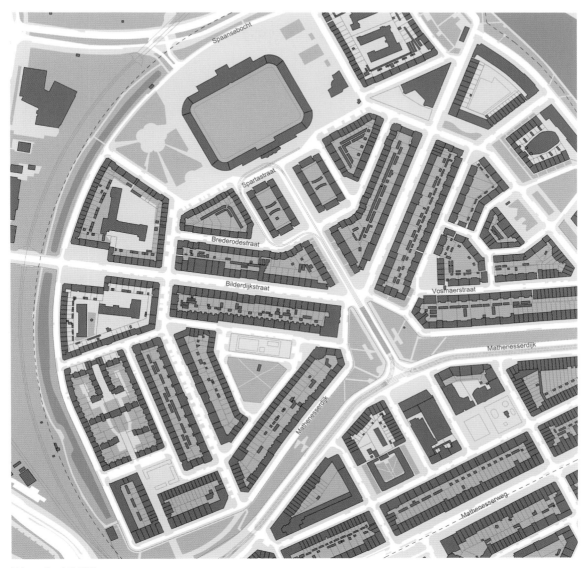

Urban plan 1:5,000

ones, he was able to turn the prevalent spatial logic inside out. The interior revealed itself to the public through several generous openings in the facade. In contrast to Oud's neighbouring square-shaped blocks with their interior schools, slightly cramped and reminiscent of an industrial infill in a 19th-century block, these openings are experienced as a genuine design intention, if not as an exhibitionist statement. For reasons of efficiency the traditional, privately developed blocks – like those in De Pijp (see Sarphatipark case study) – were narrow, and had no communal interior spaces. Just like the blocks created by the repetition of the English terraced house, their cross section was made of two mirrored gardens or backyards that were

attached to the street-fronting terraced houses. Most blocks in the Spangen scheme, as well as those of Berlage's contemporaneous Amsterdam Zuid, followed the same logic, even though the large-scale ownership by housing associations made the subdivision of the block interior theoretically obsolete.

This crucial change in horizontal structure was accompanied by an even more spectacular innovation in the vertical organisation of the scheme. For the four-storey buildings, Brinkman eliminated communal interior staircases by adding an open gallery to the second level of the development. Based on the repetition of building sections, each section hence comprised two entrances on the ground floor – one

leading through a private staircase directly up to the first-floor apartment, the other giving access to the ground-floor apartment – and two entrances on the second floor. The third floor does not feature any entrances as it contains the upper level of the duplex apartments which are accessed through the second-floor gallery. Interestingly, the gallery's primary access occurs through a separate staircase from the street, establishing a certain notion of contradiction and hierarchy with the ground- and first-floor apartments that can only be accessed through the block interior. Situated next to and between the semi-public walkways, the green spaces of this open courtyard are attributed to the ground and first-floor apartments as private gardens, establishing an element of personal responsibility and allegedly encouraging residents through the visual exposure to maintain them.

The scheme's emphasis on galleries recalls J-B Godin's Familistère in Guise (1856), a famous French archetype of philanthropic housing, but does not share its radical introversion. The cut-outs of the building envelope for the gallery are an important and unusual detail in this context: they isolate the longitudinal parts from the corners and therefore emphasise the development's slab character at the expense of the block character. In using them to allow a view from the outside into the gallery, Brinkman creates a sense of porosity and legibility that stands in stark contrast to the 19th-century separation of private and public realms.

CONCLUSION

Seen from today's point of view, Spangen leaves an ambiguous impression. This relates to its social downfall

in the 1960s and 1970s, when it became one of the city's drug-dealing hotspots, as much as to more formal questions of how to combine a large-scale programme and development approach with the creation of a diverse and attractive streetscape. Compared with Berlage's Amsterdam Zuid on the one hand, this project displays a certain heaviness in the assemblage of the newly created superstructures as a result of the massive social housing programme. Compared with the traditional Dutch urban fabric on the other hand, with its juxtaposition of independently erected terraced houses, it leaves a taste of sterility that cannot only be attributed to the often unfortunate renovation measures of the last 20 years. If the successors of Berlage in Amsterdam Zuid partly managed to solve this problem through the exceptional treatment of carefully designed brick facades and the appointment of even more architects to implement the urban plan – hence faking a diversity that could not be a natural consequence of a piecemeal development process – Spangen's marked austerity rather underlines the issue. It appears that this type of urbanism, neither piecemeal collage nor monumental *Gesamtkunstwerk*, is relatively fragile and has from an aesthetic point of view a small margin of success. This suggests that the increasing rupture of urban coherence experienced over the following decades in the form of the tower-in-park and *Zeilenbau* urbanism was as much a programmatic phenomenon as it was a formal one (see also Stuyvesant Town case study).

Spangen hence appears as a farewell to an urbanism that had just been invented, in which the political and social claim collides with a traditional understanding of the city structure, aggravated by an insufficient mix of

ABOVE LEFT: The square at the intersection of Spaansebocht and Bilderdijkstraat was created through symmetrical recesses of the two framing residential blocks, co-designed by JJP Oud.

ABOVE: From the square, an entrance leads to the interior of the block that accommodates a state school.

RIGHT: One of the new developments on the eastern boundary of Spangen, along Nicolaas Beetsstraat.

BELOW: Public green square between Bellamystraat and Betje Wolffstraat.

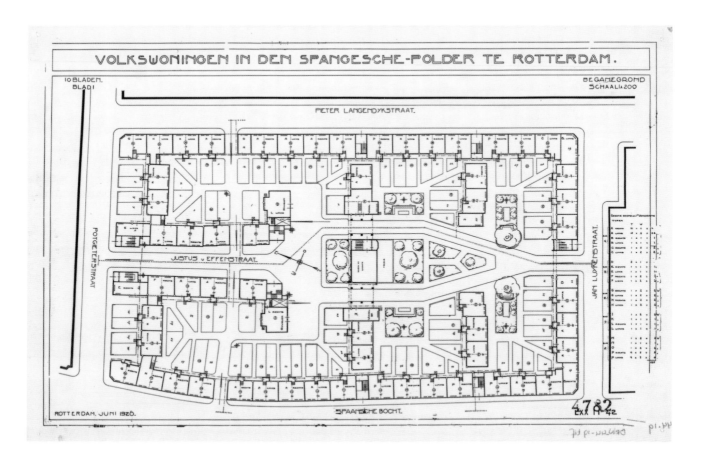

ABOVE: Ground-floor plan of Michiel Brinkman's Justus van Effen Complex.

RIGHT: Historic illustration of Brinkman's Justus van Effen Complex.

uses. In the context of this book, the Kirchsteigfeld in Potsdam and Ricardo Bofill's Antigone (see separate case studies) show alternative housing proposals that address fundamentally the same problem while utilising a 'traditionally inspired' urban fabric. The former project proposes a more radical subdivision strategy, focusing on the issue of design process, and the latter an exuberant neoclassicism as a formal way to provide civic dignity and social order. It should not be forgotten that in all these schemes the academically trained designer – architect and/or urbanist – became the driving force for all formal decisions, something that cannot be said for the pre-20th-century city where most residential structures were developed by craftsmen and builders. As one of the first social housing developments, Spangen's historic importance lies therefore above all in the discovery of mass housing as a noble architectural and urban discipline. In the decades between then and now, the question has been whether these two disciplines should be separated or not, and if the scale of intervention should be the house or the block.

The brick facade of Brinkman's famous Justus van Effen Complex (1922).

Belgravia

LOCATION: WESTMINSTER, LONDON, UNITED KINGDOM
DATE: 1812–50
SIZE: 80.9 HECTARES (200 ACRES)

Probably the purest of London's Great Estates, Belgravia has hardly changed in over 150 years of existence. As a private development that is still in the hands of the family that conceived it, it challenges the rules of time and remains one of the country's premier addresses to this day.

Floor area ratio: 1.32
Residential population: 6,300
Mix of uses: 47% offices, 41% residential, 12% retail and others (these figures exclude the mainly residential freeholds that no longer belong to Grosvenor Estates)

Belgravia is just one of the Duke of Westminster's many London Estates which include the district of Mayfair, parts of Knightsbridge and, until its sale in 1953, the district of Pimlico. These enormous holdings – today still the crown jewels of one of Britain's largest private fortunes – had comparatively little value when they were acquired by the Duke's ancestor Sir Thomas Grosvenor in 1677 through marriage to the 12-year-old heiress Mary Davies. The Manor of Ebury, at that time essentially farmland, was bounded by today's Oxford Street to the north, the Thames to the south, and the

(now dried-up) streams of Westbourne and Tybourne to the west and east. Comprehensive development did not begin until half a century later, with the design of Grosvenor Square in Mayfair and its surroundings. Still under ownership of the same family, Belgravia followed another 80 years later and a first masterplan was drawn up by John Soane's pupil James Wyatt in 1812.

Though especially large and well known – partly due to the existence of the eponymous and directly related development company – the Grosvenor Estate is just one example of a large-scale ownership type, the Great

Estates, which has defined the shape of London and many other British cities. More than the size in itself, it is the continuity of ownership, the prevention of partitioning, and the relative freedom of development initiative, that define the specificity of the London case compared with most other cities of similar importance. A condition for this is the leasehold system, through which a landowner can lease, rather than sell his property, and therefore keep it in ownership of his family for future generations. Often for a length of 99 years, he grants development rights to a so-called lessee or leaseholder, who will build houses according to a masterplan and agreed aesthetic rules, usually within a fixed time frame. After expiry of the lease, not only the grounds, but also the built structures erected upon it return in ownership to the freeholder.

It would however be a simplification to attribute the emergence of the Great Estates and their consequences on the nature of London's fabric solely to the existence of a free- and leasehold system, which, at least in related form, appears in most planning systems around the world. Equally relevant to their development were, on the one hand, the early obsolescence of defence walls, and on the other, the continuity of a strongly stratified socioeconomic order through the avoidance of any major property shift after Henry VIII's Dissolution of the Monasteries in 1536–41. Together these factors explain how large-scale and long-term urban

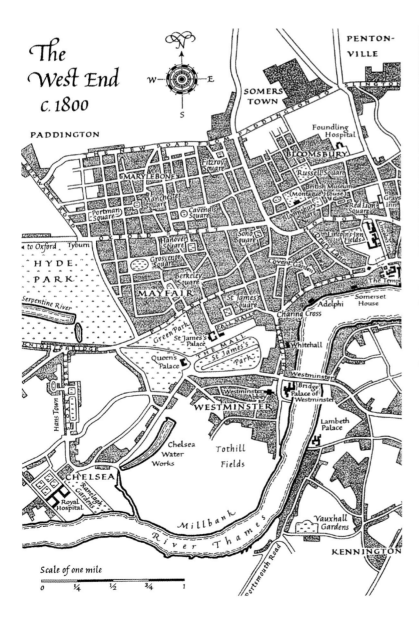

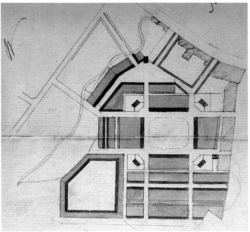

LEFT: Map of 1800 showing London's West End and the Grosvenor Estate. At that time, only Mayfair had been developed, Belgravia and Pimlico still remaining open land.

ABOVE: James Wyatt's plan for Belgravia of 1812. Though not realised, it already featured some principles that were kept in the final scheme, including the layout of Belgrave Square and its detached corner buildings.

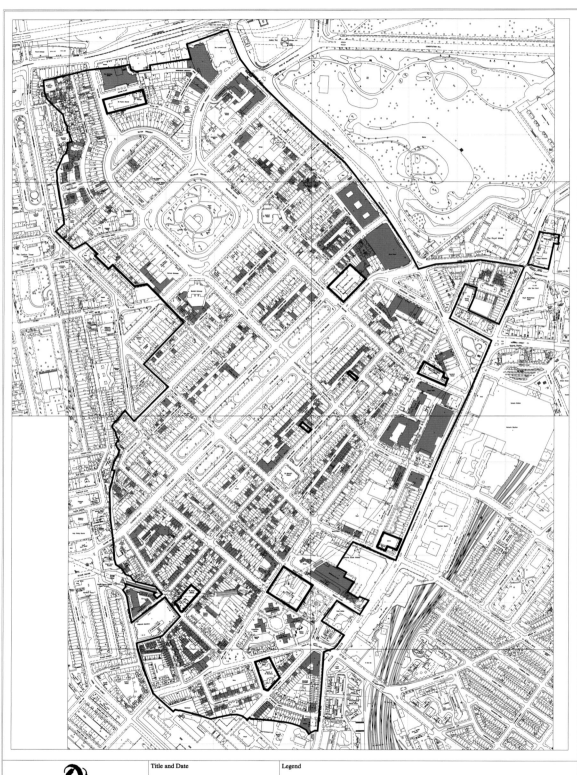

	Title and Date	Legend
GROSVENOR BELGRAVIA	**Properties Rebuilt Since 1945** (March 05)	● PROPERTIES REBUILT SINCE 1945

development could become the major source of income for an aristocratic class that might have invested differently in other parts of the world. The long-term effects of a growth perspective of many generations is interesting in the sense that it is not only a cause for the current situation, but also a result of the fact that real-estate development had been accepted from an early stage as a noble activity for a class that was already well off and therefore not necessarily in need of the quickest possible return. Calculated for just one generation, it would very probably have been more profitable to sell the freeholds and to get rid of the responsibility for such vast holdings.

A quick comparison with Paris makes clear how different the situation was in most countries of the Continent. Not only was the French capital the stage of the 1789 revolution and of the following confiscations and dispossessions, but the growth of its urban fabric had since the Middle Ages been deeply marked by the consecutive construction of town walls, the last of which – the Thiers wall – dated only from the 1840s. Very large estates in central locations were rare, and their development scheme usually included the sale of the plots, rather than a lease. A well-known aristocratic example is the estate around today's Odéon theatre (1780s), and a more recent one the development of the fashionable quarter around Parc Monceau (1860s). As Baron Haussmann's monumental breakthroughs made clear, massive public intervention was necessary in order to assure the cohesion of an old and predominantly small-scale fabric with new development initiatives. While a generous network of avenues was forcibly imposed over Paris's streets, the London case highlights rather the opposite approach. Here, generous dimensions and a holistic design control characterised the privately developed estates, while relative confusion was found on their fringes. Major thoroughfares typically and somewhat uninspiredly follow the line of the medieval or even

Roman roads, as is the case of Oxford Street, the Strand, Edgware Road and Bishopsgate. In view of the capital's vast dimensions, the scattered examples of more comprehensive planning, such as Regent Street, Shaftesbury Avenue, Kingsway and Aldwych, are therefore rather exceptions to the rule of privately developed pockets.

As a consequence of London's residential development logic since the early 17th century, strongly accelerated through 1666's Great Fire in the City's centre, the most fashionable Great Estates can be found to the west of its historic Roman nucleus. Covent Garden and its surroundings, developed by the Earl of Bedford in the 1630s, is the oldest and most central example, proving that the westward dynamic had already begun before the devastating fire. Great Estates still existing today also include, to mention just a few, the Portman, Cadogan, Howard de Walden and Crown Estates.

PROJECT ORGANISATION / TEAM STRUCTURE

In reality, and especially in the case of the larger estates, the leasehold system was slightly more complicated than a simple contract between a single freeholder and one lessee for a length of 99 years. In Belgravia, and later on an even grander scale in Pimlico, Thomas Cubitt – one of English history's most important developers – leased large pieces of land from the Grosvenors. His role varied from one plot to the other, acting sometimes as a builder, and sometimes only as a middleman who would commission third parties to erect houses. Another possibility was the direct sublease or sale, the latter of which was arranged between Cubitt and a consortium of two bankers and the architect George Basevi for the area of Belgrave Square. Once built, the houses themselves were usually for rent, or were at times sold to real-estate investors on the basis of the remaining lease duration. Similar to the contemporary development logic in most parts of the world, the first

View of a block of terraced houses with mews, situated between Eaton Place and Belgrave Square.

OPPOSITE: Map of Belgravia in 2005, highlighting the properties that have been rebuilt since 1945. With the exception of the southwestern corner, the proportion is fairly low.

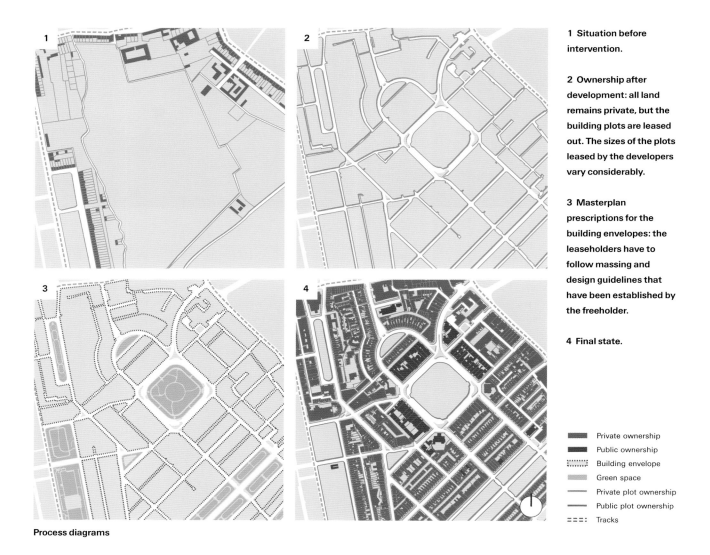

Process diagrams

1 Situation before intervention.

2 Ownership after development: all land remains private, but the building plots are leased out. The sizes of the plots leased by the developers vary considerably.

3 Masterplan prescriptions for the building envelopes: the leaseholders have to follow massing and design guidelines that have been established by the freeholder.

4 Final state.

▬▬▬ Private ownership
▬▬▬ Public ownership
⋮⋮⋮⋮ Building envelope
▬▬▬ Green space
──── Private plot ownership
──── Public plot ownership
==== Tracks

leaseholder therefore did not follow the same long-term approach as the freeholder, and tried to part as early as possible from the construction process. Only in the case of the most valuable plots would a private individual buy the lease for his own use, still obliged to the freeholder's design and use guidelines as attached to the lease agreement. In order to limit the leaseholder's financial risk, which was highest in the first years after signature of the contract when no physical value had yet been created, the freeholder usually accepted the payment of a so-called 'peppercorn rent', afterwards raised to the full extent of the agreed ground rent. It would be a mistake to assume that the 99-year extent of most leases still leads to a cyclical management logic for the whole estate. The signature of individually negotiated lease extensions, and the occasional prolongation in order to help the lessee out of a difficult financial

situation, are measures that have levelled the exchange and renewal rhythm since the early stages of the development.

The advantage of the leasehold system for the freeholder was not only the retention of a long-term interest in the development's success, as stated above, but also the fact that it removed any need for detailed knowledge of the real-estate profession. In the early years, the management style of the Grosvenor Estate seems to have been fairly hands-off, with only one single full-time employee, the 'London Agent', and even the Estate's surveyor and principal lawyer being employed on just a part-time basis. Lease conditions varied considerably, as did the amount of ground rent. In 1845, on the succession of the second Marquess of Westminster, these business policies were considerably modernised. A variety of measures were taken including

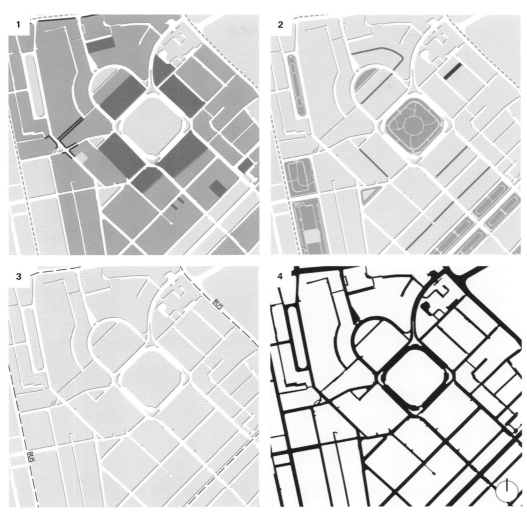

Analysis diagrams

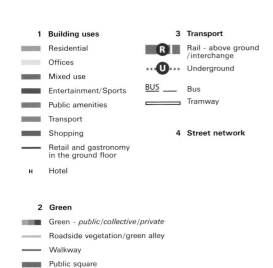

1 Building uses

▬ Residential

▪ Offices

▬ Mixed use

▬ Entertainment/Sports

▬ Public amenities

▬ Transport

▬ Shopping

— Retail and gastronomy
in the ground floor

H Hotel

2 Green

▰ Green - *public/collective/private*

▭ Roadside vegetation/green alley

— Walkway

▬ Public square

3 Transport

▪ⓇR▪ Rail - above ground
/interchange

••Ⓤ••• Underground

<u>BUS</u> ___ Bus

▭ Tramway

4 Street network

the right to void all former contracts that were found to
be imprecise or were lacking in suitable safeguards.
Gradual modernisation occurred not only on the
freeholder's side: Thomas Cubitt has been attributed
with the invention of the developer's profession as
opposed to the at that time common practice
undertaken by small-scale builders. Though personally
competent in many fields, including design, Cubitt
started to separate the profession of the contractor
from that of the developer, architect, agent and investor,
and, in so doing, enabled his company to undertake
ever-larger projects.

URBAN FORM / CONNECTIVITY

James Wyatt's 1812 proposal for the northern part
of Belgravia was eventually significantly modified by
the Estate's internal surveyor, probably under the

**Centrepiece of a terraced-
house development
fronting Belgrave Square.**

influence of Thomas Cubitt and Seth Smith, the major leaseholders. Yet many of the urban principles for Belgrave Square can already be recognised in this early sketch: the square's approximate position and orientation, the decision to underline its highest social status through the construction of freestanding town palaces at its four corners, and the existence of service streets, so-called 'mews', in the middle of the generous urban blocks.

The urban specificity of Belgravia is linked to three major points: its coherence as an almost museum-like example of mid-19th-century planning, the richness of its urban layout, and an unusual sense of architectural and spatial generosity. More than any other of the inner-city estates, it has retained the introverted character of this development style. Of comparatively low density due to the large size of the individual terraced houses and the abundance of open spaces, it still appears as it was planned: a decidedly upper-class and mainly mono-functional suburb in a (now) central location. More than just an accumulation of houses and squares in a grid-like layout, the elegant sequence of spaces like Wilton Crescent, Belgrave Square and Eaton Square reinforces this impression of singularity. It might be argued that it is this quality of an ensemble, rather than the city's building conservation policies, that has provoked the preservation of almost all its built structures until today. The far greater changes experienced in Mayfair – the northern part of the Grosvenor Estate – could be attributed to the fact that

TOP: The green park in the centre of the square was initially only accessible to residents. It is now open to the public.

ABOVE: Late Georgian and early Victorian facades on Eaton Place.

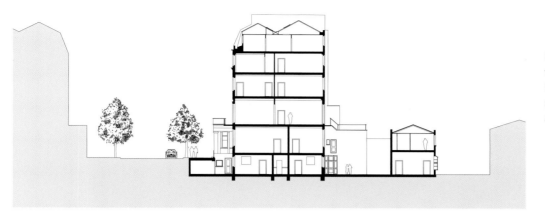

Section of a typical terraced house on Eaton Place. For further plans see *The Urban Housing Handbook*.

LEFT: View from Eaton Square down Lyall Street. Eaton Square is a continuation of King's Road, and connects Sloane Square with Buckingham Palace.

BELOW: Terraced houses on Eaton Square, one of London's most sought-after addresses.

OPPOSITE: View from the interior of one mews into another. Historically built as service roads, they are now mostly used as secondary streets, and the former carriage buildings have been transformed into separate houses or private garages.

Aerial 1:10,000

Mayfair was developed on a simpler model with less homogeneity between urban design and architecture, making new interventions less disruptive there than they would be in Belgravia.

ARCHITECTURAL TYPOLOGIES
The buildings around Belgrave Square, designed by Basevi, are especially impressive examples of a style that John Nash had only recently used for the construction of the Regent's Park terraces. Instead of simply juxtaposing terraced houses along their party walls, Basevi designed the front facade of the whole terrace as if it were a single structure. Emphasising the centre and the angles with theatrical colonnades, the result achieves the desired monumental effect and frames the square in almost perfect symmetry. Historically, the relationship between the houses and the square was much closer than it is today, since only direct residents received the keys to open the square's gates. While this arrangement is still in place at some other estates, for example the Portman Estate on the northern side of Oxford Street, the Grosvenor Estate has opened the interior of its squares for public access. Given the lack of private outdoor spaces for each house and the English aristocrats' ambivalence about urban life, the existence of these communal green spaces was of great importance for the attraction of some of the country's most distinguished citizens, used to the

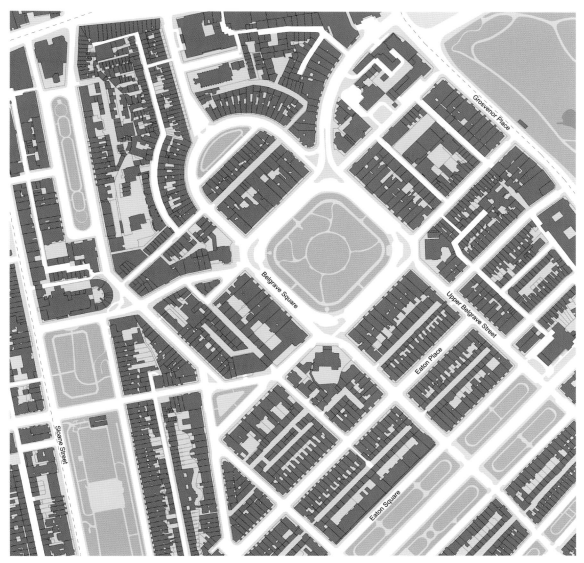

Urban plan 1:5,000

bucolic character of their country estates. The houses as such are slightly larger and taller than the average middle-class terraced house, but the major sign of social distinction is given through the mews buildings which are attached to the back of the property. Today in many cases individual dwellings, they initially housed the carriages and offered additional accommodation for the masters' servants. The resulting hierarchy between 'clean' and service streets is one of the most intriguing features of British urbanism, the one-family counter-model to the European apartment building and its inner courtyards. In the case of Belgravia, the transition between these two networks is particularly successful and solved through magnolia-white arches at the

entrances of the mews. Mostly cul-de-sacs and residential-only, they do not have the same impact as in other parts of London where shops and pubs have inserted life in spaces that were planned as socially underprivileged service zones.

CONCLUSION

In the context of this book, in addition to the singularity of the British leasehold system, Belgravia is relevant from several points of view. First of all, despite its central location, it is the only example to be consistently built up with a single-family typology. Even if a majority of houses have now been converted into stacked apartments, the architectural form as such has not

changed. In several cases wealthy owners have even consolidated the original configuration as a single unit, reattaching the mews building as a garage. While the limited density of such a configuration might be questionable as an all-round inner-city solution, it is still an excellent example of how to attract the upper classes and their buying power into the city's central core. In London, with its wealth and long-established urban history, this might not be such an issue; but in economically less fortunate cities, Berlin included (see Potsdamer Platz case study), or in cities whose centre has recently only been used for offices, as is the case in many American downtowns, such proposals can support and complement an inner-city renewal that primarily relies on medium-density apartment buildings.

A second interesting point addresses the social issue from an urban rather than architectural angle, and deals in the widest sense with the question of gated and segregated communities. It is hence intriguing to realise not only how the strong typological repetition and formal coherence leads to an obvious social homogeneity, but also how simultaneously well-connected and remote a district can be as part of an urban agglomeration. Without any gates, Belgravia still feels like a world of its own: although only minutes away from major thoroughfares like Sloane Street, Buckingham Palace Road or Knightsbridge, it has to be searched for in order to be found. To the south, the green spaces of Eaton Square serve as an effective buffer zone and hence the heavy traffic of King's Road is channelled through, rather than brought into the noble district. Interestingly, though socially the counterpoint of a project like Spangen in Rotterdam (see separate case study), the combination of large-scale landownership and quasi mono-functionality have in this respect produced some similar urban outcomes, meaning the formal coherence and relative remoteness.

ABOVE: The western part of Wilton Crescent, with Thomas Cundy the younger's St Paul's Church (1843) in the background.

OPPOSITE: View of the northern part of Wilton Crescent.

False Creek North

LOCATION: DOWNTOWN VANCOUVER, CANADA
DATE: 1987–2020
SIZE: 83 HECTARES (204 ACRES)
      (67 HECTARES (166 ACRES) FOR THE SUBZONE CONCORD PACIFIC PLACE)

With Vancouver aiming to become the world's greenest city by 2020, the example of False Creek North and its residential towers shows that density plays a major role in this complex equation. Situated 'on the edge of wilderness', the high-rises help – paradoxically, as some might say – to retain a strong relationship to the city's magnificent natural setting even in the midst of intense population growth.

Floor area ratio: 1.65
Residential population: 20,000
Mix of uses: 69% residential, 16% office, 4% retail, 7% mixed-use around stadium, 4% others (including stadium)

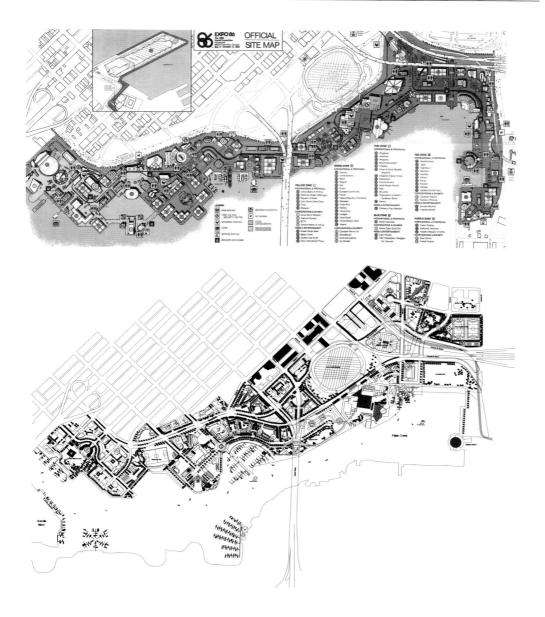

LEFT: Map of the Expo '86 site, held on land that had been acquired by the Province of British Columbia.

BELOW: Masterplan for False Creek North, as illustrated in the city's ODP (Official Development Plan). Most of the area consists of Concord Pacific Place, the northeastern edge being developed separately.

The development of the 67 hectares (166 acres) of the Concord Pacific Place site is an important chapter in the history of the entire False Creek inlet which delimits the southern edge of Vancouver's Downtown Peninsula. Since the city's founding in 1886, its proximity to protected waters predestined the creek's use for port and industrial activities, sawmills being the region's major employers for many years. Beginning in the 1950s, along with Vancouver's development from a railhead and resource-exporting economy to a provincial corporate centre, these activities started to recede and during the 1960s discussions were opened about restructuring the whole zone. In order to facilitate these renewal efforts, a massive land trade between the Canadian Pacific Railway, the City and the Province resulted in almost all of the north creek being in private, and all of the south creek being in public hands. In 1974 an ODP (Official Development Plan) was approved for the southern half of the creek, and the construction of a housing district in the spirit of Christopher Alexander's 'pattern language' started a couple of years later. Granville Island, bearing Vancouver's historic name, was part of this ODP and developed by its landowner, the federal government, into a mixed-use leisure zone and a national park.

For the northern shore, Marathon – the real-estate branch of the Canadian Pacific Railway (CPR) – surprised the city in 1969 with a radical high-rise

Section through the
Aquarius block (2000),
designed by James KM
Cheng.

BELOW: View from the
waterfront promenade
of the towers along
Marinaside Crescent
and the Quayside
Neighbourhood. The
three towers on the left,
including a mid-rise, are
part of the Aquarius block
(see plans).

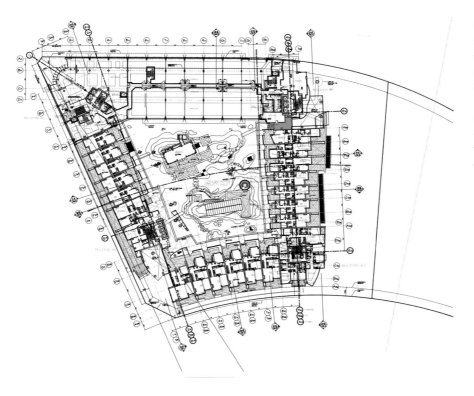

Podium level of the Aquarius block, with townhouses on the block perimeter and an elevated communal garden.

BELOW: Typical floor plan of tower 4a, situated in the southwestern corner of the Aquarius block.

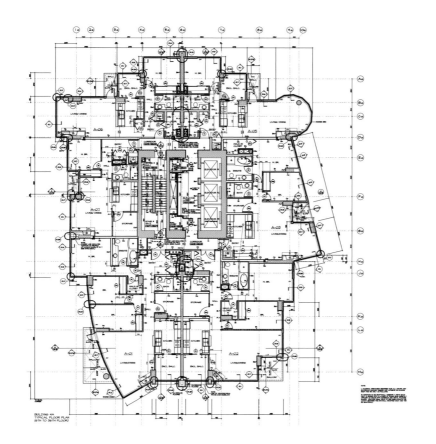

LEFT: The Beach Neighbourhood and George Wainborn Park, designed by PWL Partnership.

BELOW: Panoramic view of Cambie Street Bridge (1985) and the Downtown Peninsula from Mount Pleasant on the south side of the creek. The retention of mountain views influenced the position and height of the towers.

redevelopment scheme of pure CIAM inspiration. Though vehemently rebuffed, it had the virtue of further intensifying discussions about and speeding up development momentum for a zone that obviously would have a major impact on the future of Downtown. In 1974, under Marathon's pressure, 38 hectares (94 acres) of its False Creek holdings were re-zoned by the city for residential development. As the re-zoning prescriptions required a one-third share of non-market housing, the project was not considered profitable and was never implemented.

Beginning in the mid-1970s, ideas were floated for using the area for a major exhibition, eventually resulting in the 1986 World's Fair 'Expo '86', and the entire site was hence acquired by the Province of British Columbia. After several planning setbacks, Marathon was happy to leave the stage. In 1980 the Province founded a dedicated development company, British Columbia Place Ltd, that started to elaborate designs for the exhibition and a new multifunctional stadium (inaugurated in June 1983 under the name BC Place Stadium), the most lucrative development of the whole site.

Acting according to a mixture of political and economic interests, BC Place's plans collided with the city's vision, and led in 1981 to the city's unilateral adoption of 13 planning principles for False Creek North. Even in these early stages the high-rise component – not in the Modernist version of a slab-in-park configuration, but as part of a contemporary and more pragmatic vision of slender point towers – was not unknown to the local planning community and had already been tested in the Downtown Peninsula's West End since the late 1960s. In the aftermath, the area of Granville Slopes, situated between Burrard Street Bridge and Granville Bridge, just west of the BC Place site, was re-zoned, and urban design principles were established that can be considered as the predecessors of the guidelines for Concord Pacific Place: namely the protection of view corridors, the reduction of shadows and the improvement of solar access, the connection of high-rise to the historic street layout, the definition of maximum building heights and the formal idea of slender towers. More importantly, Granville Slopes, and later on City Gate, on the very eastern edge of the False Creek North area, helped to define a collaborative and participatory planning culture for which the city has now become famous. It is referred to as a discretionary zoning system, combining typical European and American planning principles in a three-step planning process. The city's aim is to control and guide private intervention, rather than to intervene itself in building works. This is in marked contrast to projects like Puerto

Madero (see separate case study) or Paris Rive Gauche (see Masséna Nord case study), where the public sector took – usually through the means of a dedicated legal structure – the responsibility and risk of building infrastructures and parks.

PROJECT ORGANISATION / TEAM STRUCTURE

The Chinese-born architect and developer Stanley Kwok played an important role in the further development of this collaborative approach. After emigrating from Hong Kong in the late 1960s, Kwok became a board member of BC Place in 1983. Among other tasks, he led the North Park project east of the stadium in which 28 hectares (69 acres) of former industrial land were successfully re-zoned in 1986 in a process that involved an unusual number of public presentations and hearings. Again, construction was eventually not implemented as planned, due to decontamination issues, but the efficiency of the collaboration between the city, the developer and the public was considered exemplary.

After the conclusion of the well-regarded and image-lifting Expo '86, BC Place decided to sell the site and in the summer of 1987 invited three developers to submit their bids for November of the same year. In a cunning coup, the famous Hong Kong businessman and developer Li Ka-shing and his son Victor hired Stanley Kwok several weeks after his resignation from BC Place, leaving him just enough time to prepare the concept

View from the waterfront promenade into Drake Street and the Roundhouse Neighbourhood.

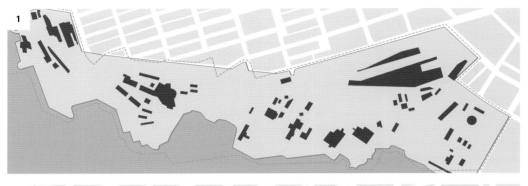

1 Situation before intervention and before Expo '86, when the site was owned by Canadian Pacific Railway.

2 Plot subdivision and ownership after redevelopment through Concord Pacific Place.

3 Masterplan prescriptions for the building envelopes.

4 Final state.

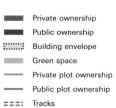

Private ownership
Public ownership
Building envelope
Green space
Private plot ownership
Public plot ownership
Tracks

Process diagrams

design, a mandatory component of the bid. Kwok quickly and secretly set up a small task force assembled from three architectural companies (Rick Hulbert, Downs/Archambault, Davidson & Yuen) and elaborated with this team the so-called Lagoons scheme which would be part of the winning bid. It envisaged the creation of several artificial residential islands in front of the northern shore and Pacific Boulevard. With a sales price of 320 million dollars and only 50 million dollars down payment, it has subsequently been argued that the vast site lost its public ownership for too little money, a claim that was underlined when the decontamination costs of over 60 million dollars were assumed by the government. However, Li Ka-shing's offer for Concord Pacific Place was considered to be the best out of the three submitted, and had – through

the prominence of the purchaser – the positive side effect of further accelerating the massive influx of Hong Kong Chinese capital into Vancouver. Today, as a result of this and earlier emigration waves, over a quarter of Vancouver's population speaks Chinese as the first language. Shortly after the site's purchase, Li Ka-shing had already paid for its initial investment through the re-sale of two sub-sites south and east of BC Place Stadium. During the 1990s and early 2000s the ownership structure changed, and the Hui family, initially only minority stakeholders in Concord Pacific Place, purchased further shares from the Li family and took the listed company private.

The city did not appreciate the Lagoon scheme. Through its exclusiveness and detachment it felt that it contradicted several of the urban principles that

View from the marina towards False Creek South.

1 Building uses

- Residential
- Offices
- Mixed use
- Entertainment/Sports
- Public amenities
- Transport
- Shopping
- Retail and gastronomy in the ground floor
- H Hotel

2 Green

- Green - *public*/*collective*/*private*
- Roadside vegetation/green alley
- Walkway
- Public square

3 Transport

- R Rail - above ground /interchange
- U Underground
- BUS Bus
- Tramway

4 Street network

Analysis diagrams

it had previously defined. The aim was to imagine the development of the site as an extension of Downtown, to provide publicly accessible and pedestrian open spaces, and to offer a socially and functionally rich mix of uses. Over the next several years, interdisciplinary collaboration and over 200 public presentations led to the adoption in 1990 of an ODP for False Creek North that fulfilled all of these demands, including the provision of 20 per cent non-market housing, 1.1 hectares (2.7 acres) of open space per 1,000 inhabitants, and 25 per cent family-sized apartments, featuring at least two bedrooms. During this intense process, the city planning team was led by Ray Spaxman and Johnny Carline until 1989 and later by Larry Beasley. Stanley Kwok represented the interests of Concord Pacific Place until 1993. The design team, assembled from numerous local practices, was paid by the developer alone.

The plans for False Creek North were not disconnected from the rest of the city, and a Central Area Plan (CAP) – developed between 1987 and 1991 – situated the area in its wider context. Against the background of a commercial real-estate crisis, it also grounded the conviction that a predominantly residential use would be the best opportunity to create wealth on such a promising, but difficult site.

URBAN FORM / CONNECTIVITY

It is interesting to note that the prescriptiveness of the early design guidelines was considerably relaxed in the course of the project which comprised the consecutive development of four major subdistricts. This should not be understood as a sign of declining design quality, but rather as a recognition of the efficiency of the public-private process and the fact that overly restrictive design guidelines do not fit the development time frame of such a vast site.

Most important for the successful public conquest of these former industrial and inaccessible holdings was the extension of the city's grid across Pacific Boulevard towards the waterfront. Beach Crescent and Marinaside Crescent are excellent examples that highlight how a meaningful link has been established between Downtown's grid, a new waterfront promenade – reminiscent of Battery Park City (see separate case study) – and a series of generous open spaces. As the Lagoons scheme and its artificial islands show, the 'retention' of the site's shoreline was not an evident feature, and the ODP hence included a chapter that clearly defined the areas in which landcuts or -fills could be undertaken.

Since Expo '86, the site has been connected to the city centre and the eastern part of Vancouver through

A lonely beach along Vancouver's West End with 1960s mid-rise towers in the background. The idea of using height to combine population growth with the retention of natural features has a long tradition in Vancouver.

Aerial 1:10,000

the Expo Line of the SkyTrain, a driverless light rapid transit system. The Millennium Line reinforced these links in 2002, as did the Canada Line in 2009. The latter one marked a considerable improvement, not only serving the more centrally located Yaletown–Roundhouse Station – as opposed to the older and more peripheral Main and Stadium–Chinatown stations – but also offering fast connections to south Vancouver and the airport.

ARCHITECTURAL TYPOLOGIES

In the context of this book, this case study is, next to the 'Haussmannisation' of Paris (see Avenue de l'Opéra case study), the only one to involve planning developments that have coined a term: Vancouverism. Without being an official designation, it can roughly be defined as consisting of mixed-use tower-on-base schemes, sometimes covering a whole city block, that are characterised by the low rise of the base part and the medium height of usually 25- to 35-storey towers. Vancouverism is today a well-marketed export product and has influenced recent developments all around the world, including Roppongi Hills in Tokyo and Dubai Marina (see Downtown Dubai case study).

If the tower-on-base typology is certainly not new (see La Défense Seine Arche case study), the specificity of the local type is its grounding and insertion capacity in a 'traditional' urban fabric, notably Vancouver's block-

Urban plan 1:5,000

defined grid. The combination of vertical and horizontal elements here is not linked to the concept of functional separation – pedestrians on top and cars underneath – as is the case for the Modernist visions of this configuration, but rather is an attempt to achieve density through tall buildings without compromising the quality of the streetscape. In terms of high-rise typology, it therefore marks the opposite of the slab-in-park type which represented a sudden break from a traditional urban logic with streets as clearly designated negatives of the built mass. The aim is not necessarily the production of excessive densities – with approximately 200 inhabitants per hectare (80 per acre), False Creek North's density is comparable to that of Paris – but the

possibility of creating considerable profits and valuable views despite the generous provision of 25 per cent of open spaces, a figure that the average Parisian fabric and its cramped structure of low- to mid-rise buildings cannot provide. In addition to clearly defining the space of the streets and pavements, the building bases adopt commercial uses and/or function as townhouses, a crucial feature that the modern freestanding tower always had issues providing. The interiors of the blocks which are delineated by these fairly narrow building elements are often landscaped, covering the underground parking. In contrast to the development logic of the 'traditional' urban block, the smallest planning and development unit of these constructions

LEFT: Townhouses along the waterfront promenade as part of a tower-on-podium development.

BELOW: View from the promenade into Davie Street.

is usually the whole block and not the single building. In order to respect view corridors towards the sublime natural setting, the positioning of the tall elements is precisely masterplanned and, unlike the typical American downtown, does not work as a generalised extrusion of single-building plots. Some of the site's purest examples of this typology can be found on Marinaside Crescent (see plan and section of the Aquarius block).

CONCLUSION

The development of Concord Pacific Place, and False Creek North in general, is considered to be a great success, for the developer in financial terms, but also for the city that was able to force through the majority of its self-declared urban principles and the provision of major public amenities. Large-scale landownership might be one reason for this success, and personal involvement through gifted communicators like Stanley Kwok, Larry Beasley and Mayor Gordon Campbell another. The development's positive image rests on specific urban qualities that – though partly still to be proven in the long term – are the result of a consistent urban design vision. Goodwill for the project was further enhanced by the fact that its initial circumstances were not that promising: how many professionals would have expected that a high-rise megaproject, privately financed by a foreign billionaire investor, would turn out as an acclaimed example of international practice?

In the context of growing public deficits and voter expectations, False Creek North features very pragmatic reasons for being appreciated. It allowed for the politically accepted urban renewal and residential densification of a key downtown site at a lower public cost than most other examples in this book. Critics might argue that this very convenient truth overshadows the fact that no design competitions were held and that the process – fairly unusually for such a key location – was in the end controlled by a single private entity. It is true that extensive public consultation work with over 25,000 attendees, as exemplary as it might be, does not ultimately alter these facts. It is also true that a piecemeal development process would have offered the opportunity to create more diversity through the involvement of more numerous landlords, but to what public cost and over how long a time span? In the context of this book it is unfortunately impossible to further examine these issues, but the question is raised of how a democratic planning process can be defined, and if it is at all implementable or even desirable. The example of Concord Pacific Place shows just one option, in which the result of collaborative work between the city and the developer's hand-picked design team was openly and extensively discussed with the public. This cannot be claimed for most similar projects in other parts of the world, where the public's influence is essentially nonexistent.

Magnified view from Cambie Street Bridge into Davie Street, with the Aquarius tower to the right, highlighting the fact that the extension of the Downtown grid into the False Creek North development became a driving principle of the masterplan design.

Sarphatipark

LOCATION: DE PIJP, AMSTERDAM, THE NETHERLANDS
DATE: 1865–1900
SIZE: 101.5 HECTARES (251 ACRES)

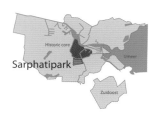

The northern part of De Pijp, situated around Sarphatipark, was the object of several masterplan initiatives for the planned extension of Amsterdam to the south. Beginning in 1870, the area was eventually developed in a piecemeal way through private small-scale initiatives. It exemplifies a development method that – mainly for ownership reasons – is based on the highest common denominator, rather than on a blueprint and on comprehensive public or private control.

Floor area ratio: 1.84
Residential population: 23,850
Mix of uses: 84% residential,
7% retail and restaurants,
4% office, 5% others

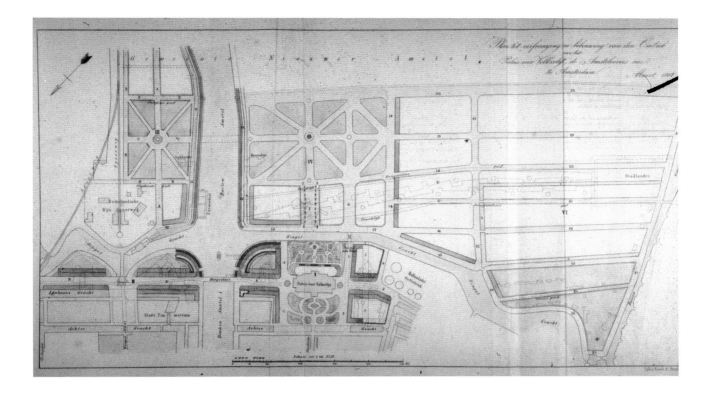

For over two centuries, until approximately 1850, the city of Amsterdam experienced modest population growth. This was largely the consequence of developments in earlier centuries, linked to the Netherlands' seafaring conquests of the 17th century, and a comparatively late industrialisation process. As in many other European cities, the demographic boom of the late 19th century hence exerted considerable pressure on the city's planning services and the city engineer who was in charge of supervising building activity on behalf of the municipal authorities. For financial reasons, the conservative body was reluctant to expand the civil service, and the city engineers were thus allowed to act as private consultants to development corporations, in addition to their public duty. As just another sign of the characteristic mix of public and private interests, many investors and directors of development companies were members of the municipal council.

Amsterdam resumed its process of spatial growth in the 1860s after its fortifications had lost their defensive function in the Napoleonic era. Until then, vacant land on the abandoned ramparts had been used for the construction of plantations, factories, a prison and barracks for the garrison. Land on the outskirts of town, outside the ring canal, was taken by a hotchpotch of roads, drains, ponds, sawmills, factories, country estates, landfills, hovels and small blocks of recently constructed cheap dwellings.

A new era of expansion started with the ambitious plans of Samuel Sarphati, a medical doctor and developer. In 1862, inspired by modern urban planning and the great exhibitions of Paris and London, he proposed an extension plan that covered parts of the former fortification grounds and the city's southern suburbs. Combined with the construction of a 'Palace for the People' and a large hotel along the River Amstel were several residential areas, meant to solve the city's increasingly problematic health conditions. Welcomed by the city fathers, the plan was accepted, and Sarphati founded the Nederlandse Bouwmaatschappij (Dutch Development Company). Since the avant-garde character of the 'Palace for the People' project – inspired by Hyde Park's Crystal Palace of 1853 – skilfully addressed patriotic feelings, early money-raising efforts were extremely successful. However, moneylenders' expectations for the hotel project and the residential scheme were less optimistic. By the time Sarphati died in 1866 he had not managed to build much more than the palace itself (which was destroyed in 1929 by a fire), and a considerably downsized version of the hotel. His development company also built some of the more exclusive houses in today's De Pijp, but resold most of the land that it had previously acquired to individual

Masterplan proposal by Samuel Sarphati of 1862 for the northeastern edge of De Pijp and the 'Palace for the People'.

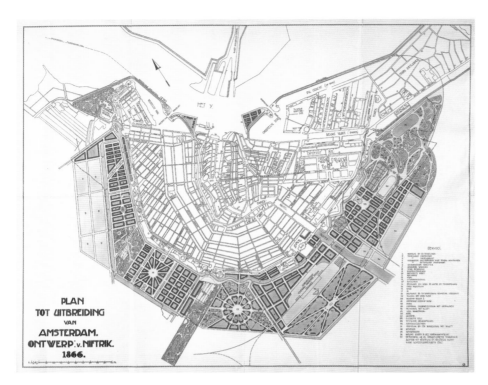

LEFT: Masterplan proposal by Jacobus van Niftrik of 1866.

BELOW: The masterplan by J Kalff of 1875.

ABOVE: Due to their privileged situation, the buildings with a view on Sarphatipark were more elaborate than most other constructions in De Pijp.

FAR LEFT: The steep communal staircase that links the second entrance door with two or three apartments on the upper floors in a building on Sarphatipark's northern border.

LEFT: These buildings on Ferdinand Bolstraat testify to the fact that most of the area has been developed in a small-scale manner.

investors or small-scale developers. It was not able to implement the urban plan that its founder had envisaged.

In 1866 a new attempt was undertaken, and the then city engineer Jacobus van Niftrik presented a comprehensive plan for the whole ring of Amsterdam outside the built core. This proposal, explicitly inspired by the large-scale modernisation works for Vienna, Paris and Brussels, was soon repudiated. This rejection was linked less to the mediocre quality of the plan as such

than to obstinacy in the municipal council, whose newly elected administrators were stern advocates of the free market. They deemed it morally improper and harmful from a budgetary perspective to call on state legislators to use the constitutional right of eminent domain. Only some 30 per cent of the land on and just outside the old fortifications was in the hands of the municipality or corporations controlled by the municipal authorities. Formally, the masterplan's allegedly low development efficiency and the positioning of a new central railway

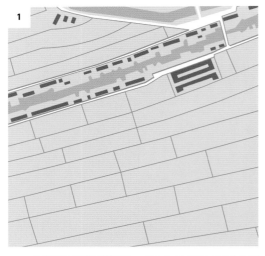

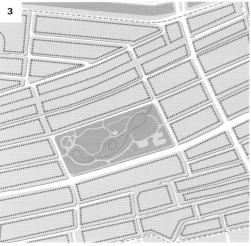

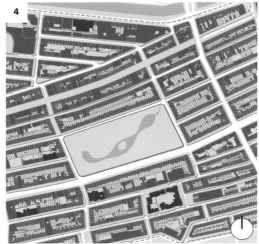

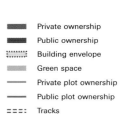

1 Situation before intervention in the mid-19th century.

2 Plot subdivision and small-scale ownership after redevelopment.

3 Kalff's masterplan prescriptions, defining closed perimeter blocks and the position of the new streets.

4 Final state.

▬	Private ownership
▬	Public ownership
▦	Building envelope
▨	Green space
—	Private plot ownership
—	Public plot ownership
≡≡≡	Tracks

Process diagrams

station on the site of today's Sarphatipark were played up as devastating arguments for the proposal's final refusal. The latter point was considered to have a detrimental effect on the evolution of the centre, and the station was finally built in the 1870s on the northern boundary of the centre, in direct relation to the port.

PROJECT ORGANISATION / TEAM STRUCTURE

In order to understand Amsterdam's development logic during the period in question, it is important to note that the city did not need a statutory plan in order to grow. The rejection of van Niftrik's plan as an official document did not mean that development activities stopped. It did not even mean that the plan's content had no impact on what was actually built. The city of Amsterdam exerted its influence and control until the beginning of the 20th century in a fairly liberal way,

and usually signed concessions of private law with developers, instead of elaborating large-scale planning documents. Of crucial importance, however, were the respect of safety regulations and the assurance that the ground, situated below sea level, was well prepared.

The result of this mixture of laissez-faire mentality and strict technical controls was a complex development procedure in which the city was responsible for the delivery of building permits, the construction of roads and sewers and the provision of street lighting, and was hence accustomed to constantly intervening on a small-scale basis. This was done through the services of the city engineers, and explains how van Niftrik – in his role as city engineer rather than that of an aspiring masterplanner – was still able to take an active role in the implementation of the northwestern part of De Pijp, the grid characteristics of the executed work being vaguely reminiscent of his

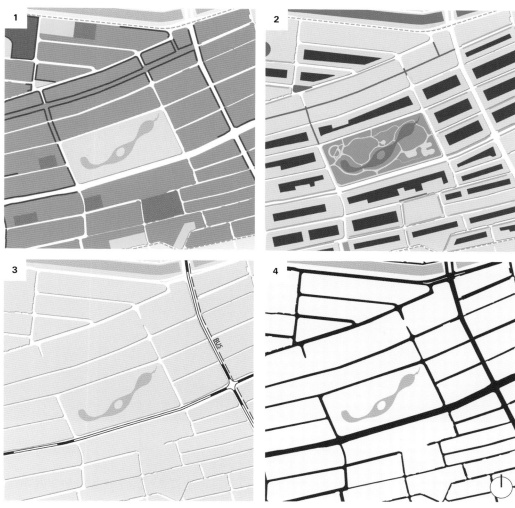

Analysis diagrams

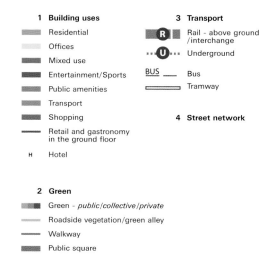

1 Building uses

Residential
Offices
Mixed use
Entertainment/Sports
Public amenities
Transport
Shopping
Retail and gastronomy in the ground floor
H   Hotel

2 Green

Green - *public/collective/private*
Roadside vegetation/green alley
Walkway
Public square

3 Transport

R   Rail - above ground /interchange
U   Underground
BUS   Bus
Tramway

4 Street network

1866 design. A good example of this kind of early and informal development was the quickly expanding Heineken beer business, founded in 1864 with the purchase of an already existing brewery on Stadhouderskade. In an increasingly hopeless residential market, Heineken could no longer wait for the city planners' decisions and started to build houses for his workers. The city had no reason to stop such an initiative and, until the commissioning of the Kalff plan in 1875 (see below), van Niftrik's drawings appeared as the most appropriate basis for discussion. A more detailed comparison of van Niftrik's masterplan and the built reality north of Gerard Douplein shows, however, that the developers insisted on higher densities than he had initially envisaged, and the green block interiors have eventually been compressed to allow for the construction of more streets and therefore more dwellings.

ABOVE: View from Hobbemakade to the western edge of De Pijp.

FAR LEFT: The buildings in one of the calmer streets. Almost all houses have one entrance for the ground-floor apartment, and another one for the staircase that leads to the upper floors.

LEFT: A café in the ground floor of a corner building on Ferdinand Bolstraat.

URBAN FORM / CONNECTIVITY

In 1875 burgomaster and aldermen made a promise to the newly elected municipal council that they would inform them about the guidelines used in the negotiations with aspiring developers. Until then it was through the above-stated hands-off procedure that the city engineer discreetly exerted his official function and professional prestige. The new council felt it appropriate to adopt a more coherent policy framework, and this politically sensitive project was confided to J Kalff, the director of the newly established Public Works Department. He used an assemblage of van Niftrik's alignment schemes and a collection of planned and partly already ongoing development proposals for the compilation of a comprehensive municipal development plan. The draft of this fairly anti-utopian document was intensively discussed by the board and the council committee for public works, and was finally adopted in 1877.

For the southern extension of Amsterdam, with the exception of the aforementioned triangular area that had since 1870 already been developed on the basis of van Niftrik's artificial grid, the plan proposed to follow the geometry of the existing drainage channels which had determined the shape of the city's outskirts since the Middle Ages. In so simplifying the subdivision and ownership question, usually determined by the drains, it deferred for almost 30 years the necessity for the city to develop a new strategy of land control and expropriation. Private investors or small development companies could easily purchase land from the former owners, negotiating with the city the share of the plots to be given over for the construction of the streets. Sometimes, in order to solve tricky situations, the city intervened directly, bought up properties that were incompatible with a local plan, demolished and rebuilt them. In contrast to the Spangen development (see separate case study), the ground of the building plots had to be elevated by up to 80 centimetres (31 inches). This requirement, part of the building regulations, was a health measure against the soil's humidity. In addition, it lowered the potential impact of inundations: if the medieval drainage of former moorland had enabled the ground's use for farming and construction, it had also led to its sagging well below sea level.

Sarphatipark itself as a green infrastructure was the result of the city's negotiations with the developers, and part of its territory had been ceded to the public by Samuel Sarphati's Dutch Development Company before it had to abandon the whole undertaking and sell its holdings to other parties. The relatively important size of Sarphatipark today, compared with its designation in the Kalff plan, shows, however, that the

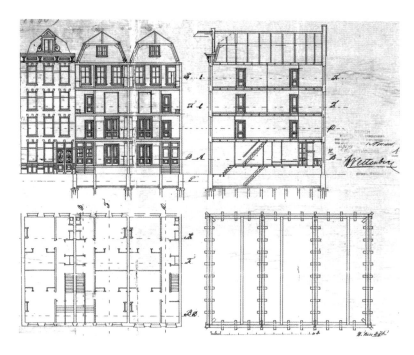

city was able to gather further grounds for its extension, probably as a compensation for the district's overall high density and lack of open spaces. The modest park, while of great importance on the scale of De Pijp, symbolises the district's simple and pragmatic origins compared with the Vondelpark district to its west, developed as a completely private enterprise about 10 years earlier. If the beauty of Vondelpark was a reason for the bourgeoisie to move house, Sarphatipark was just a way to make De Pijp acceptable for the working and middle classes.

ARCHITECTURAL TYPOLOGIES

The comparison of these two almost contemporaneous projects explains indirectly why the city had, in the long term, no other choice but to change its housing policies. The private sector was apparently not able to satisfy the residential needs of the less privileged classes other than through overcrowding. Just like in New York, Paris or London, the privately developed houses in De Pijp – architecturally of more than acceptable quality – contributed to the solution of the housing problem only through the subletting of individual rooms to multiple people, a practice that created hygienic problems and in the end could provoke social unrest. Large-scale public housing and the creation of housing associations, a predominantly Northern European specificity (see again Spangen case study), have been since 1902 the country's answer to the increasingly desperate and politically preoccupying situation.

Plan, section and elevation of a typical building in De Pijp, situated in Jan Steenstraat.

Aerial 1:10,000

Typical for Dutch architecture, and not only for the houses of this specific period, is the avoidance of communal staircases and entrance doors. As a mixture of a one-family terraced house and a small apartment building, the narrow constructions comprise at least two, but mostly four units. One door serves the ground-floor duplex including the lower basement, while the other door serves a communal staircase and the three or four upper floors. In the case of De Pijp, due to its socially relatively modest population, the upper levels are often designed in order to be rented as single-room apartments, and the attic – if not rented as a unit in itself – is reserved for communal uses and storage. Quite often in this district, one building was

commissioned by a single person, a widow for example, who occupied the lower unit with its own entrance and made her living in renting out the upper surfaces in the most dense and profitable way. The outdoor spaces in the block interior were attributed to the lower unit and, like in many English terraced houses, were situated on a lower level than the street. The width of these terraced houses was a function of land prices and building techniques, and usually reflected the 5- to 6-metre (16- to 20-foot) bearing length of wooden beams. Compared with the deep buildings of the 17th-century ring canals, the depth of these houses was, at 12 metres (39 feet), fairly modest, but still allowed for the provision of two

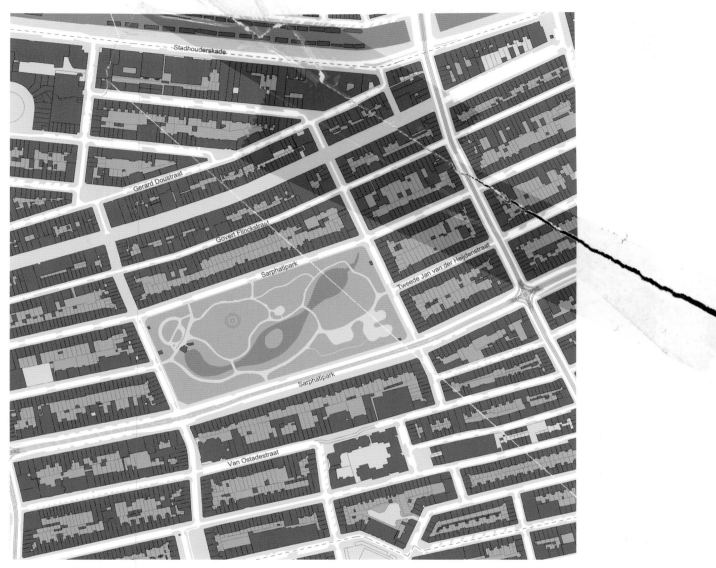

Urban plan 1:5,000

back- and front-oriented spaces including two central sleeping alcoves. The latter feature was hygienically problematic for light and ventilation reasons, and became strongly discouraged in the Dutch Housing Act of 1902. In corner buildings and along the major thoroughfares the ground floors were used for retail, leaving the first floor for the owner's private rooms.

The actual origin of the district's name 'De Pijp' still remains shrouded in mystery, but is probably a popular saying for the house plans' and the building blocks' simplicity, being aligned like narrow pipe boxes. Recently this etymology has been contested, and the word could designate in 17th-century Dutch a long drain opening to a river.

CONCLUSION

If 'masterplanning' is the activity through which the future urban form of a site is fixed and its development controlled by a single entity over a long period of time, then the story of De Pijp is one of failed masterplanning. This becomes especially clear if we compare it with the neighbouring districts of Vondelpark and HP Berlage's 1897–1917 plans for Amsterdam Zuid (see *The Urban Housing Handbook*, pp 244–9). It is exactly this quality that makes the project interesting, and it highlights one of the lowest possible levels of comprehensive planning, if not the counterpoint to projects like Stuyvesant Town, Dubai Downtown or even Antigone (see separate case studies).

This, however, does not mean that it is a rare case, and until the dawn of the 20th century the majority of urban development – as opposed to the then emerging, academic discipline of 'urban planning' – occurred in a similar manner, through private initiative that was more or less informally connected to initiatives undertaken by other parties in the same area. The particularity of this case study goes back to the Netherlands' exceptional topography and the geometry of the drainage channels. The resulting grid, 'organic' rather than strictly orthogonal, has a slightly different shape than developments that followed the lines of former agricultural subdivisions. These latter ones tend to be less repetitive in form, not having the background of the drainage techniques which were by definition a community affair and a question of national safety. In terms of process, both cases follow essentially the same logic as an orthogonal grid development, where clear and simple rules are overlaid on an existing ownership pattern, with Manhattan's Commissioners' Plan of 1811 as a famous and radical example. Kalff's idea was to further facilitate this overlay, and to essentially match existing ownership boundaries with

the position of new circulation spaces. A glance at the actual detailed overlays makes clear that in reality this match was hard to establish – streets being often positioned off the boundaries – and this might answer the question why the system was not applied to greater parts of the city's extension. Interestingly, our study area around Sarphatipark includes on a small surface both development types: the artificial grid around the Heineken Brewery as a remnant of the Niftrik plan on the one hand, and the drainage-channel geometry of the Kalff plan on the other.

In the context of this work, it is tempting to make judgements about the success of the urban form on the basis of the level of sophistication in the masterplan, which was low in the case of De Pijp. However, the uninventiveness of the urban layout does not necessarily imply a low quality of architectural design or even urban design on the intermediate scale of the block; the same Manhattan grid has produced tenement quarters of dubious reputation as much as it has created the Upper East Side with its beautiful apartment towers. Time does not simplify the equation and, just like other working-class districts in New York

ABOVE: Typical streetscape along one of the former drainage channels, with Sarphatipark in the background.

or elsewhere, De Pijp has experienced since the mid-1970s a major gentrification phenomenon, proving that the relative simplicity of the urban layout and architecture represents a desirable quality for an increasing proportion of the population. Such an insight did not come by chance: in the case of Amsterdam, it was the result of fierce political fights calling into question the city's tabula-rasa policy that threatened to tear down the whole district. Seen from this angle, De Pijp represents an imaginary development alternative for the Gashouse District in New York's Lower East Side that was replaced by Stuyvesant Town (see separate case study) as a 'one-client, one-architect' type of development.

Gerard Doustraat marks the boundary between the artificial grid of Jacobus van Niftrik's 1866 plan and the drainage-channel layout of J Kalff's 1875 plan.

BELOW: A street view with superblock in Amsterdam Zuid, masterplanned from the end of the 19th century by Hendrik Petrus Berlage. The change to a large-scale development logic is clearly visible and highlights a fundamental feature of modern housing architecture.

Marunouchi

LOCATION: CHIYODA DISTRICT, TOKYO, JAPAN
DATE: 1988–PRESENT
SIZE: 120 HECTARES (297 ACRES)

One of the most valuable pieces of real estate in the world, Marunouchi represents the fairly rare example of a district undergoing major planned redevelopment without a notable change of ownership. The main reason for this is the existence of a strong private initiative whose origins reach far back in time.

Floor area ratio: 5.63
Residential population: 0
Mix of uses: predominantly offices, hotels and exhibition space, with approximately 2% retail and restaurants

The intriguing history of Marunouchi starts with the sale of a large plot of land by the Japanese state. Earlier in time, the *daimyos* (lords) and other members of the high aristocracy lived in this neighbourhood surrounding Edo Castle, seat of the Shogun as the country's political leader. Inside the protecting (and enclosing) moat, these powerful feudal lords remained under attentive supervision of the Shogun who obliged them to spend every other year with him away from their territories and regional strongholds. After the Meiji Restoration in 1867 and the abolition of the Tokugawa shogunate, this obligatory arrangement became redundant, and under foreign pressure Japan's political structure was forever altered. In 1890, after several years of use as army barracks and parade grounds, it was hence decided to sell the land on the private market. Due to its size and the allegedly high asking price, the offer found little interest. The estate was finally sold to the businessman Yanosuke Iwasaki, brother of the Mitsubishi founder Yataro Iwasaki. By that time, the former Edo Castle had already been the seat of the Emperor for over 20 years, and Marunouchi as its direct eastern neighbour

LEFT: Portrait of Yanosuke Iwasaki, who bought the Marunouchi site in 1890 from the Japanese government. He was the brother of the Mitsubishi founder, Yataro Iwasaki, and the company's second president after his brother's death.

BELOW: Postcard view from the early 1920s of the area called 'London Block', due to its architectural features.

remained an area of highest symbolic esteem. Iwasaki agreed to pay a high price, because he was the only one to have a clear development vision of what was to become one generation later the country's wealthiest business district and until 1991, before its move to Nishi-Shinjuku, also the seat of Tokyo's city hall.

Paradoxically, Marunouchi's early success as the headquarters of a large part of Japan's booming economic power also made it vulnerable: beginning in the late 1970s, it found itself under increasing pressure to modernise its offer. The quickly growing companies on site needed more floor space and expected the latest building technologies to be provided. Such demands were easier to fulfil for newer developments like the high-rise district of Nishi-Shinjuku, built from scratch in the western part of the city on the site of disused waterworks. At least as important as the local competition was the affirmation of the district's status on the world scene, and the need to offer real-estate products that were comparable to Downtown Manhattan, Canary Wharf or La Défense, with international financial institutions rather than manufacturing companies as increasingly powerful tenants. Marunouchi's location in the direct vicinity of the Emperor's palace was in this context revealed to be of ambiguous character, representing the only place in the capital that is subject to aesthetically driven height restrictions. All others are caused by flight corridors.

The challenge therefore lay in organising a radical but piecemeal renewal process that would neither endanger the district's achieved status through inactivity, nor compromise the retention of a coherent urban environment.

PROJECT ORGANISATION / TEAM STRUCTURE

In 1988 the Otemachi–Marunouchi–Yurakucho (OMY) District Redevelopment Project Council was founded as a structure that would defend the interests of the 70 landowners of the 120-hectare (297-acre) site. This happened under the initiative and leadership of Mitsubishi Estate which controls about one third of the area's real estate, making it by far the largest landlord. Indirectly, the name Mitsubishi controls a much larger stake of the site, but this only holds true if the different parts of Japan's formerly largest conglomerate are still considered to be an entity, a fact that at least legally is not accurate. The 'group' therefore owns – in addition to the holdings of Mitsubishi Estate – buildings of Mitsubishi Corporation, Mitsubishi Electric and the Bank of Tokyo-Mitsubishi. Before the Second World War, these companies and many others still belonged to the Iwasaki family, which had started its fortune in shipping. Under pressure from the Allies, due to the family's involvement in the arms business, its overpowering national influence and the company's

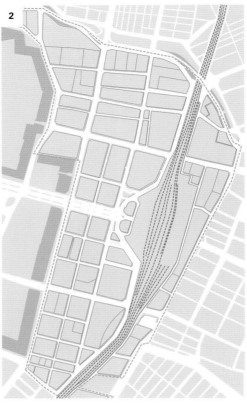

1 Situation before intervention.

2 Plot subdivision and ownership after redevelopment, essentially unchanged.

3 Masterplan prescriptions for the building envelopes. Aside from a slight increase of publicly accessible spaces on the ground, the main change to the building envelopes is in terms of height.

4 Final state.

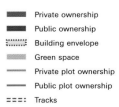

▬▬ Private ownership
▬▬ Public ownership
⋮⋮⋮⋮ Building envelope
▨▨ Green space
── Private plot ownership
── Public plot ownership
≡≡≡ Tracks

Process diagrams

use of slave labourers, the group along with other similar cases was dissipated and the Iwasaki family expropriated. The different branches of the group do, however, still exist, and an estimated number of approximately 500 independent companies today employ over 50,000 workers. Interestingly, despite the members' legal and economic independence, all Mitsubishi companies still officially honour the three principles established by the Conglomerate's last Iwasaki president: corporate social responsibility; integrity and fairness; and international understanding through trade.

The new vision for the redevelopment of Marunouchi has been elaborated by an advisory committee which, in addition to the OMY District Redevelopment Project Council, is comprised of the next-largest landowner, the East Japan Railway Company, together with the Tokyo Metropolitan Government and the Chiyoda District as public bodies. The resulting design guidelines that were developed in conjunction with external consultants and advisors do not have any statutory authority as such. Nevertheless, as a 'gentlemen's agreement', they constitute the basis of Chiyoda District's allocation of building permits.

URBAN FORM / CONNECTIVITY

The most interesting point in terms of urban form is the fact that it has hardly changed since the beginning of the redevelopment works. The general concept is to rebuild and modernise existing structures and to raise the amount of available floor area. Even the site boundaries are historically very clearly defined, and offer an easy reading of Edo Castle's former shape. To the west, the site still borders the interior moat of the Imperial Castle, and to the north, east and south, several large infrastructures have redrawn the curved line of the former outer moat. Due to these very limited modification options and the impossibility to conceive any 'grand design', the project's public-space strategy has gained major importance and become its most remarkable urban feature.

This can most emphatically be observed in the alteration and landscaping works of Naka-Dori, the area's central thoroughfare. Considerable change has been established by the widening of the pavement, and by the attraction of high-end retail and restaurant activities in the surrounding buildings' ground floors. Historically, the street was lifeless, and the ground floors were occupied by office entrances or bank branches. These interventions may appear modest in relation to the district's size and wealth, but they reflect a major shift in the understanding of corporate urbanism. If the development aim was formerly limited to the

quantitative supply of efficient office space, the market today asks for 'more': employees want to be entertained during their lunch break, to do some shopping, and to be part of a special community that surpasses the frame of their company. These demands are obviously not only a question of architectural design or building uses, and the notion of 'soft masterplanning', including the organisation of special events, sport contests and morning lectures, has over time achieved an important position in the project's curriculum. It has eventually helped to rejuvenate Marunouchi's overly conservative reputation. Due to Mitsubishi Estates' strong economic interest in the provision of a promising strategy, essentially the basis for the city administration's concessions in terms of allowable floor area and

View of Hopkins Architects' Shin-Marunouchi Tower (2007) and the red Tokio Marine & Nichido Building (1974, by Kunio Maekawa). The picture is taken from Hibiya-Dori along the moat towards the east.

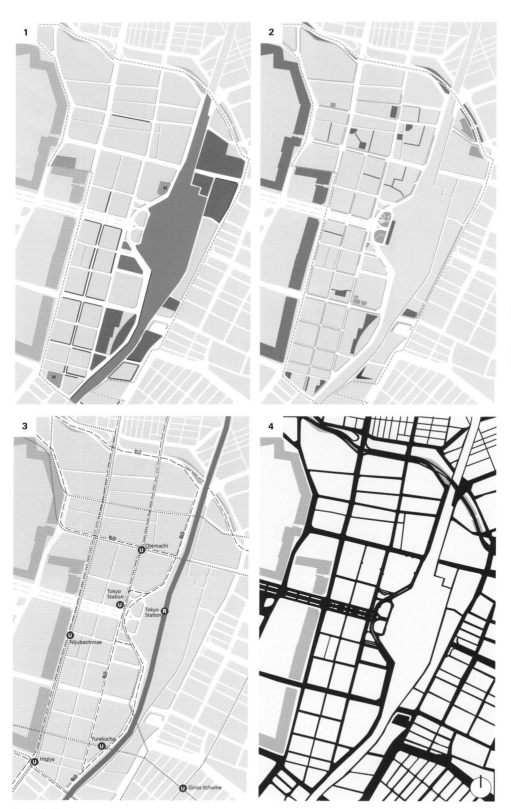

1 Building uses

- Residential
- Offices
- Mixed use
- Entertainment/Sports
- Public amenities
- Transport
- Shopping
- Retail and gastronomy in the ground floor
- H Hotel

2 Green

- Green - *public/collective/private*
- Roadside vegetation/green alley
- Walkway
- Public square

3 Transport

- **R** Rail - above ground /interchange
- **U** Underground
- BUS Bus
- Tramway

4 Street network

Analysis diagrams

View from the square in front of Tokyo Station towards the Industry Club of Japan which has been incorporated in the new development of the Mitsubishi UFJ Trust and Banking Building (2003, by Mitsubishi Jisho Sekkei).

maximum building heights, the majority of these interventions – including their management and planning costs – have been incurred by the developer with a modest participation of the area's other landowners. This can also be explained by the fact that these other landowners are often owner-occupiers who, unlike Mitsubishi Estates, do not consider real estate to be at the core of their business activity.

Marunouchi's statutory floor area ratio (FAR) is, at 1,300 per cent, the highest in Tokyo. For some plots it even surpasses this level, if such an exception is considered to be in the public's interest. This bonus system, distinctive for all of Tokyo and not only Marunouchi, explains the frequent appearance of small public squares on the corner of building plots: the provision of publicly accessible open space on private grounds enables the developer to build more

floor area. It is important to understand that the status of the land remains private, and that a potential redevelopment of the plot could preclude public access. Above 1,000 per cent, at least half of the additional floor area has to be used for activities of public interest, including shops, restaurants, museums or sports grounds.

Transport links are essentially the project's major trump: with several underground stations and the city's central train station, it is probably Tokyo's best-connected area. More as a marketing tool than as a response to real needs, an additional bus shuttle service has been installed in order to avoid the short walk to one of the underground stations. An extensive pedestrian network of underground tunnels offers a choice of alternative routes and the opportunity to reach other buildings and transport connections in a comfortable

ABOVE LEFT: As part of the new masterplan philosophy, the spaces between the at-times intimidating buildings have been carefully landscaped.

ABOVE: Entrance of the Maruzen shopping mall, part of the Marunouchi OAZO development (2004), designed as a joint venture between Mitsubishi Jisho Sekkei and Nikken Sekkei.

Aerial 1:10,000

climate. Featuring retail and restaurants, the tunnels are especially popular during the hot humid summers and cold windy winters.

ARCHITECTURAL TYPOLOGIES

The renewal plan's main architectural and repetitive feature is the tower-on-base typology, which applies to many of the new generation of high-rise buildings. The use of this form here was a response to several factors: the impossibility of considerably raising the height of existing block-buildings without loss of spatial qualities; the desire to maintain a vestige of the area's historic cityscape by showing the massing outline of the former perimeter blocks; and – directly connected

to the former point – the actual construction above preserved historic buildings, the Industry Club of Japan being just one example. Similar to Manhattan's 1916 zoning laws, which led to the famous wedding-cake shape of most pre Second World War high-rises, another obvious reason for this disposition is the aim to avoid an overly intimidating shadow effect on the streetscape and neighbouring buildings.

In terms of plan layout and architectural style, an emphasis on space efficiency rather than originality seems to be a common denominator. For the foreign observer, the calm and sometimes austere elegance is reminiscent of older Japanese car design. Such utilitarian expression is emphasised through the fact

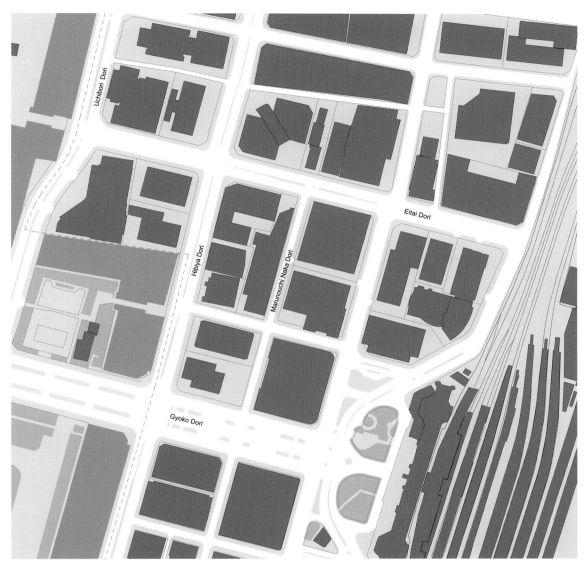

Urban plan 1:5,000

that the corporate architectural market is controlled by a small group of large companies, Nikken Sekkei and Mitsubishi Jisho Sekkei being the area's most prominent performers. The latter is a division of Mitsubishi Estate, and has therefore been responsible for the design of many of the developer's own buildings. The case of Hopkins Architects' Shin-Marunouchi Tower (2007) represents a specific development type, in which international architects are asked to collaborate on key projects for mainly aesthetic reasons, the plan layout being more or less predetermined by national designers. Another architectural highlight of the area is the Tokyo International Forum, built in 1996 by Rafael Viñoly who had won the international competition for its design.

CONCLUSION

The high profile of the scheme and its national importance can also be understood as a burden: Marunouchi is in the uncomfortable situation of having more to lose than to gain. Compared with most other urban interventions of such dimension, Mitsubishi Estate's initiative is proactive and not the result of ongoing decay or dropping real-estate values. This also means that the inclination to take risks, and to distinguish the area through somehow iconic and hazardous interventions, would be of economically dubious motivation. If the renewal of Marunouchi comes indeed with a considerable increase of office space and a stronger emphasis on the financial sector,

FAR LEFT: View down Naka-Dori after complete renewal of the streetscape. The pavements have been widened and the traffic has been minimised.

CENTRE LEFT: Due to the district's high density and the existence of many cross-connections at ground level, the tracks leading to Tokyo Station are not considered to be a major nuisance.

BOTTOM LEFT: View of the area from its southern edge at the main crossing of the fashionable Ginza district.

LEFT: Pavement design on Hibiya-Dori, the area's western edge. The moat and the Imperial Palace's Outer Gardens are situated to the left.

the clients are, generally speaking, already on site. There is no need for overly loud publicity, and so it is not surprising that the area is, unlike other parts of Tokyo, not famous for its architectural attractions.

In terms of land use, and within the scope of this work, Marunouchi, despite its claim to be an ABC (amenity business centre) and no more a CBD (central business district), is most comparable to La Défense

and Broadgate (see separate case studies) as 'competing' schemes of corporate urbanism. As the latter London case has only recently been attained by redevelopment thoughts based on the modification of height restrictions, La Défense and its futuristic podium urbanism remains an obvious counterpoint of similarly critical national importance. Conceived on completely different urban principles, dating from the end of the 1950s rather than the 1890s of Marunouchi, it shares today the same strategy of raising building heights in order to remain competitive. In terms of project set-up, it is difficult to judge whether the Japanese collaboration of 70 lobbying landowners is a more complex or simpler construct than La Défense's national status, spread over three politically separate municipalities. Despite the existence of masterplan documents in the Japanese case, both find themselves today essentially in a logic of piecemeal renewal, rather than ad-hoc redevelopment. Marunouchi can therefore be perceived as an excellent case study of a masterplan's development over time, rather than just a recent example of urban renewal. Over 120 years after the initial sale of land, the area's ownership structure and cadastral logic still has a major impact on the organisational set-up of its evolution.

OPPOSITE: The central part of Naka-Dori has been transformed into a luxury shopping location. Street art is an important element of the area's 'soft masterplanning'.

BELOW: Plan of
Marunouchi's
underground network.
It accommodates many
retail and restaurant uses
and is directly connected
to the city's train and
metro system.

RIGHT: Section of the
Marunouchi tower
opposite Tokyo Central
Station. Designed by
Mitsubishi Jisho Sekkei
and completed in 2002,
it is one of the area's
largest developments
and a typical example
of the tower-on-podium
architecture of the new
masterplan.

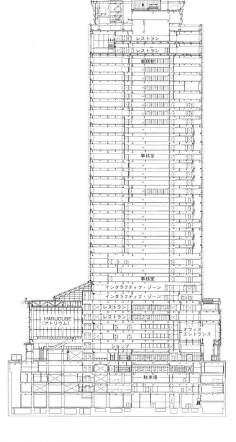

Euralille

LOCATION: LILLE, FRANCE
DATE: 1987–2012
SIZE: 126 HECTARES (311 ACRES)

It would be difficult to find a project that is more closely linked to the topic of transport than Euralille. Its development would have been unimaginable without the decision to make the centre of Lille a major node in a new European network of high-speed trains. Euralille marked the hopes of a city whose reputation, despite major successful structural changes, still suffered from the comparison with a glorious industrial past.

Floor area ratio: 0.82
Residential population: 8,000
**Mix of uses: 43% office,
27% residential, 16% retail
and restaurants, 10% public
amenities, 4% hotels**

In 1981 France and Britain signed an agreement to undergo advanced studies for the construction of a high-speed train link that would connect London and Paris, Europe's largest metropolitan zones, through a tunnel under the Channel. By 1986 these studies had proven technically and financially feasible, and a treaty was signed that transformed an old dream, originating in an 1802 proposal by French engineer Albert Mathieu-Favier, into reality. Pierre Mauroy, Prime Minister under François Mitterrand at the time of the treaty's signature in 1981, immediately sensed a once-in-a-lifetime opportunity to use a portion of the project's expected urban and economic dynamics for the revitalisation of the city of Lille, of which he had been mayor since 1973.

The special importance of the train's stop in northern France was the connection of the London–Paris Channel Tunnel line with the TGV towards Brussels and the Netherlands, making it the network's most strategic and truly European knot. As the precise location of this stop had not been identified with the 1986 signature, Mauroy threw all of his political weight into making sure that it would be built in Lille and not in Amiens, the major competitor. Furthermore, he wanted to secure the stop in the city's centre and not just somewhere in an arbitrary place on the territory of its urban agglomeration. This agglomeration, the political entity of Lille Métropole, third largest of France, comprises the historic textile cities of Lille, Roubaix,

BELOW: Early conceptual sketch for Euralille by OMA.

BOTTOM: The three zones of the current Euralille masterplan.

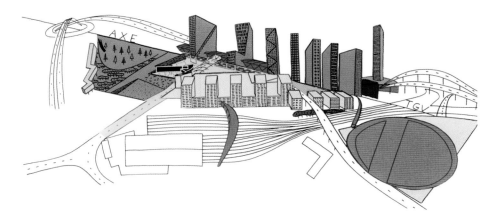

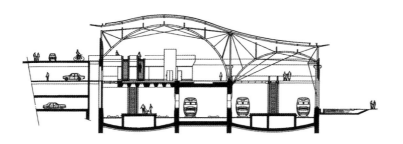

Section through Lille Europe Station. The details of the roof structure were designed in collaboration with Peter Rice from Arup.

LEFT: South entrance of Jean-Marie Duthilleul's Lille Europe Station (1994). The plaza has been sunken to allow a visual connection of the exterior with the underground high-speed trains.

BELOW: View from the interior of the station to the west.

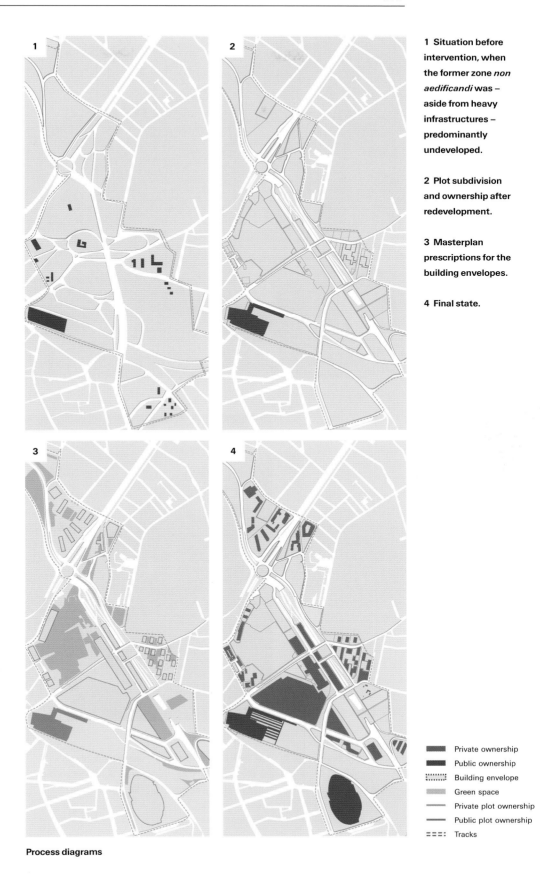

Process diagrams

1 Situation before intervention, when the former zone *non aedificandi* was – aside from heavy infrastructures – predominantly undeveloped.

2 Plot subdivision and ownership after redevelopment.

3 Masterplan prescriptions for the building envelopes.

4 Final state.

- Private ownership
- Public ownership
- Building envelope
- Green space
- Private plot ownership
- Public plot ownership
- Tracks

Tourcoing and 82 surrounding communities. Seen as an urbanised region with existing transport connections and intense economic exchanges, its official population of over 1.1 million inhabitants can be further raised by at least 500,000 people, extending over the directly adjacent border with Belgium. However, calculated on the basis of a 90-minute train ride, Lille suddenly appeared in the centre of an urbanised zone with over 50 million inhabitants, raising it to much more than a provincial city to the north of Paris.

As mayor of the city of Lille and not yet of Lille Métropole – an additional position that he would hold only after the election of 1989 – it was politically not evident for Mauroy to claim that the station should be best positioned in the centre of Lille and not somewhere in between the Métropole's three major conurbations, as previously planned. Technically, placing the station at the heart of the city also produced complications and additional costs that the French national rail company SNCF estimated at 800 million francs. Mauroy therefore set up a private company in order to make his case and to elaborate a feasible financial scenario. His lobbying against positioning such an important new interchange in the hinterland was finally successful and in 1987 the decision was made to build the new station right next to the old terminal – Lille Flandres – on the eastern border of the inner city. This vast fringe zone of approximately 130 hectares (320 acres) was already owned by the city and had remained unbuilt after destruction of the

TOP: View from above the tracks behind Lille Flandres Station of Jean Nouvel's Euralille Shopping Centre (1994) and Claude Vasconi's Tour Lille Europe (1995).

ABOVE: Interior of Jean Nouvel's Euralille Shopping Centre.

Vauban fortification that had encircled all of Lille since 1668 when Flanders became part of France under King Louis XIV. At the time of the project, the former zone *non aedificandi* therefore did not contain much more than train lines and the city's peripheral ring road.

PROJECT ORGANISATION / TEAM STRUCTURE

After signature in 1987 of the agreement to build the station in Lille, the clock started ticking: the station would have to open in 1994 and it had to be accessible by foot and by the local tram and metro networks. Adding to the considerable financial pressure, the city of Lille had to assume 133 million of the above-mentioned surplus of 800 million French francs, as claimed by SNCF. For a short time, it therefore seemed sensible to sell the whole site to a single investor. The city, however, eventually refused the offer from the influential French construction and development company Bouygues who had approached it with a scheme designed by Ricardo Bofill (see also Antigone case study). Euralille-Métropole, the successor of the private company founded by Mauroy, proceeded with the planning on its own, and invited eight teams – four French (Yves Lion, Claude Vasconi, Jean-Paul Viguier, Michel Macary) and four foreigners (OMA, Vittorio Gregotti, Oswald Mathias Ungers, Norman Foster) – to submit proposals. Since the programme had to be developed in parallel with the actual scheme, consisting initially of not much more than the idea to combine the construction of the new station with the development of an international business centre, the teams were asked to present a vision and attitude rather than a physical proposal. Not a single drawing or sketch was accepted, and each of the candidates had to endure a 90-minute discussion with the jury. An uncontested master of conceptual work, the Dutch architect Rem Koolhaas of OMA was unanimously chosen, despite his at that time minimal built experience. His speech raised the issues that the management team had previously been contemplating. He was also the candidate who best understood the potential impact of the high-speed train, intellectually justifying the enormous effort and ambition given to something that others might secretly have considered as provincial megalomania. As just one indicator of the project's complexity, the existing ring road had to be moved and adjusted to the train tunnel's given alignment; otherwise, any meaningful relationship between the station and the city would have been impossible.

As already mentioned, the first two years of work were undertaken by private companies under Mauroy's initiative – first Lille Gare TGV and then Euralille-Métropole – with banks as major risk-taking stakeholders.

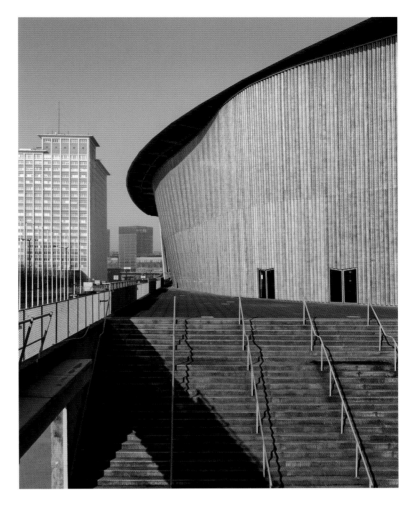

Then, from 1990 onwards, the project followed the common French development set-up and became steered by the SAEM (*société anonyme d'économie mixte*) Euralille, a public-private development company. With Mauroy serving as president and Jean-Paul Baïetto as general manager, work began with the acquisition of the studies that had previously been undertaken by the aforementioned independent structures. Unlike most other companies of that type, Euralille was a genuine mixed company, with the public sector holding only 51 per cent of the shares. From the total investment of approximately 5 billion euros, 3.8 billion were private.

The strong dependence on the private sector and the still vague ideas for the programme made it especially important to engage the local, national and international community and to maximise the project's communication efforts. Several open tables were set up in which business leaders and community representatives discussed specific topics during regular meetings. Euralille was a voluntarist action, a vision for

OMA's Congrexpo with a tower of Jean Nouvel's Euralille Shopping Centre in the background.

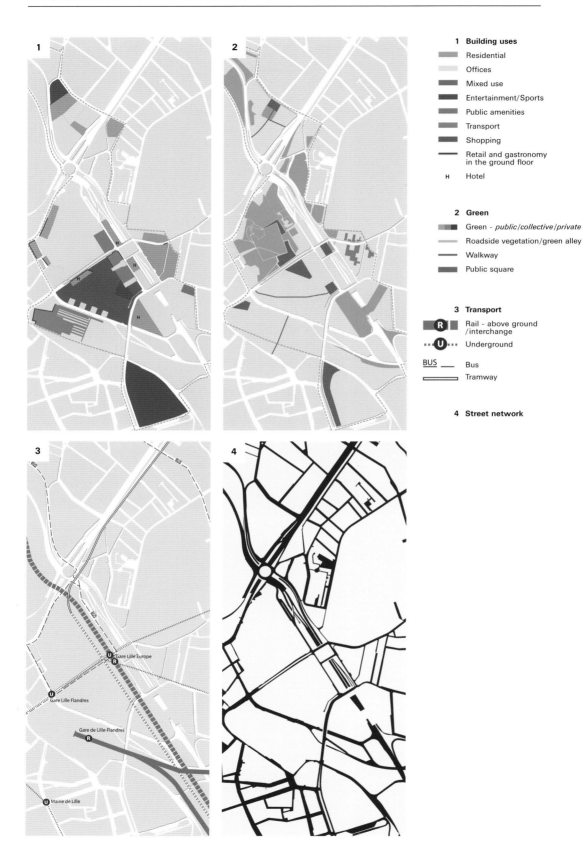

1 Building uses

Residential

Offices

Mixed use

Entertainment/Sports

Public amenities

Transport

Shopping

Retail and gastronomy
in the ground floor

H   Hotel

2 Green

Green - *public/collective/private*

Roadside vegetation/green alley

Walkway

Public square

3 Transport

R   Rail - above ground
     /interchange

U   Underground

BUS   Bus

Tramway

4 Street network

Analysis diagrams

and of the future, and not a reaction to specific and calculable demands, as is the case of most urban projects presented in this book. The assumption that brilliant transport connections would convince national and international companies to settle in Lille or Lille Métropole was economically sound only if such a claim could be made heard. The customers had to actively choose Lille, and such a choice was less obvious than the decision to settle in Brussels, Paris or London, all established members of a global community.

URBAN FORM / CONNECTIVITY

The Euralille project, as it exists today, is in its entirety developed by the SAEM Euralille, but consists of three legally separate integrated development zones (*zones d'aménagement concerté* (ZACs)): Euralille 1, masterplanned by OMA; Euralille 2, masterplanned by Dusapin Leclercq; and Porte de Valenciennes, also masterplanned by Dusapin Leclercq. The total area counts 126 hectares (311 acres) and over 880,000 square metres (9.5 million square feet) of mixed developments, with 360,000 square metres (3.9 million square feet) of offices being the primary use. Our description focuses on the first and most commercial phase, the second and third ones still being in progress. Moreover, they can arguably be seen as separate pieces of the city and follow a different set of urban principles, partly due to their distance from the infrastructural hub and the predominance of residential uses.

Euralille is one of the most-published urban projects of the late 20th century and, despite a strong temptation to participate in the discussion about the concept's validity and success, there seems little point in repeating arguments that have already been made elsewhere.

It may be more worthwhile to examine the project's relatively low density in relation to its fringe position, the existence of major traffic arteries, and the first phase's commercial character. If the scheme was to act as a marketing tool for a city that had gradually lost its attraction as a major textile and metallurgic centre of the 19th century, it had to be big. The interest of the built result is that it has been able to provide monumental character, as austere as some might define it, to a vast and problematic site that was suffering from the existence of overbearing infrastructures. This has been accomplished with an ultimately fairly modest development programme which, in terms of numbers, does not fit the claim of bigness. OMA's apparently flexible concept has not only been able to uphold meaning after pruning of its content, but has also succeeded in accommodating uses that the small-scale fabric of the inner city would have struggled to swallow. In this respect, the fringe position of the site was as much an opportunity as a burden. The commercial towers and megastructures of Euralille appear as the pillars of a huge tent that spans the whole eastern edge of Lille, offering under its cover and label not only a series of high-quality residential developments, but also a selection of stunning open spaces, including work by Gilles Clément, François Grether and Duncan Lewis. The palpable tension between global aspirations and local realities seems therefore well expressed.

ARCHITECTURAL TYPOLOGIES

OMA's masterplan mission did not include the choice of the architects, and neither did it define the programme. The Dutch firm could, however, give advice, and the selection of architects as much as their final designs

BELOW LEFT: Parc Matisse, by Gilles Clément, Empreinte and Claude Courtecuisse.

BELOW: The Giants' Garden, designed by Mutabilis and Duncan Lewis.

Aerial 1:10,000

were the results of discussions that took place in the Urban and Architectural Quality Circle, chaired by François Barré. Founded for the Euralille project, this body regrouped celebrated and less well-known members from all sorts of backgrounds, its aim being, as Jean-Paul Baïetto noted, 'not to leave the masterplanners alone'. It also provided a helpful link between the French architectural establishment, the development world, the local community and the Dutch design team. In addition to the masterplan mission, OMA also received the architectural commission for Congrexpo, and provided the spatial concept for the Piranesian space which links the train station to the parking and metro network. Lille Europe Station itself,

heart and engine of the whole undertaking, was designed by Jean-Marie Duthilleul, head architect of SNCF, with the support of Peter Rice from Arup for the design of the delicate roof structure.

The site's main challenge was turned into one of its most striking features, as large portions of the design (and financial) efforts went into the elaboration of the best strategy to unearth the station from its tunnel position and to project its interior life to the outside. The two towers of the international business centre, remnants of the more ambitious earlier plans, are positioned on top of it: the Tour Crédit Lyonnais (1995; now Tour de Lille) by Christian de Portzamparc, and the World Trade Center (1995; now Tour Lille Europe) by

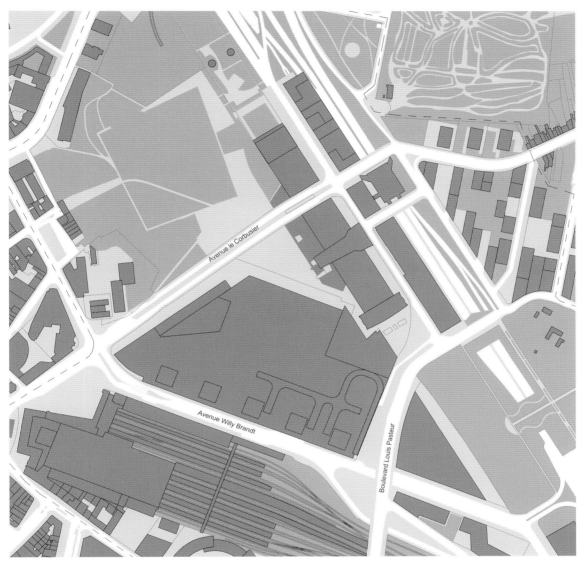

Urban plan 1:5,000

Claude Vasconi. The architectural language of both towers, as different as it may be, has proven to be as timeless as that of the station. Portzamparc's so-called 'ski-boot' is probably the masterplan's most outstanding construction.

Jean Nouvel's Euralille Shopping Centre, incorporating additional uses in small towers along Avenue Willy Brandt, is marked by its vast tilting but inaccessible roof, intended to create a formal unity between the two stations. In its broad outline a result of OMA's masterplan efforts, it is probably this roof's gesture that appears from today's point of view as the project's weakest element. As a conceptual leftover of an early design phase, it cannot hide the fact that the interior mall design, the

planned connection to the World Trade Center and the unearthing of the western station entrance through a downward-sloping square have produced technical imperatives that eventually were difficult to reconcile.

CONCLUSION

Due to its prominent position in the city's recent history, it is an especially complex task to measure the success of Euralille, and such an assessment cannot be the aim of this book. Like many urban projects of equally ambitious size, it went through major turbulence, and experienced a strategic shift after a financial restructuring in 1999, the simultaneous recovery of the French real-estate market and the appointment of

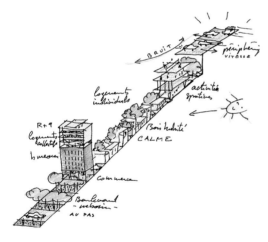

Jean-Louis Subileau as general manager of the SAEM Euralille, following the sudden death of Jean-Paul Baïetto in January 1998. The fact that the sale of four buildings to Bouygues in 1999 was the area's first office transaction in seven years shows how serious the economic pressure must have been. After this painful, but successful termination of the project's heroic first phase, dismissed by critics as a post-1970s transport exaltation, the new management focused on the elimination of its major flaws, and Euralille – including its extension to the south – has only recently become perceived by its inhabitants as a genuine component of the city of Lille. The early economic expectations that many international companies would settle around the high-speed train station did not materialise, but on the national level Lille Métropole has proven its attractiveness as a regional business centre. The city has also been able to draw considerably more foreign

tourists than previously anticipated. Due to the nature of the project and the communication activities around Baïetto's and Mauroy's frantic leadership, an intense team spirit was created that led to the city's application in 1995 for the Olympic Games of 2004, lost in 1997 against Athens, and its successful nomination as European Capital of Culture in 2004. It would go too far to claim that the credit for these important image activities can be traced back to the radical nature of Euralille's urban design, but it can indeed be imagined that a quieter approach might not have produced the same international marketing effect or have released the same human energy that OMA's controversial scheme was somehow able to generate.

The topic of human energy and effort leads to another interesting finding: the fact that the amount of personal initiative cannot directly be linked to the legal nature of a project. By intuition, it might be expected that a private developer would show more interest in the creation of a specific urban product than local electives and civil servants; but the impressive, and at times stubborn investment of people like Pierre Mauroy and Jean-Paul Baïetto in Euralille does not uphold such a notion. Eventually, the pressure of the market seems to have a more levelling effect on a private developer than the political pressure of the voters, assuming that the latter exists. To complicate things further, the French example must be understood against the background of the decentralisation process that began with a general law in 1982 and was extended to the field of urban planning in 1983 and 1985. Euralille is therefore part of an early generation of projects that were initiated and implemented by local collectives and not by the French state.

The Bois Habité district in the Euralille 2 zone, masterplanned by Dusapin Leclercq.

LEFT: Hand-drawn section for the Bois Habité district: the residential zones in the centre of the development are protected from the surrounding heavy infrastructures.

OPPOSITE: A Piranesian space structures the inside of the interchange next to the northern entrance of Lille Europe Station.

Puerto Madero

LOCATION: BUENOS AIRES, ARGENTINA
DATE: 1991–2015
SIZE: 131 HECTARES (324 ACRES)

Río de la Plata
City center Puerto Madero

Of all the projects discussed in this book, Puerto Madero probably had, together with Euralille, the strongest impact on the city in which it is situated. As a new mixed-use centre, its generous and airy urban layout drastically contrasts with Buenos Aires' dense inner-city grid, and symbolises the country's entry into the 21st century.

Floor area ratio: 2.00
Residential population: 21,800
Mix of uses: predominantly residential and office use, with abundant retail and restaurants, hotels and museum

The early history of Puerto Madero, more than its recent redevelopment, provides a lesson in the risk and complexity attached to the development of large-scale projects. In principle, the idea of constructing an efficient and centrally located port goes back to the city's foundation, and is inherently linked to its strategic position on the estuary of the River Plate. But why did it take so long to build it? The answer largely relates to the estuary's very shallow waters, and to the considerable effort and coordination it would require to dredge a canal deep enough to allow for ships to discharge in a more or less central location. For centuries, cargo had to be transferred to small barks or it had to be transported by land. For as long as there was no local trade competitor, and as the complicated transport chain was not too costly – being supported through the use of cheap slave work until its abolition in 1813 – the motivation for the start of such an ambitious undertaking was low.

Since the end of the 18th century the upgrading of the natural port of Montevideo increasingly challenged these circumstances, and the city fathers realised that the future of Buenos Aires – the official capital of the Viceroyalty of the River Plate since 1776 – could hardly

be envisaged without the existence of a modern port facility. The first implemented improvements began in 1802 with the construction of a modestly sized quay of 35 metres (115 feet) in length, and its extension to over 200 metres (650 feet) in 1855. Fundamental to the history of this site is the discussion of two opposing port designs, proposed during the 1870s and early 1880s, by the engineer Luis Huergo on the one hand and the businessman Eduardo Madero on the other. After years of hesitation, fierce political battles and financial bottlenecks, the Congress selected the European-inspired concept of Madero and a contract was signed by President Roca in late 1884. In 1889 the first dock was inaugurated, followed in 1898 by four docks and two entrance and exit canals in the north and south of the development. Madero's plan was inspired by the design of major ports like London or Liverpool, but it tragically suffered the same destiny: the inability to adapt to the explosive growth of trade and the similarly explosive growth of ship sizes. Only a decade after Puerto Madero's opening, the inefficiencies due to the restrictions of the design forced the city officials to begin planning the construction of a new port. Puerto Nuevo, following many ideas of Huergo's initial competing concept, was finished in 1925 and led to the drastic decrease of loading activities in Puerto Madero.

In the following decades many ambitious plans for the redevelopment of Puerto Madero were proposed by a large number of investors and consultants, including Le Corbusier; but none was implemented, and the perfectly located site suffered from increasing decay. The nature reserve to the east of Puerto Madero is itself a remnant of an abandoned development project: it formed over the years as river deposits added to the area of land that had been reclaimed for the scheme before it foundered. An important biotope in an extraordinarily central location, over 348 hectares (860 acres) in size, it has the disadvantage of impeding the direct relationship between the river and the city – a relationship that had existed relatively briefly in the early years of the 20th century, when there was a major waterfront promenade and beach along Costanera Sur.

PROJECT ORGANISATION / TEAM STRUCTURE

In November 1989 the Corporación Antiguo Puerto Madero SA (CAPMSA) was founded as a company of private law, with the National Government and the City of Buenos Aires as equal shareholders. The company's goal was the development of the Puerto Madero site, and its only starting asset was the land itself, signed over from the national port company, the national train company and the national grain company, among

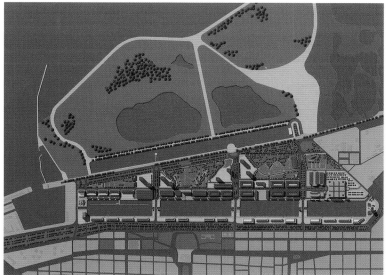

TOP: Aerial view of Puerto Madero at the very beginning of the 20th century, when it had just started operating. The nature reserve did not yet exist, and the city had a direct relation to the river along Costanera Sur.

ABOVE: The masterplan in the early 1990s, showing the urban principles that were to be implemented over a period of approximately 15 years.

LEFT: View across the second dock from the third floor of a new office building in the direction of the historic centre. The brick buildings on the other side of the dock are historic structures that have been converted as part of the first redevelopment phase of Puerto Madero.

BELOW: View down the docks from the northwestern limit of the site. From this perspective, the two tower clusters appear as a single entity.

others. These state agencies had previously used parts of the former port for warehousing, and contributed to the start-up finances of the new company in renting back their former property. Another immediately available source of income was generated through the sale of old material and through parking spaces that are positioned along the western limit of the site, between Plaza de Mayo and the brick buildings of the four docks. Several television series were shot within the district, as well as scenes for movies such as *Highlander* and *Evita*, a welcome happenstance that aided CAPMSA's marketing efforts. After a comprehensive analysis of several comparable schemes like Battery Park City (see separate case study) and the London Docklands, and with the support of the planning office of the City of Barcelona (with its recent experience in comprehensive urban renewal), an ideas competition was organised in June 1991. The three prize-winning practices sent

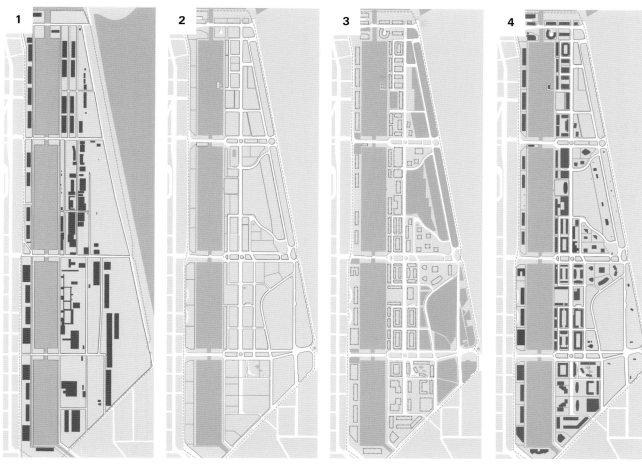

Process diagrams

1 Situation before intervention.

2 Plot subdivision and ownership after redevelopment.

3 Masterplan prescriptions for the building envelopes.

4 Final state.

▬▬ Private ownership
▬▬ Public ownership
∷∷∷ Building envelope
▬▬ Green space
── Private plot ownership
── Public plot ownership
≡≡≡ Tracks

three members each into a dedicated team that would establish the official masterplan in mixing the elements of their initial ideas. As is common practice in such circumstances, the development corporation had decided not to nominate a single winner through a binding competition. Against the initial protest of the local architectural community, it preferred to keep long-term control of the design process and to achieve a greater degree of diversity and flexibility. The size of the estate, the estimated development time and the high political profile of the project made constant adjustments seem probable, and allegedly these could be better met by a larger team of professionals than by a single practice.

More problematic than the definition of urban principles for the masterplan was the instigation of development momentum. The extraordinary situation of the site was not a guarantee for success, and many of the larger investors were reluctant to commit to an undertaking that they could not comprehensively control. Not only was the site unusually large, but the

development structure, with the corporation as central element, was also uncommon. The idea of selling the whole site to a single private developer had previously been discussed on the political level, with Donald Trump having been an avid applicant, but eventually the opinion prevailed that such a lack of diversification might involve an even higher risk than the smaller-scale approach of the CAPMSA.

In order to showcase quick progress and to improve the corporation's feeble financial situation, the western part of the site, with its brick warehouses originally built by British architects, was separated from the actual masterplan initiative and sold on a piecemeal base. The tendering process for the redevelopment project attracted more bids than expected, and the corporation was able to choose the best programmes and architectural projects while still making considerable profits. The applicants were restricted in their ability to alter the existing facades, and the retention of historic character was probably the determining decision for the future success of the ambitious scheme. Grounded

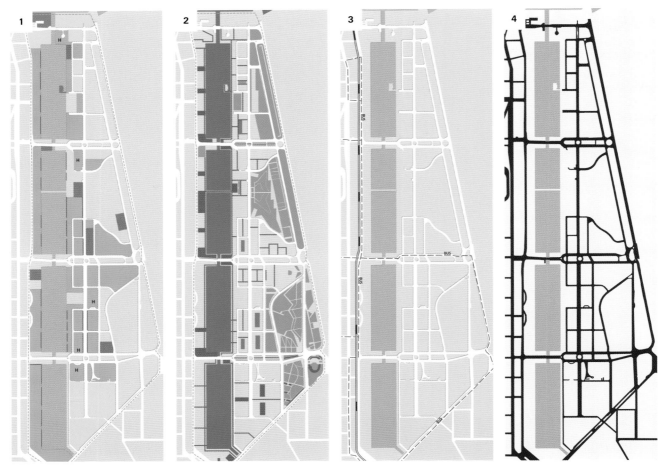

Analysis diagrams

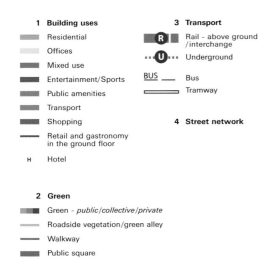

1 **Building uses**

     Residential

     Offices

     Mixed use

     Entertainment/Sports

     Public amenities

     Transport

     Shopping

     Retail and gastronomy
     in the ground floor

H   Hotel

2 **Green**

     Green - *public/collective/private*

     Roadside vegetation/green alley

     Walkway

     Public square

3 **Transport**

     Rail - above ground
     /interchange

     Underground

BUS   Bus

     Tramway

4 **Street network**

in the city's collective memory, this strategy supported the acceptance of a new district that socially, culturally and architecturally had little in common with its surroundings. The sales process began in the northern extremity of the site's triangle, using the proximity to the city's financial core as a major marketing advantage. Today, Puerto Madero appears as the corporate heart of Buenos Aires, accommodating projects of several large players like Repsol YPF, Tishman Speyer and the Faena Group. In this context it is therefore interesting to note that the foundation was laid by smaller development companies who discovered in the brick buildings and the port heritage a potential for future growth.

URBAN FORM / CONNECTIVITY

Technically, the main reason for the area's particularity is its completely different cadastral logic, obviously linked to the infill background and the former use as a port. On the eastern side of the docks, CAPMSA decided to subdivide the site into plots that fitted the interests of the office market, which is notable for the construction of

View from the pedestrian part of Olga Cossettini street towards the dock. These office buildings were part of Puerto Madero's first new-built projects (see building plans).

Elevations of the Porteño Plaza office building (2000), designed by MRA+A. It is a good example of the first generation of new developments on the eastern site of the docks, and is situated between the waterfront and Olga Cossettini street, not far from Santiago Calatrava's Puente de la Mujer.

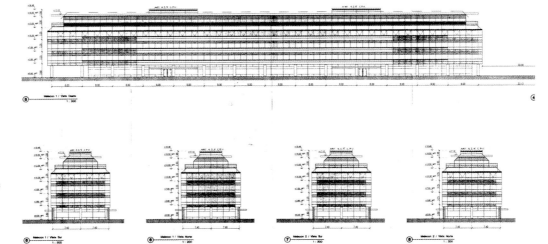

Aerial 1:10,000

low-rise buildings with large floor plates. The availability
of such plots in a central location was an attractive
novelty for developers who usually had to concentrate
their programme on the small and narrow plots of the
typical Buenos Aires block. The new development unit
hence grew larger and the block itself smaller. Crucial
for the rationale of the whole project, and one of the
reasons for the public's interference in the development
process, is Puerto Madero's potential to constrain and
minimise the flight of investment from the centre to
the outskirts. The city officials tried to strengthen the
status of the city centre, hoping that the benefits of
investments from wealthy individuals and companies
would also profit the urban renewal of the less

privileged surroundings. It is important to understand
that Puerto Madero has not been planned as a new
CBD (central business district), and that its mix of
uses, though socially homogeneous, also includes
apartments, restaurants, shops, hotels, museums and
a university. The physical connection to the city centre
and Plaza de Mayo is at the same time obvious and
ambivalent. On the one hand, it can be seen as just a
five-minute walk away from the Casa Rosada as the
seat of the government, incorporating Santiago
Calatrava's pedestrian bridge, El Puente de la Mujer,
as a direct extension of Avenida de Mayo. On the
other hand, this proximity cannot hide the city's historic
closure to the sea, as Puerto Madero still suffers from

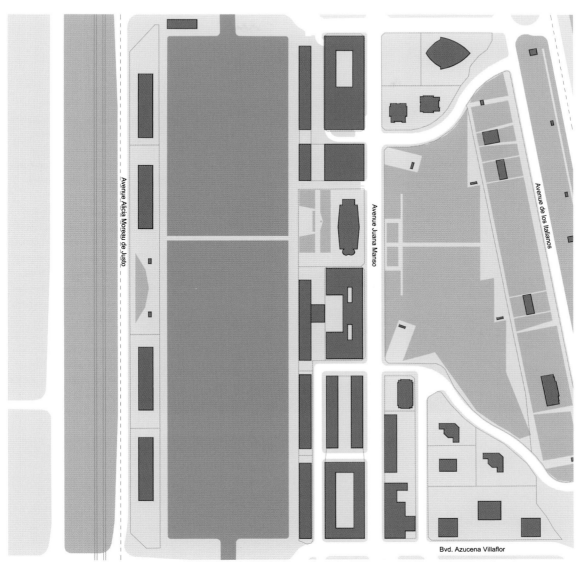

Urban plan 1:5,000

being positioned on lower grounds and cut off from the core through a belt of infrastructure, comprising tram tracks, car parks and two streets with heavy traffic.

The masterplan itself defines a very clear and simple layout. Its main development axis follows the geometry of the four docks and transforms the areas around the water into a major urban attraction. The large zones to the east of the site adopt a triangular shape and feature four major parks as well as two tower clusters, the northern one being predominantly commercial and the larger southern one predominantly residential. Symmetrically positioned off the central axis of Avenida de Mayo, these two clusters, referred to as 'clouds', play an important role in the wider context

of the city. They are the only elements that can be seen from the historic core.

ARCHITECTURAL TYPOLOGIES

It is interesting to compare the choice of block structure for Puerto Madero with alternative proposals that were developed in other parts of the world during the same period. In the section east of the docks, most buildings stand free and form smaller blocks on their own: party walls and narrow spaces are avoided as much as possible, seemingly in an effort to avoid overcomplicating the urban and architectural rules. Compared to some contemporaneous Parisian projects like the Front de Parc in Bercy or the residential

FAR LEFT: The wide pavement on the western side of the converted brick buildings. Trees protect pedestrians from the noise of the street.

LEFT: The northern end of Olga Cossettini street, with a residential block to the left and the Fortabat Art Museum (2008, by Rafael Viñoly) to the right. The street runs parallel to the docks.

BELOW: View from Cesar Pelli's Repsol YPF Tower (2008) in direction of Plaza Mayor and Casa Rosada, seat of the government.

developments around the New National Library (see Masséna Nord case study) – both explicitly studied models – the scheme commits similarly to an urbanism of perimeter blocks and active street fronts, but does so in an urbanistically less sophisticated way. In contrast to the development machinery of the French model, refined and tested over decades, with an often-significant implication of public housing corporations, the CAPMSA could not rely on the same understanding from the local client's side in the context of a completely exceptional project. It is therefore the stratification of public space that holds the simple block structures closely together and successfully manages to create a strong spatial tension between main roads, service roads, pedestrian, semi-pedestrian, public and communal spaces. Density and changing surfaces manage to create an atmosphere that is reminiscent of more complex urban fabrics. In several cases, spaces that could have been internal courtyards of a perimeter block have been externalised and transformed into small public squares, situated between two simple slabs. This is specifically true for the northern and older part of the development, the southern area following an increasingly large-scale approach.

LEFT: Typical floor plan of the Aleph building, developed by Faena Properties and designed by Foster + Partners.

BELOW: Artistic representation of Foster + Partners' mainly residential Aleph project, part of the Faena Arts and Technology District which is still under construction (expected to open in 2013). A covered market square is the centrepiece of a new urban plaza.

CONCLUSION

The study of the history of Buenos Aires and its relation to the river illustrates how a change in lifestyle and urban economy can impact the shape and development dynamics of a city. While the Argentinian capital's example appears to be particularly paradoxical – a port city without a natural harbour, a strategically perfect position without an actual view of the river – the difficult relationship of many coastal cities to the water is a recurrent theme in the history of urban development. Demanding sophisticated embankment, dyke and transport solutions as technological starting conditions, public health improvements and the redundancy of military protection have finally opened a dramatic array of possibilities of how to use the city's coastal fringes in the most efficient way.

Today, with an understanding of the city as a competitive knowledge centre in constant need of reinvention, rather than an inert industrial machine, water features are seen as a unique opportunity of differentiation compared with settlements which are situated inland. Just like Barcelona, Marseilles or Vancouver, Buenos Aires has grasped this precious opportunity and consolidated its position as one of Latin America's most attractive and diverse capitals. It does so in emphasising its morphological differences, based on the port heritage, rather than through the adoption of the city's rigid grid.

OPPOSITE: The Faena Hotel is a 2004 Philippe Starck conversion of a formerly industrial building. It is situated to the southeast of the site, on the level of the third dock.

LEFT: The Mujeres Argentinas Park seen from the Repsol YPF Tower. Buenos Aires' old fortifications were chosen as a design theme, but were historically positioned further inland.

BELOW LEFT: The nature reserve seen from the Repsol YPF Tower. It is the result of natural deposits that occurred after the beginning of reclamation works for a failed development project.

Hammarby Sjöstad

LOCATION: STOCKHOLM, SWEDEN
DATE: 1996–2017
SIZE: 160 HECTARES (395 ACRES) (40 HECTARES (99 ACRES) WATER EXCLUDED)

Principally marketed as a sustainable district, Hammarby Sjöstad has also proven to be a highly attractive and desirable environment. Less than 3 kilometres (2 miles) south of the Stockholm Royal Palace, the site offers its over 20,000 inhabitants an opportunity to profit from its idyllic location around Hammarby Lake while enjoying a more relaxed and less formal atmosphere than that of the city's historic core.

Floor area ratio: 1.43
Residential population: 24,000
Mix of uses: 80% residential,
18% office and public amenities,
2% retail and restaurants

The area was not always this bucolic. Up to the 20th century it was indeed a mainly untouched leisure zone, but in 1917 it was purchased by the City of Stockholm in order to establish a new harbour and industrial park. The site's proximity to the city centre, abundance of water and connection to the Baltic Sea via a canal were perfect reasons to do so, and one of the first occupants was actually a General Motors plant. When redevelopment plans started in the early 1990s, industrial operations were still ongoing. At that time, however, the city chose to prioritise the satisfaction of housing needs above the development of partly heavily polluting activities in what could now be considered a central location.

One of the main arguments for the choice of the site was the fact that it was to a large extent already owned by the city. Furthermore, it accommodated only a very small number of listed buildings. This facilitated the implementation process and allowed the city to avoid much of the time loss linked to lengthy expropriation measures, even though Swedish municipalities – in addition to their planning monopoly – implement especially efficient pre-emption and expropriation rights. The project really gained momentum in 1996 with Stockholm's bid for the 2004 Olympic Games. The proposal already included the idea of a highly sustainable development model for Hammarby as site of the Olympic Village. Despite the candidature's failure in favour of Athens, announced in 1997, this principle was maintained and became the major theme for the continued planning of the new family-oriented residential district.

PROJECT ORGANISATION / TEAM STRUCTURE

The 'Project Hammarby Sjöstad' was created in 1997 as an organisation within the Stockholm City Development Administration. Together with the City Planning Administration, it is responsible for designing and implementing the area's masterplan, including urban planning, finances, land decontamination and construction of bridges, pipes, streets and parks. The public control of the whole development is therefore tight, but not consistent in time and direction. Several political changes led to major modifications of the project's principles, as the tenure of the conservative coalition between 1998 and 2002 was followed by a red–green coalition. Public versus private landownership, rental properties versus cooperatives, and the number of parking spaces per household, are just a few of the issues that became the focus of political battles. Even the sustainability goals as such, defined somewhat vaguely as having to be 'twice as

good as a usual development', changed status in becoming a recommendation rather than a statutory obligation.

The design process and development of the masterplan was closely managed by the public sector. A first draft was internally developed by a group of architects under the supervision of Jan Inge-Hagström from the Stockholm Town Building Office. In the next step, the large site was subdivided in 12 sectors, and each of them given over to a team of three or four directly commissioned private architectural practices who were asked to test and further develop the first draft. After the city harmonised these proposals, with direct input from architects and developers, this knowledge was translated into design guidelines for each sector and its typically four to 11 plots. Due to the early involvement of implementing professionals,

TOP: Idyllic painting by Ehrenfried Wahlqvist of Hammarby Lake in 1864, approximately 50 years before it became a major industrial park.

ABOVE: Aerial view of Hammarby Lake before redevelopment, looking east towards Nacka municipality.

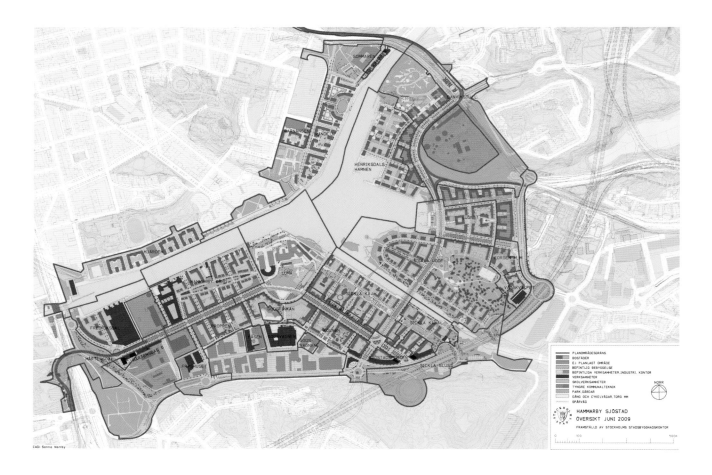

CAD: Sanna Norrby

these guidelines are very detailed and cover all aspects of urban and architectural form, parking spaces, open spaces and even the maximum distance between apartment entrances and rubbish chutes. In a concluding step, the plots were distributed to public or private developers and their architects who proceeded to create the final design within the margins left by the guidelines. Due to the considerable size of the development, the planning process spanned approximately a decade. As part of the aforementioned political disagreements, the land is sold or sometimes only leased, the former being a preference of the right-wing parties.

It is important to understand that the guidelines' *raison d'être* is the avoidance of specification changes during the lengthy development process, rather than the enforcement of individual design ideas by the municipal planning services. In most cases, the guidelines are based on the (team)work of the same architects who will later on apply for the individual building permits. This is a different approach from the one chosen in most of the other examples in this book, where the masterplanner defines guidelines without

any input from the architects who will, in a subsequent step, design the actual buildings (see, for example, Masséna Nord case study). It is obvious that the Swedish model relies on a collaborative work attitude that might not easily be established in other political cultures. Such discipline can at least partly be explained by the fact that the developers pay for the amount of floor space that they build, at the beginning of construction, and not for the plot itself. In conjunction with the above-mentioned planning monopoly, this means that they can hardly expect to achieve any gains without the city's approval. In the worst scenario, the city could repossess the site, the developer holding only a conditional contract until approval of his project.

The Sickla Udde peninsula in the eastern part of the perimeter was the first plot to be developed, partly before termination of the 'Hammarby Model' with its overall sustainability agenda. Sickla Udde was one of the most challenging sites, as it was heavily polluted and initially not in public ownership. The strength and specificity of the Hammarby Model is its early and integrative approach, developed by the energy provider Fortum, Stockholm Water Company and the Stockholm

The 2009 version of the official masterplan and its 12 subdistricts. These areas have been detailed by different architectural teams, and are not only the result of a phasing strategy. The design authority for the masterplan lies, however, with the city planning services, and not with the private architectural practices as temporary consultants.

Waste Management Administration. Approaching the question of sustainability from a consistently cyclical point of view, the plan aimed not only to use a minimum of resources through energy-saving construction, but also to recycle locally all waste, water and energy. Heat from the incineration of efficiently collected and sorted waste is, for example, used for the production of electricity and district heating. The heat of purified waste water feeds into the same system, and the remaining cold water is used wherever air conditioning is needed. As a result of these and other measures, approximately 50 per cent of the site's electricity and heating consumption can be covered through regeneration measures. Most of these techniques did not have to be reinvented, and Sweden and especially the Stockholm area have for a long time been consistently developing sustainable infrastructures in the form of district heating, district cooling and a high degree of waste incineration. Nowadays, these systems are often owned and operated on a commercial basis.

URBAN FORM / CONNECTIVITY

In the larger urban context, it was decided to preserve the site's natural features and green corridors and to compensate any necessary losses through the creation of new green space. To this end, the city embarked on the decontamination of the brownfield sites, as well as more generally promoting retrofit through further densification of already developed land rather than urban sprawl. It might be useful to add that – in contrast to many other countries, especially the United States – the sprawl problem in Sweden, though existing, rarely relies on the one-family typology.

Early discussions about the most sustainable urban form had highlighted Stockholm's traditional inner-city block structure as the most promising and preferred model. The designers therefore oriented their proposals towards similar urban dimensions, densities and heights. The final products, however, were significantly altered to reflect the demands of the contemporary market. Vestiges of those early ideas remain not only in the existence of block structures as such, but also in a certain notion of homogeneity and repetition. Despite its subdivision into 12 subdistricts, Hammarby indeed appears as a coherent whole. This can be attributed to the rapid pace of development, the teamwork approach, and the general attitude that Hammarby's success did not depend on the originality of 'signature architecture', but rather on the thoughtful and collaborative exploitation of a very privileged setting. The lack of input of any foreign design firm further underlines this attitude, as it does the fact

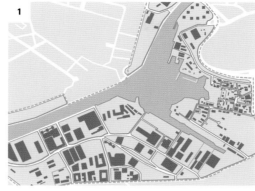

Process diagrams

1 Situation before intervention.

2 Plot subdivision and ownership after redevelopment.

3 Masterplan prescriptions for the building envelopes.

4 Final state.

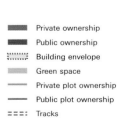

Private ownership
Public ownership
Building envelope
Green space
Private plot ownership
Public plot ownership
Tracks

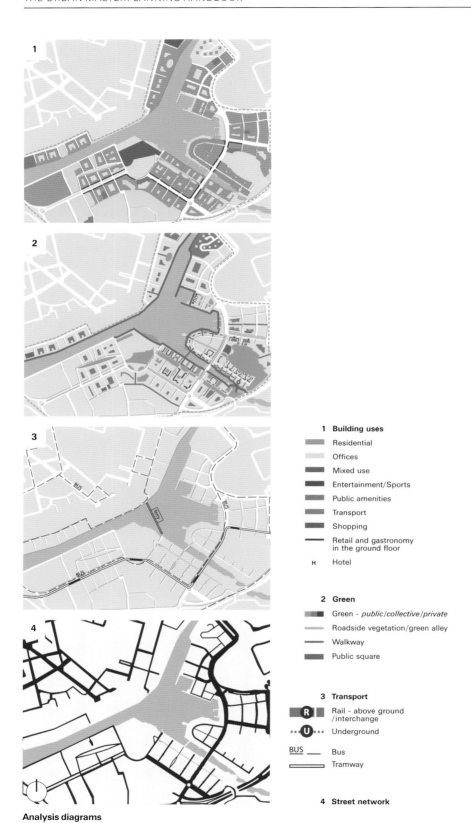

Analysis diagrams

1 **Building uses**
   Residential
   Offices
   Mixed use
   Entertainment/Sports
   Public amenities
   Transport
   Shopping
   Retail and gastronomy
   in the ground floor
H Hotel

2 **Green**
   Green - *public/collective/private*
   Roadside vegetation/green alley
   Walkway
   Public square

3 **Transport**
R Rail - above ground
   /interchange
U Underground
BUS Bus
   Tramway

4 **Street network**

OPPOSITE TOP: View from the southeast of the site towards the northern shore of the lake. These buildings are part of Hammarby, but were developed earlier than the recent masterplan initiative following the sustainable 'Hammarby Model'.

OPPOSITE BELOW: View from the pedestrian bridge of the town-villa typology along the waterfront of Sickla Udde.

that the local development world is a fairly manageable community.

Glancing at an aerial image of the site's surroundings shows a great diversity of urban and architectural typologies, and suggests that the city's decision to focus on different variations of the block type was neither an accident nor a foregone conclusion, but a result of comprehensive and comparative research.

In order to limit commuter car use to 20 per cent of the total number of journeys, it was crucial to offer efficient means of public transport. This has been achieved through the extension of a tram line (Tvärbanan), good bus links and two ferry routes. There is also a car-pool system called 'city-car' that is used by private individuals and professionals alike. More controversial was the presentation of the Southern Link, a motorway project with almost 5 kilometres (3 miles) of tunnels in the southern suburbs around Hammarby, as a sustainability feature. Easing the traffic pressure on the city's core, it is part of the ambitious plans for a new ring road, and indirectly a condition for the development of the area's largest subdistrict, Henriksdalshamnen.

As a result of the traffic redirection through the tunnel, this part of the Hammarby sector became available for redevelopment which would not have been legally

ABOVE LEFT: The publicly accessible courtyard of a residential development.

ABOVE: The green courtyard of one of the U-shaped developments in the Sickla Kaj subdistrict.

LEFT: View from the elevated terrace of the back-building in the same courtyard. Town villas close the space loosely on the open edge of the U.

ABOVE LEFT: Parallel to the waterfront walk, a path leads through the openings in the residential buildings.

ABOVE: Beautiful landscaping on Sickla Kaj, parallel to the waterfront.

LEFT: View from the new tram line into a residential street of Sickla Udde.

possible formerly, when the existing road was considered to produce an unacceptably harmful residential environment.

ARCHITECTURAL TYPOLOGIES

Compared with the closed blocks of the historic centre, the Hammarby types are airy and discontinuous. This design allows more natural light to reach the courtyard-oriented parts of apartments and, in this special case, also optimises real-estate values by maximising the number of lake views. Fairly often, the blocks are therefore U-shaped, with one or two smaller and lower detached buildings loosely delimiting the open edge. In the case of the Sickla Kaj subdistrict, opposite the Sickla Udde peninsula and east of the converted Luma Light Bulb Factory, the back-buildings are taller and the lateral buildings feature convexities in order to increase the same visual effect of optimised lake views.

Interestingly, the masterplan's design guidelines also explicitly address stylistic issues, and situate the desired

Aerial 1:10,000

outcome in between the traditional block model and a distinctively local and new type that offers larger floor plates and more exterior spaces. In relation to the country's Modernist period, air, light, nature attachment, flat roofs and light colours are mentioned as inspirational features, but must be combined with higher densities, clearer spatial hierarchies and a place-specific expression. The architecturally and commercially attractive reality of large floor plates, glazed surfaces and generous balconies shows how the aim for sustainability and energy efficiency partly collides with the demands of the contemporary client. At least for the first phases of the development, the energy consumption of the buildings remained over

100 kilowatt-hours per square metre per annum (9 kilowatt-hours per square foot per annum), far above the target of 60 kilowatt-hours per square metre per annum (5.5 kilowatt-hours per square foot per annum). The project's overall energy efficiency is therefore due to the above-mentioned recycling methods rather than to the building's thermal insulation. With time, it can be expected that the architectural solutions will equal the excellence of the site's integrative engineering, but this is more difficult to achieve if smaller windowpanes are not accepted by the market. The question of apartment sizes reflects a similar market logic, and is supplemented by that of the ratio of dwellings to inhabitants. Due to the

Urban plan 1:5,000

country's prosperity, long life expectancy, high divorce rates and the generally early age of children leaving the parental home, the number of dwellings per inhabitant in Sweden is among the world's highest. In this context of middle-class developments, the aim of high living densities in terms of population per hectare is therefore especially difficult to meet, and clearly surpasses the technical realm of sustainable urbanism.

CONCLUSION

Almost unanimously considered a positive example, Hammarby is one of the few new urban districts that appeal to most strata of the population, as long as they consider apartment living as an option. The teamwork

approach, the high quality of Swedish architecture and an early involvement of developers and architects have produced a mainstream result whose rapidly increasing real-estate values are a reliable measure of success. Four times larger than Freiburg's Vauban (see separate case study), a recent German example of ecological planning, it appears as an inherently urban alternative, despite similar residential densities of around 130 to 150 inhabitants per hectare (50 to 60 inhabitants per acre). At first glance surprising, these figures cannot only be explained by the higher amount of commercial activities of the Swedish example, and its indeed higher overall density. They are also based on the existence of more substantial infrastructures and several larger green

spaces – actual parks – that are spatially opposed to the comparatively dense constructions on the building plots. In Vauban, such typically urban tension does not exist, and the whole site appears as a densified villa-district or eco-village rather than a city extension. The need for public green space is less pronounced and less expensive. Both projects therefore represent two opposed alternatives for an otherwise comparable starting situation, both under initial public control and ownership – one in the context of a European capital of 800,000 inhabitants (over 2 million for the urbanised area), and the other of a regional centre of only 200,000 inhabitants. If such comparison is made, Hammarby's urban layout has significant financial implications through the construction of major public infrastructures.

Another difference between the two schemes is the residents' degree of influence: in the 'bottom-up' German example, the smaller building sizes and the frequent use of the specific legal form of building groups enabled a very direct, if not causal relation between building design and the population's characteristics. In Hammarby, this was not possible, as apartments were sold on plan or rented after construction through public or private developers. This explains one of the project's few criticisms, namely the fact that the quest for maximal sustainability is not always supported by the inhabitants' lifestyle. Surveys have, for example, shown that the relatively low number of parking spaces, symbolic for a change of consumer patterns, was considered by a fairly large percentage of the population to be a disadvantage. In Vauban's homogeneous green community – admittedly less representative of the development logic of large cities – it was considered to be a strong point.

Open space next to the tram station on Lugnets Allé.

OPPOSITE: View from the Mjärden subdistrict towards Henriksdalsberget to the east. See line drawings for the plans of the buildings to the left. The whitish gables belong to the independent constructions that loosely delimit the courtyards of the blocks to the south.

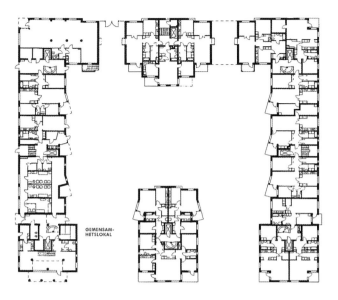

GEMENSAM-
HETSLOKAL

FAR LEFT: Ground-floor plan of a U-shaped residential block in Mjärden (see also photograph), on the northwestern border of Hammarby. These constructions – designed by White Architects – date from the mid-1990s, and are precursors of more recent developments in Hammarby that follow a similar spatial configuration.

LEFT: Detail of a three-bedroom apartment in the same building. The angled shape of the balconies maximises lake views for the units that are oriented towards the interior of the U.

Downtown Dubai

LOCATION: DUBAI, UNITED ARAB EMIRATES
DATE: 2004–13
SIZE: 200 HECTARES (494 ACRES)

Presented as 'The Centre of Now', Downtown Dubai marks a new qualitative step in the emirate's explosive urban growth. Its emphasis on open spaces, a comprehensive mix of uses and the connection to the public transport network are competitive advantages that have helped the development to survive a severe real-estate crisis.

Floor area ratio: n/a
Residential population: 30,000
Mix of uses: predominantly residential, with an abundant offer of retail, restaurants and hotels; some office buildings

For the average European or American citizen, Dubai is essentially a new travel and shopping destination, entertaining the world for now over a decade with a multitude of breathtaking building projects including the first seven-star hotel (Burj Al Arab (1999)), an island version of the earth (The World (2008)), the world's largest shopping mall (Dubai Mall (2008)), and the planned opening of an oversized theme park (Dubailand). Expressing an apparently insatiable ambition, every building project seems to be a superlative, and Dubai has long led the 'best of' lists in almost all conceivable fields of construction.

The aggressive and highly successful tourist strategy, raising visitor figures from just 600,000 in 1990 to over 6.5 million in 2007, tends to overshadow the emirate's considerable achievements in other economic sectors. However, unlike its neighbour Abu Dhabi – the only member of the seven United Arab Emirates besides Dubai to hold the right of veto – Dubai's economy does not rely on oil exports, which currently account for less than 5 per cent of GDP. This is the lowest figure of all Gulf States, and explains why Dubai's relation to the exterior, its openness and relative liberalism so fundamentally differ from the still very conservative attitude of the surrounding countries, Saudi Arabia being the most powerful and extreme example. The need to produce wealth through international trade and business rather than through oil exports has a long tradition, and started before the realisation, at the end of the 1980s, that production would quickly decrease. The oil reserves were discovered fairly late, in 1966, but they were never considered vast enough to assure the city-state's prosperity over several generations. Under the stable rule of the Al Maktoum family since 1833, Dubai therefore developed in a fairly strategic way from a village of pearl-fishers to a genuinely global hub, acting as a reliable haven of opportunities for the wealth of the whole Middle East. The transition from a pre-industrial to industrial to post-industrial economy happened within approximately 50 years – much more quickly than in most Western cities.

Out of many different interventions to stimulate economic activity, two have been especially important and have a legal background. They illustrate how the small emirate was creating loopholes in order to attract foreign capital and knowledge. Initially against the intentions and economic principles of its neighbours, especially Abu Dhabi, these ingenious measures have since been copied in the whole region. The first initiative is linked to the spectacular development of Dubai's port activities. Starting on a modest level with the natural creek, the birthplace of the settlement, Dubai became

the region's and one of the world's most important ports through the construction of Port Rashid in 1972, one year after foundation of the UAE and the independence from Britain, and the subsequent construction of Jebel Ali Port in 1977. Next to Jebel Ali Port, situated in its own municipality 35 kilometres (22 miles) to the southwest of the creek, a free zone was created in 1985 that permitted the foundation of fully foreign-owned companies. Previously, such a practice was forbidden under UAE law, foreigners being forced to use structures whose majority share was held by local nationals. The instant success of this derogation, initially presented as being solely linked to the specific activities of the port, has since led to the creation of 20 more free zones, covering approximately one third of the city's surface.

TOP: View from Burj Park towards SOM's Burj Khalifa (2010). The 1.5-hectare green space is positioned on an island in the artificial lake in front of the world's tallest construction.

ABOVE: The waterfront promenade with the Burj Khalifa to the left, The Address hotel (2008, by Atkins) to the right and the Dubai Mall (2008, by DP Architects) in the background.

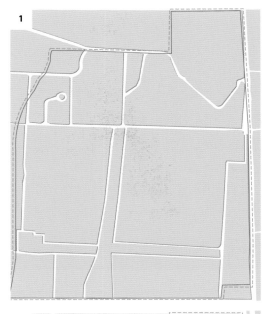

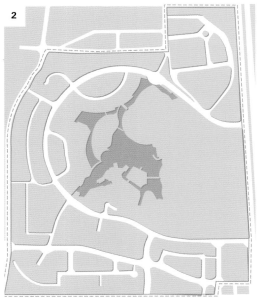

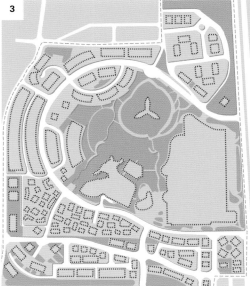

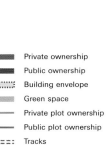

1 Situation before
intervention.

2 Plot subdivision
and ownership after
redevelopment.

3 Masterplan
prescriptions for the
building envelopes.

4 Final state.

Process diagrams

	Private ownership
	Public ownership
	Building envelope
	Green space
	Private plot ownership
	Public plot ownership
	Tracks

PROJECT ORGANISATION /
TEAM STRUCTURE

The second crucial step of economic reforms, creating
the basis for an allegedly unlimited real-estate boom,
was the enabling of freehold landownership for
foreigners. Beginning on shaky legal ground, until
final clarification in 2006, the early schemes offered a
99-year lease that would most probably be renewed for
a single dollar, circumventing the at that time impossible
official mention of a freehold. Traditionally, the ruler
would grant land to his nationals in order to build their
private family homes, and sell, to a rather limited extent,
land outside of the settlements to local development
companies. With the new legislation, first implemented
by the development company Emaar and its founder
and chairman Mohamed Alabbar in 1997 for the
Emirates Hills suburban villa district, Dubai reached
another dimension in its economic possibilities: in an
immensely wealthy but frequently unstable region, it
was finally able to offer, in the form of real estate, the
most conservative investment opportunity to a queuing
crowd of avid buyers. The relevance of this opening

becomes even clearer if we take into consideration the city's exposure to foreigners, the local Emirati population making up only 17 per cent of the current total of 2.3 million inhabitants. The market was enormous and so attractive that many investors did not hesitate to speculate, with little concern about who the end users of the buildings might be.

If the latter initiative explains the sudden growth of the emirate's building ambitions, the former one, in relation to the free-zone status, partially explains the complexity of the planning system and the 'leapfrog' nature of the urban fabric. Despite the existence of the Dubai Municipality as a planning body, following a US-inspired zoning system, a large percentage of the city's territory is developed according to exceptional standards which makes the emergence of a coherent urbanism difficult. The emirate's breathtaking speed of development and the explosion of its urbanised area from 150 square kilometres (58 square miles) in 1993 to a projected 605 square kilometres (234 square miles) in 2015 further underlines this issue, the result being an often still limited connectivity between the different subzones, or cities-within-the-city. This is valid not only for the pedestrian connections, unsurprising in view of the region's harsh climate, but even for the street network which heavily relies on Sheikh Zayed Road as the backbone of the whole city.

The Downtown Dubai project, developed by the publicly listed Emaar Properties Group, is not a free zone, and several features like setbacks, permissible floor area ratio (FAR), parking standards, maximum heights and fire regulations were the result of negotiations with the Dubai Municipality. The project's site, right next to the huge interchange between Doha Street and Sheikh Zayed Road, was previously a military ground. Emaar bought the site and developed it on its own, selling apartments in mid- and high-rise buildings, but rarely subselling the land to other development companies. Emaar, through subsidiaries, also operates the Dubai Mall and several hotels, the most famous ones in Downtown Dubai being The Address and the Armani Hotel in the Burj Khalifa. The latter one is the result of a joint venture with the Italian fashion group, and there are plans to establish similar hotels in other exclusive locations around the world.

URBAN FORM / CONNECTIVITY

Like most recent developments in Dubai, Downtown does not follow the grid logic on which the older parts of the city north and south of the Creek were built. In the spirit of an oversized garden city, it creates a strongly centralised notion through the construction of a ring road around a landscaped centre of impressive dimensions, featuring the world's tallest tower as the

The landscaped zone framed by SOM's Burj Khalifa to the right and one of the new office towers of Aedas's Boulevard Plaza development (2010) to the far left.

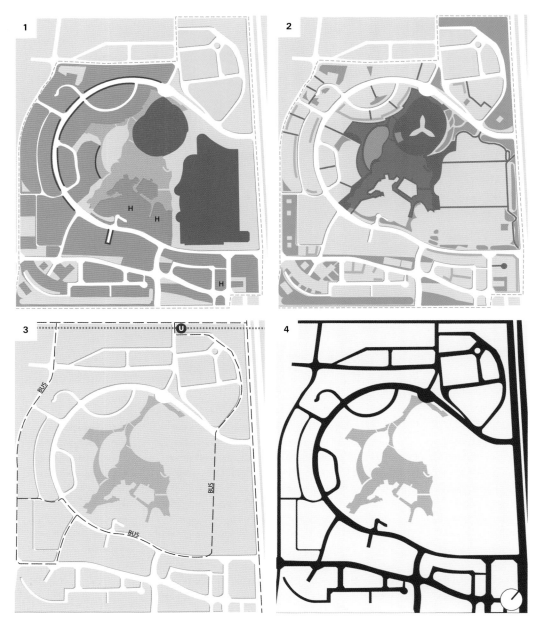

Analysis diagrams

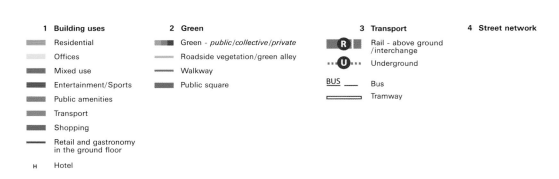

1	**Building uses**	2	**Green**	3	**Transport**	4	**Street network**
	Residential		Green - *public/collective/private*	**R**	Rail - above ground /interchange		
	Offices		Roadside vegetation/green alley	**U**	Underground		
	Mixed use		Walkway	BUS	Bus		
	Entertainment/Sports		Public square		Tramway		
	Public amenities						
	Transport						
	Shopping						
	Retail and gastronomy in the ground floor						
H	Hotel						

focus of all attention. Both the extensive use of artificial landscaping and the urban form itself are reminiscent of large golf developments in which private houses are nestled around beautifully designed pedestrian and open spaces. Comparisons may be drawn with the above-mentioned Emirates Hills scheme, developed by the same client approximately 10 years earlier, with similar street network form and connectivity. However, the parallels end there, as extensive mixed use and high densities contribute, in the case of Downtown Dubai, to the creation of an urban experience that is obviously not comparable to that of a suburban villa district.

The ring road itself, with a diameter of almost a kilometre (two-thirds of a mile), has been designed as an urban boulevard and is intended to accommodate a thriving pedestrian life. Named Emaar Boulevard, it is essentially a distributing loop for the new district's predominantly residential tower-on-base developments, connected to Doha Street and parallel to Sheikh Zayed Road, and is marketed as an alternative to major thoroughfares like the Champs-Elysées in Paris, the Ramblas in Barcelona or Park Avenue in New York. A key difference between these spaces and the Emirati iteration is that in Dubai the retail and restaurant offerings of the bases' ground floors will have to compete with the world's largest shopping mall, situated nearby on the northern limit of the loop. Emaar Boulevard's success as a lively urban space is hence dependent on very high densities and the users' active

ABOVE: Streetscape of Emaar Boulevard including public art, with the Old Town district to the right and Old Town Island district to the left.

LEFT: Unlike numerous tower developments, the Old Town district takes its inspiration from the local building tradition.

LEFT: Old Town Island and the lakefront promenade. Next to the Burj Khalifa in the background is one of the Boulevard Plaza office towers by Aedas.

OPPOSITE: The world's tallest tower is only the centrepiece of a whole district: these tower-on-podium developments in The Residences subdistrict (2007), designed by Woods Bagot, are especially reminiscent of Vancouverism (see False Creek North case study).

choice to have an experience different from that offered by the central spaces around the artificial lake, like the Burj Park, the Burj Steps and the Burj Plaza, which are frequently animated through the play of the world's most sophisticated water fountains. However, the real revolution of the Downtown development, and its advantage compared with numerous local competitors, is the sheer existence of these attractive outdoor spaces, be they along the boulevard or in the centre. Even before the district's final completion, the high numbers of visitors show that most former developments have underestimated the value of these exterior and pedestrian components. Emaar itself had built one of the few projects that could be considered a local predecessor: Dubai Marina.

With the opening of its first metro line in September 2009, Dubai has reached a new stage in its urban development, in the technical as much as social sense. Downtown Dubai features its own station along Sheikh Zayed Road, and is now efficiently connected via public transport to the city's main attractions and the airport. From the station, bus lines offer a frequent service along Emaar Boulevard and towards the southernmost parts of the development which are too far away to be accessed on foot. In addition, there are plans for an air-conditioned travelator – the Dubai Mall Metro Link – between the station, Burj Khalifa and the mall.

ARCHITECTURAL TYPOLOGIES

It goes without saying that the Burj Khalifa, 828 metres (2,717 feet) tall and designed by Adrian Smith of Skidmore, Owings & Merrill (SOM), is the district's most spectacular architectural construction. In the context of this study, it is especially interesting to realise that its highly elegant and subtle spine shape relates directly to the predominantly residential use. This feature stands in stark contrast to the majority of the world's tallest towers, which are built for corporate office uses to offer as many large floor plates as possible. Financially the tower is of much higher value than its own profitability, because it marks the viewpoint, centrepiece and major marketing trump for the whole Downtown area, all of which was developed by the same owner. This again is a previously unknown case, highlighting the immense ambition and large-scale character of the Downtown undertaking, comparable only with projects like the Roppongi Hills development by Mori in Tokyo (2003; see *The Urban Towers Handbook*, pp 120–25) or the Rockefeller Center in New York (1939; see *The Urban Towers Handbook*, pp 88–93), although the latter does not include residential uses.

Due to an extensive application of the tower-on-base typology, Dubai Marina and Downtown Dubai have in recent literature repeatedly been compared to the architecture and urbanism of Concord Pacific Place in

Aerial 1:10,000

Vancouver (see False Creek North case study). It is indeed true that several collaborators of the Canadian project have been hired by Emaar, including Stanley Kwok, and that a fairly similar notion of high-rise architecture has evenly been combined with the provision of large open spaces and a generous waterfront promenade. It is somehow representative that the crucial relation to the water is, in the case of Dubai, artificially created around interior waterways, as the seafront, due to its lack of prominence and mountain views, does not offer the same natural attraction as its acclaimed Vancouver counterpart.

Two important testimonies of Downtown's typological diversity are the Old Town and Old Town

Island districts on the southern border of the lake. Low-rise, dense and traversed by a multitude of narrow pedestrian lanes, designed by the South African office DSA Architects, they provide a link to the region's traditional architecture that the emirate's obsession with high-rise often ignores. The charming character of a labyrinthine spatial experience recalls the fact that the tower typology, despite its obvious advantage of (potentially) high densities and spectacular views, always had issues creating complex spatial hierarchy and diversity. The aforementioned podium feature considerably improves this flaw, but cannot reverse it. In addition to the Burj Khalifa and the Old Town projects, Emaar's growing attention to architectural excellence

Emaar Boulevard

Urban plan 1:5,000

can be recognised in the hiring of international and award-winning offices like RMJM, DP Architects and Woods Bagot. A particularly good example of the interest in iconic shapes can be contemplated in the northern part of Downtown, next to the metro station: if the six first mid-rise buildings of the Emaar Square office development feature a very simple and conventional architecture, the two recent Boulevard Plaza additions by Aedas impress with their elongated elegance and the towers' quaint shape of a layered veil.

CONCLUSION

Downtown, the allegedly most advanced project that has yet taken place in Dubai, is especially difficult to

summarise. The slogan 'Centre of Now' somehow underlines why, because the extreme pace of the emirate's development is unique from several points of view, making forecasts of future changes and adjustments appear hazardous. The question is not only how the new district will be used once it is completed, but how the population's urban life will change once Dubai has established and secured its status as a world city and the population influx has become stable. How many users will be foreigners, how many just tourists? Where will the lower and middle classes live? How many citizens will be willing to use public transport? How easy will it be to directly interconnect the often self-sufficient compounds in order to eliminate cul-de-sac urbanism,

LEFT: An interior space in the Dubai Mall.

BELOW: The futuristic design of the Burj Khalifa / Dubai Mall metro station, situated along Sheikh Zayed Road.

View from an apartment in the Old Town district towards the centre of Downtown Dubai.

other than through the major motorways? Comparisons with other places or earlier periods might be helpful, but Dubai will have to find its own solutions in a constantly changing economic framework. The consequences of non-industrial growth in which the influx of new population is strictly controlled is interesting in comparison with the European boom towns of the late 19th century. This also explains why overcrowding is not an issue, or at least not in the areas that are accessible to tourists and planned for the middle and upper classes. As an inverted phenomenon compared with the industrial city, Dubai's urbanism is a masterplanned magnet and creator of wealth, and not a consequence of such creation. To a certain extent, overcrowding in the sense of densification and city life is an aim rather than a threat, and the Downtown project with its spectacular open spaces an important element in this quest.

OPPOSITE: View to the north from a tower on the southern limit of the district. The building on the left is actually a disguised cooling station.

Beijing Central Business District

LOCATION: BEIJING, CHINA
DATE: 2000–20
SIZE: 399 HECTARES (986 ACRES)

One of the largest of the projects presented in this book, Beijing's new Central Business District is essentially an accumulation of subdistricts rather than a single site. The constant modifications and adjustments of the initial masterplan are an expression of the tension that exists between the project's economic aim, the attraction of the world's most important financial institutions, and its formal one, the creation of a specific urban setting with distinctive place-making qualities.

Floor area ratio: 2.51
Residential population: 62,500
Mix of uses: 50% office, 25% residential, 25% retail, restaurants and public amenities

The decision to create a financial district in China's capital was part of the Beijing Urban Master Plan of 1993, and several large enterprises opened offices in the area in the years following this announcement. It was only in 1998 that the site boundaries were officially delimited by the City Planning Bureau. This rather uncoordinated kick-start changed nature and pace when, in 2000, a public development company was founded and tasked with steering the process of change. In the first year of its existence the company organised an international masterplan competition, for which eight teams were invited to submit their ideas. Only two of these teams were Chinese.

Beijing's CBD is simultaneously a typical and atypical example of urban planning in the booming People's Republic of the early 21st century: on the one hand, as a case study, it symbolises the increasingly liberal competitiveness between the country's major cities and the ongoing transformation from an industrial to a service economy, but on the other hand it also

LEFT: Model representation of Johnson Fain's winning masterplan proposal of 2000.

BELOW: Illustration of Pei Cobb Freed & Partners' winning proposal for the CBD Core Area (2006).

embodies an exceptional demonstration of power. As the planned CBD of the new superpower's capital, it holds a special status and level of prestige. This does not, however, mean that its development logic follows completely different rules than similarly sized projects such as Shanghai's Lujiazui on the Pudong Peninsula (begun 1990; see *The Urban Towers Handbook*, pp 170–77). Since the introduction of a market economy,

the Chinese municipalities have experienced a major shift in the composition of their budget: previously, they covered most of their expenses through the profits of the nationalised industries; today, in contrast, the exploitation of real estate has come to play a key role in public finances. As Chinese land has traditionally been public, the government sells leaseholds, rather than freeholds, and allows the private utilisation of land for a limited period of time. Afterwards, it falls back under public control. In the present regulations, the length of these leases has been fixed to 40 years for commercial uses, 50 years for offices, and 70 years for residential uses. Although municipalities are now forced to sell their land by auction, the allocation process was previously less transparent. Prior to 2003, it was possible to negotiate direct non-competitive agreements between the cities and interested buyers – a fact that explains why the well-connected SOHO Group was able to secure not only one, but five plots on its own, all without falling into the CBD's actual target group of international investors and leading financial companies.

For the wider public, both national and foreign, the new CBD might not be specifically well known, but it has indirectly gained worldwide prominence through the construction of the Chinese Central Television's headquarters, the CCTV building. Designed by Dutch star Rem Koolhaas of OMA (see also Euralille case study), this uniquely shaped megastructure has become one of the most successful examples of urban marketing through architecture, comparable in Beijing only to Herzog & de Meuron's so-called 'Bird's Nest', the Olympic Stadium for the 2008 Games.

PROJECT ORGANISATION / TEAM STRUCTURE

The CBD development company gathers the sites, demolishes the existing structures, builds new infrastructures, prepares the land and manages the sale process to private developers. Only in special cases, such as the construction of public amenities and landscaped elements, does the company itself

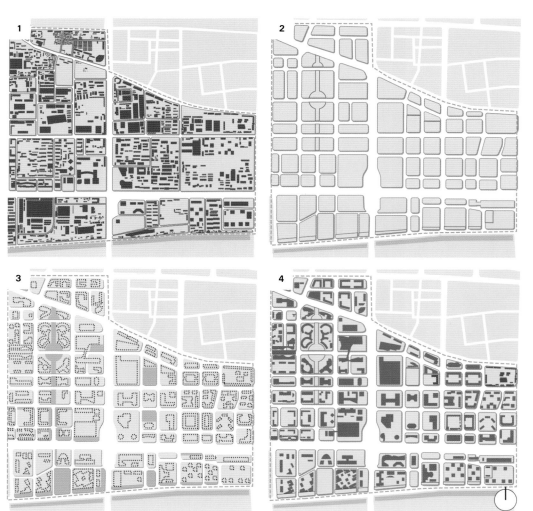

1 Situation before intervention, when most of the site was covered by state industries and workers' housing.

2 Plot subdivision and ownership after redevelopment: the CBD Authority sells the properties by auction.

3 The prescriptions for the building envelopes are internally defined and nurtured by the initial masterplan, later proposals for each subsite, and the demands of the purchasers.

4 Final state as expected in 2010.

▬▬▬ Private ownership
▬▬▬ Public ownership
⋮⋮⋮⋮⋮ Building envelope
▬▬▬ Green space
——— Private plot ownership
——— Public plot ownership
==== Tracks

Process diagrams

1 Building uses

Residential

Offices

Mixed use

Entertainment/Sports

Public amenities

Transport

Shopping

Retail and gastronomy in the ground floor

H Hotel

2 Green

Green - *public/collective/private*

Roadside vegetation/green alley

Walkway

Public square

3 Transport

R Rail - above ground /interchange

U Underground

BUS Bus

Tramway

4 Street network

carry out development. A particular feature compared with most other examples in this book is the area's impressive size and the fact that it was already inhabited. While the closure and spatial reorganisation of partly outdated and mostly public industrial uses was a relatively straightforward process, making up approximately 50 per cent of the site, the relocation of the local residents took more time and is still ongoing. This explains why the phasing of the project's implementation may appear to be uncoordinated and piecemeal, somehow contrary to what one might expect from urban planning in an authoritarian country. Analysed within the framework of this book, the CBD bears similarities with the 130 hectares (321 acres) of the Paris Rive Gauche area and its eight subdistricts (see Masséna Nord case study), but is still over three times larger. Even Hammarby in Stockholm, with its

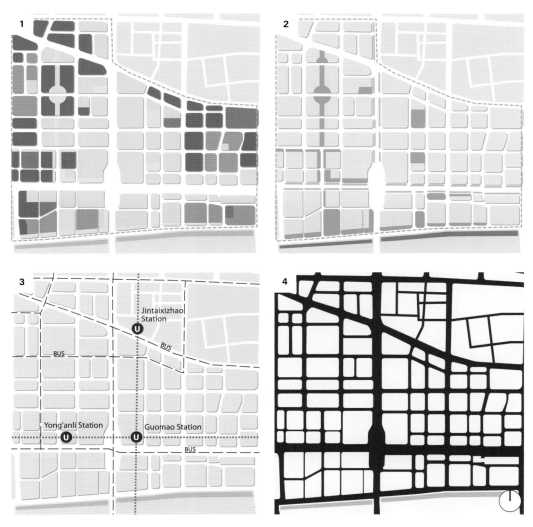

Analysis diagrams

40 hectares (99 acres) of water included, is just half the size of Beijing CBD. These scale comparisons are crucial for an understanding of the relatively indistinct character of the masterplan and the project's – by Middle and Far Eastern standards – seemingly long development time frame. Compared with the French example which had the additional planning advantage of a large stake of public amenities and social housing – hence controlling not only the offer, but also parts of the demand – one might consider that the CBD relies almost completely on private investment, having comparatively little influence on the demand side. Both the French and the Swedish projects were industrial brownfields, while this was, as previously mentioned, only the case for approximately half of the CBD. This fact draws another comparison, with La Défense business district in the western suburbs of Paris (see separate case study), for which over 20,000 people had to be displaced.

As a matter of fact, the CBD's implementation pace therefore depends on the availability of land and the progress of sales, more than on a particular phasing strategy or the attractiveness of the plots. If, despite the above explanations, the Beijing case still appears slightly weak in terms of overall urban concept, this can first and foremost be explained through the fact that, in the year 2000, when Johnson Fain won the masterplan competition, several plots had already been sold or were still in negotiation. This meant that neither the height prescriptions nor the open-space provisions or

major connections could be enforced according to the winning proposal. The CCTV tower, whose construction was decided only in 2002, now covers several blocks in the centre of the site's vast perimeter, further diluting the urban concept and blocking one of the masterplan's major green east–west axes. Similar to the planning of Lujiazui in Shanghai, where Richard Rogers' office won with a widely marketed, but never implemented vision of a concentric sustainable city, the prescriptions of the design competition were never meant to be statutory. Instead they served as a one-off inspiration for the Beijing Municipal Planning and Design Institute, the actual implementing body for the CBD's physical form.

URBAN FORM / CONNECTIVITY
Like the Paris Rive Gauche sector, but less clearly subdivided and communicated, Beijing CBD is therefore a combination of masterplans rather than a masterplan in itself. Jianwai SOHO, for example, is a 16-hectare (40-acre) site on its southern limit that was designed by the Japanese architect Riken Yamamoto for the SOHO Group. The plan was the result of a private invited competition and, unlike the CCTV tower and many of the district's other new high-rises, features a strong urban concept that surpasses the accumulation of oversized architectural monuments. Another subdistrict, at 38 hectares (94 acres) almost exactly the size of Battery Park City (see separate case study), is situated on the northeastern corner of the district's central

BELOW LEFT: View towards the east from under the canopy of The Place, an exclusive office and retail development in the northwestern part of the CBD. It also features the world's second-largest sky-screen.

BELOW: The intersection of Jianguomenwai Street and the third ring road is one of the city's most important traffic hubs.

RIGHT: Wanda Plaza (2007), designed by German architects GMP (von Gerkan, Marg & Partner). It is situated on East Jianguomenwai Street and features apartments, a hotel, offices and retail.

BELOW RIGHT: This north–south-oriented landscaped axis in the western part of the CBD follows approximately the open-space prescriptions of the 2000 masterplan by Johnson Fain. The curved buildings in the background are part of the residential Central Park development.

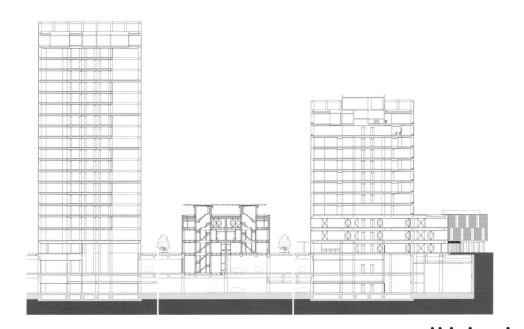

Section through two towers and a villa building of the Jianwai SOHO development.

BELOW: View from Jianwai SOHO to the north, with OMA's CCTV building in the background.

intersection between Jianguomenwai Street and the third ring road. It is called Beijing CBD Core, and was masterplanned in 2006 by the office of Pei Cobb Freed & Partners. In contrast to Jianwai SOHO, it is in itself constituted of several properties and is not in single ownership. The competition was organised by the public CBD development company in order to complement the Johnson Fain vision of the year 2000. Due to the multitude of intervening parties, it is probable that the final built result will turn out to be considerably different from the winning proposal by Pei Cobb Freed & Partners.

Before the current redevelopment, more than half of the total site was covered by industry. The remaining area was mostly comprised of low-rise slabs which had been erected as residences for the workers in a north–south-oriented logic similar to that of the 1920s German *Zeilenbau*. These structures, both the industrial and the residential ones, constituted the dense interior elements of an orthogonal grid of very large urban blocks measuring up to 1 kilometre (two-thirds of a mile) a side. On a macro level, this layout followed the city's traditional grid, with the difference that in the city's core, within the limits of the second ring road, the interiors of the megablocks were built up by a so-called *hutong* structure of narrow and winding alleys. These alleys passed along the walls of the *siheyuans*, the north-Chinese version of a one-storey courtyard house, connecting the block interiors with the major thoroughfares on their perimeter. On the site of the CBD, due to its post-war industrial heritage, this typology only exists as an exceptional element. The urban logic is nonetheless preserved since internal streets within the block did not follow any repetitive logic and were therefore – similarly to the historic *hutongs* – clearly subordinated to the city's megagrid. Through the new masterplan, this logic has changed, and the grid has often been subdivided into smaller blocks and plots. Although some spatial complexity is lost, the scheme simplifies the relationship between large built masses and the surrounding infrastructures in the most efficient way. Despite its straight rather than curved geometry, the block structure is therefore similar to the one chosen for Lujiazui in Shanghai, meant to accommodate large footprints in the middle of each block.

Crucial for the district's strategic importance is not only its position on the junction of two of the city's major roads, but also the connection to the public transport network through three planned or already existing metro lines and an extensive bus system. In parallel to the impressive building activities above ground, several underground levels allow access to the trains and will cross-connect large parts of the whole sector,

also accommodating various public amenities and emergency refuges.

ARCHITECTURAL TYPOLOGIES

Due to the lack of block perimeter definition and the – at this stage – only modestly discernible character of the urban concept, the individual architectures stand out more than the urban realm and its open spaces. In this context, and similar to most financial districts all around the world, the tower typology has been the favourite choice of most investors and developers. The China World Trade Center III, measuring 330 metres (1,083 feet) in height, is the district and city's tallest example. It will very probably be surpassed by one or several projects planned for the eastern extension of the CBD, for which a masterplan competition was won by Skidmore, Owings & Merrill (SOM) in 2010. In contrast to Shanghai, high-rise is a fairly recent architectural

The bases of the Jianwai SOHO towers (2007), designed by the French–Japanese architects Mikan, define the urban spaces and provide a rich mix of uses.

Aerial 1:10,000

feature in Beijing. In addition to the need for abundant space and excellent transport connections, this issue has also been a reason why the CBD was not built in the very centre of the city, where tall buildings are prohibited. Even more radically than in most other cities, Asian or European, Beijing's planning services therefore had to deal with a complete shift of architectural paradigm. Due to the country's political and economic past, the local built heritage offers very little substance that could have filled the gap between the vernacular courtyard typology and the current expression of corporate wealth and ambition: the tower. In the near future, new types might be developed, mixing local traditions with Western influences, but currently this is

not the case, and probably not even the goal: China's breathtaking speed of development over the past 30 years has – at least for some regions and some strata of the population – reached a level of prosperity that is equivalent to the West. It is more efficient to express this achievement through the abundant use of the same architectural symbols, than to introduce novelties that might not fit into this iconography of success whose rules have for historic reasons been defined by the capitalist West. Furthermore it should not be forgotten that the CBD targets by definition a global market with global clients and their standardised needs, a fact that considerably limits the scope of ad-hoc adjustments. In this context it is not surprising that the

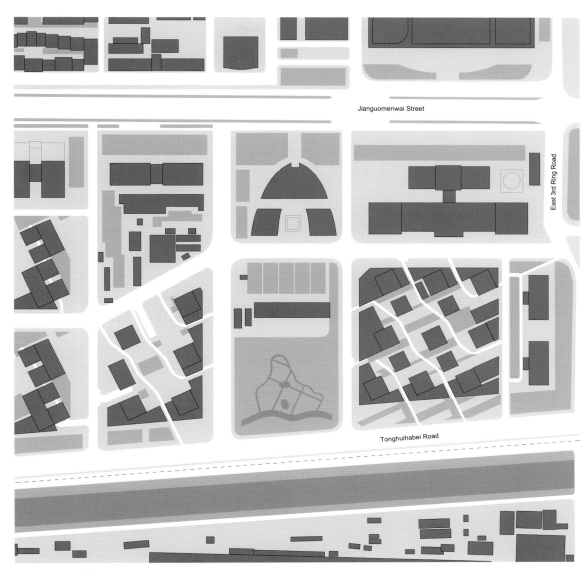

Urban plan 1:5,000

marketing of the CBD is, among other features, based on an accumulation of superlatives, reaching from 'the city's tallest tower in the 1990s', to 'the world's tallest international trade centre', to 'the building with the world's most spacious underground'.

CONCLUSION

From the Western perspective – and with the current lack of historical distance – it is tempting to perceive projects like the CBD solely in the light of drastic political and economical changes, and to overestimate differences rather than to acknowledge similarities with Western planning methods which surpass the often generic use of the word 'globalisation'. As already

mentioned, it is indeed unsurprising that the CBD Authority seems to have encountered some complications in developing and implementing a coherent urban strategy for such a large piece of land. With the tumultuous history of projects like Paris's La Défense (see separate chapter) and London's Canary Wharf in mind, the assumption could be made that these complications are an inherent ingredient of masterplanned office developments. Larger in terms of architectural scale, more prone to economic fluctuations and marked by the professionalism of not only the investors, but also the tenants and end users, these developments tend to experience more adjustments than residential schemes with their allegedly superior stability. In the French case, it should not be forgotten that the site perimeter and the vague idea of a podium urbanism were essentially the only fixed project characteristics for a stagnating period of over 15 years.

Today, after expiry of just about half of the expected development time frame, it is still difficult to identify an 'iconic' urban concept for the 399 hectares (986 acres) of the Beijing site. However, despite the fact that works are still ongoing and improvements constantly being made, it could also be claimed that such a forced coherence would be inappropriate, simplifying a potentially richer and more complex mix that will evolve naturally over a longer period of time. This soft vision of masterplanning essentially follows the model of the traditional American CBD that eventually merges with its surroundings, because it is built up on the same principles of urban form. Mid- and Downtown Manhattan and Chicago's Loop are probably the most famous examples of this type, where the specificity of the CBD district relies mainly on higher floor area ratios (FARs) and an unusually dense agglomeration of specific uses, and not on a single 'masterplan'. The problems of such a vision for the Beijing CBD are the difference in type of grid, and a history of courtyard architecture that seems almost disconnected from the current models of corporate design. In this situation, the elaboration of spatial concepts that deal with the relationship between the architectural element, the urban block and its perimeter are therefore as important as architectural innovation and landscaping. They provide exciting scope for a new type of morphological research.

TOP: Landscaping detail on the northwestern edge of the CBD.

ABOVE: View of Jianwai SOHO along Tonghuihe North Road, on the southern boundary of the CBD. The masterplan and the towers were designed by Riken Yamamoto and Field Shop.

OPPOSITE: View from the top floor of the China World Trade Center III (2007, by SOM) to the east. Many former industrial and residential structures are still standing, but will soon be replaced by modern constructions.

La Défense Seine Arche

LOCATION: NANTERRE, PUTEAUX, COURBEVOIE AND LA GARENNE-COLOMBES, FRANCE
DATE: 1958–2020
SIZE: 564 HECTARES (1,394 ACRES) (LA DÉFENSE: 160 HECTARES (395 ACRES))

Internationally known only for its 160 hectares (395 acres) of high-rise architecture – Europe's largest business district – the territory of the national development company EPADESA actually spans an area almost three times larger. As an extremely complex site, dissected by a whole range of major infrastructures, it symbolises the opportunities and challenges of the future 'Le Grand Paris'.

Floor area ratio: 0.83
Residential population: 25,000
Mix of uses: 73% office, 20% residential, 5% retail and restaurants, 2% other (these figures relate to the redevelopment programme)

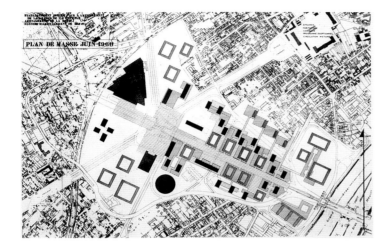

LEFT: The masterplan for La Défense in 1960.

BELOW: The territory of EPADESA today, including the TGT & Associés masterplan for the Seine Arche sector to the west and the high-rise redevelopment projects in La Défense to the east.

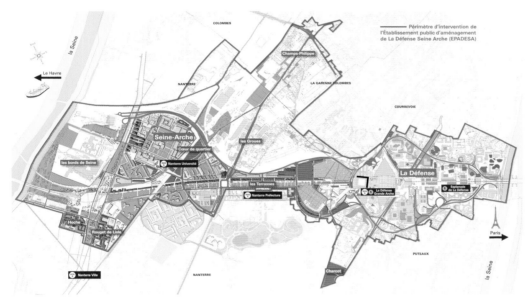

Due to its position on the historic royal axis leading from the Louvre westwards to the castle and hunting grounds of Saint-Germain-en-Laye, the elevated area around today's Grande Arche had been in the focus of the national planners for a long time prior to its development. Among many others, there had been a proposal in 1901 to create a 10-kilometre (6-mile) urban boulevard from Paris to Saint-Germain as an extension of the Champs-Elysées, with a bicycle lane and tram line at its centre. After the First World War, the specificity of the site as a planning impetus was reinforced by the development of a comprehensive national planning system, and in 1924 it was decreed that all French communities would have to establish a regional plan as a vision for future development. The reason for this law was an early phenomenon of urban sprawl, ongoing

since the 1910s, mainly through the uncoordinated construction of family houses in formerly rural areas that had not yet been zoned and protected.

The dedicated plan for the Paris region, elaborated under the leadership of Henri Prost for an area of 35 kilometres (22 miles) in radius including no less than 657 political entities, suffered several delays and was finally adopted in 1939. In addition to limiting the urbanised area and protecting green spaces, its aim was to decongest the city centre, plan transport routes and strategically organise industries. Housing densities outside the city core were constrained in order to avoid the hygiene concerns that the centre had to cope with. The extension of the *voie triomphale* ('triumphal way') through La Défense was an element of this document, but appeared essentially only in the form of a motorway

to the west. Plans became more specific through an addendum in 1956 when the area of La Défense, situated along the axis between two curves of the River Seine, was officially designated as a future office district. At that time, in the context of a housing crisis which claimed many lives during the severe winter of 1954–55, the residential component of the ambitious undertaking was still of major importance.

The first expropriations began in 1955 under the minister of reconstruction and urbanism, and friend of Le Corbusier, Eugène Claudius-Petit. They were more easily realised in the eastern part of the sector, providing a pragmatic explanation for the fact that the first and main phase of the construction of La Défense happened east of the La Défense roundabout, named after the defence of Paris in the Franco-Prussian War of 1870–71. The development's designation as an *opération d'intérêt national* (OIN – operation of national interest) and the delimitation of a specific zone obviously did not result in instant public ownership of land, and ownership questions still remain of major importance today.

PROJECT ORGANISATION / TEAM STRUCTURE

In 1958, with André Prothin as its first president, the national development company EPAD (Établissement Public pour l'Aménagement de la Région de la Défense) was founded with the mission to purchase and prepare the land, to design and build the infrastructures and public amenities, to resell developed plots and development rights, and to animate and promote the project. Its national status – rare, but not unique – is different from the other French examples in this book (see Masséna Nord and Euralille case studies), which are implemented by a mixed development company (*société d'économie mixte* (SEM)) following the initiative of one or several local authorities. Other examples of national development companies that have been created in order to implement an OIN are the two international Parisian airports, Charles de Gaulle and Orly, and the Euroméditerranée site in Marseilles. The idea behind these structures is not only the provision of more financial means than in a conventional set-up, but also the opportunity to circumvent political

The Grande Arche de la Défense (Johann Otto von Spreckelsen, 1989) with the CNIT (Jean de Mailly, Robert Camelot and Bernard Zehrfuss, 1958) to the right and the Quatre Temps shopping centre (1981, by Atelier LWD) to the left. Above the shopping centre is the Elysées La Défense office building (1982 Saubot & Jullien with Overcash).

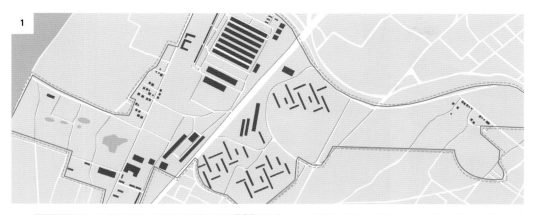

1 Historic situation in 1958 before intervention (Seine Arche site only).

2 Plot subdivision and ownership after redevelopment, according to TGT & Associés' recent masterplan.

3 Masterplan prescriptions for the building envelopes.

4 Final state.

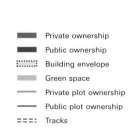

	Private ownership
	Public ownership
	Building envelope
	Green space
	Private plot ownership
	Public plot ownership
	Tracks

Process diagrams

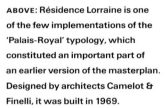

ABOVE: Résidence Lorraine is one
of the few implementations of the
'Palais-Royal' typology, which
constituted an important part of
an earlier version of the masterplan.
Designed by architects Camelot &
Finelli, it was built in 1969.

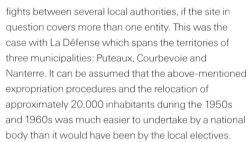

fights between several local authorities, if the site in question covers more than one entity. This was the case with La Défense which spans the territories of three municipalities: Puteaux, Courbevoie and Nanterre. It can be assumed that the above-mentioned expropriation procedures and the relocation of approximately 20,000 inhabitants during the 1950s and 1960s was much easier to undertake by a national body than it would have been by the local electives.

As an expression of the structure's rather state-authoritarian character, these local electives initially did not have full control over the destiny of their territory: of the 18 seats of EPAD's governing board, they occupied nine, including the three mayors. Today, as a result of France's decentralisation policy, these figures have changed and in the current structure called EPADESA (Établissement Public d'Aménagement de la Défense Seine Arche) the local electives represent, with nine members out of 16, the board's majority.

The creation in 2001 of EPASA (Établissement Public d'Aménagement Seine Arche) as a separate structure ensued from the City of Nanterre's desire to better control its territory, previously included in EPAD's project perimeter. It reflected discrepancies in the vision of the western sector's development as proposed in the international 'Mission Grand Axe' competition of 1991. The construction of the Grande Arche de la Défense (1985–9) by the Danish architect Johann Otto von Spreckelsen not only marked the successful termination of the district's first phase, but also, through its ingenious opening, raised the question of the axis's continuation to the west. As a physical prerequisite for such plans, the government had decided in 1990 to divert a national road, and to tunnel a section of the A14 motorway and the RER A train line. The unfortunate political separation of EPASA and EPAD ended in 2010 when they merged to create EPADESA. The original 480 hectares (1,186 acres) of territory were extended

TOP: A south section of
the Boulevard Circulaire
which delimits the high-
rise part of La Défense.
Due to the elevated
nature of the central
podium, pedestrian
connections to the area's
extensions are often
made through bridges.

ABOVE: Eve Tower (1975)
by Hourlier & Gury.
Connected to the central
podium by two pedestrian
bridges, it is one of the
district's rare mixed-use
constructions.

to a total of 564 hectares (1,394 acres), adding to the above-mentioned three municipalities a site that is part of the city of La Garenne-Colombes. Since February 2007 the maintenance and programming of the 160 hectares (395 acres) of the former EPAD estate, including the labyrinthine spaces of the podium, have been externalised. EPADESA can hence focus its attention on more strategic tasks, one of them – and its only source of income – being the sale of construction rights. This financial logic is important to understand, and explains why the extension of the official development mission, undertaken in several steps after the expiry of an initial period of 30 years that ended in 1988, is directly linked to the incremental rise of development rights.

In terms of implementation, the procedure as such is not altered through the national status of the development structure, and applies to different subsectors of the EPADESA site in the form of so-called *zones d'aménagement concerté* (ZACs – concerted development zones), which have already been discussed in other case studies in this book (see Masséna Nord, Antigone or Euralille). This is not the case for the high-rise district in which the current renewal is based on the enlargement of existing development envelopes and the piecemeal improvement of the podium's relation to the *boulevard circulaire* and its wider surroundings, rather than through the comprehensive redesign of whole neighbourhoods. These smaller interventions do not necessitate the attribution of a dedicated legal status, but have to be incorporated in the local plans (*plans locaux d'urbanisme* (PLUs)) of the municipalities they are positioned in, be that Nanterre, Puteaux or Courbevoie.

URBAN FORM / CONNECTIVITY

Much has been written about the eastern part of La Défense, situated in front of and around the Grande Arche. As one of the most extreme examples of podium urbanism, a concrete construction 1.5 kilometres (nearly a mile) in length separates a multitude of heavy infrastructures and parking levels in its centre from an artificial and pedestrianised surface on its top which gives access to a set of predominantly high-rise structures. The existence of this massive plane, in conjunction with the enclosing and symmetrical shape of the *boulevard circulaire*, immediately suggests a quickly implemented drawing-board urbanism that does not reflect the reality of the historical development. An early photomontage of 1955, prepared by the well-known architects and Grand Prix de Rome winners Jean de Mailly, Robert Camelot and Bernard Zehrfuss as a result of their appointment for the construction of the

CNIT (Centre des Nouvelles Industries et Technologies), did not actually feature any continuous podium element and envisaged a more or less symmetrical accumulation of large slab buildings on both sides of something that could be characterised as an urban motorway. At that time even the historic roundabout was preserved, but in this study was soon replaced by a small podium that unified the space around the CNIT and added a super-tall tower as the focus of the new quarter. It was only with the approved plan of 1964 that the podium became the project's structuring element. In this version of the plan the so-called 'Palais-Royal' typology of low-rise courtyard buildings, destined for residential uses, was still presented as an equally important component next to point towers with a footprint of 24 by 42 metres (79 by 138 feet) and a height of 100 metres (328 feet).

It is intriguing to realise that the voluntarist and inherently top-down character of the project's initiation

César's *Thumb* sculpture with Valode & Pistre's T1 Tower (2008) to the right and Castro Denissof's Egée Tower (1999) to the left.

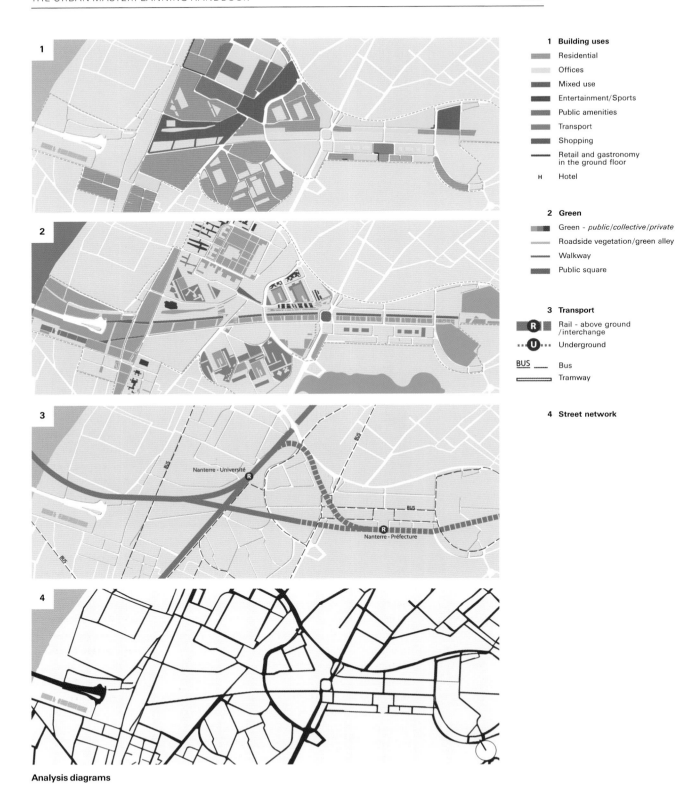

1 Building uses

- Residential
- Offices
- Mixed use
- Entertainment/Sports
- Public amenities
- Transport
- Shopping
- Retail and gastronomy in the ground floor
- H Hotel

2 Green

- Green - *public/collective/private*
- Roadside vegetation/green alley
- Walkway
- Public square

3 Transport

- R Rail - above ground /interchange
- U Underground
- BUS Bus
- Tramway

4 Street network

Analysis diagrams

phase soon collided with the interests of the market. The conception of a masterplan's coherent implementation was replaced by a piecemeal strategy that had to adjust to the specific demands of the investors. In this process of financial logic the residential uses quickly fell behind, not being able to pay for the extremely onerous construction of the podium. This was further aggravated through increasing public criticism of the district's radical urbanism, lowering the value of residential development rights much more than the commercial ones. In contrast to the modest size of apartment buildings, the large floor plates of the new corporate work culture needed space and public planning help that the government could offer. However, even under these theoretically advantageous conditions, the complexity of the project and the relative modesty of the high-rise market limited the pace of construction. By the very end of the 1960s, only three towers had been finished, Tour Esso (now destroyed and replaced) being the first in 1963. It fits into the earlier development logic that the impact of the initial masterplan team of de Mailly, Camelot and Zehrfuss, in conjunction with Robert Auzelle and Paul Herbé, diminished in the course of time. The necessity of ad-hoc changes to the 1964 plan terminated the phase of fundamental urban considerations and limited the scale of action increasingly to the implementation of architectural and engineering interventions.

The western sector of EPADESA, called Seine Arche, could hardly be more different from its corporate brother. Dissected by motorways and train lines and partly still industrial, the area was until recently considered to

ABOVE LEFT: Pei Cobb Freed & Partners' and SRA-Architectes' Tour EDF (2001) in the background, with Delb, Chesneau, Verola & Delalande's Tour Franklin (1972) to the right and Jean Balladur's SCOR building (1983) to the left.

ABOVE: View to the west of the Grande Arche de la Défense with the Jardins de l'Arche.

LEFT: View from above the Jardins de l'Arche to the east: a pedestrian bridge extends the level of the podium along the 'Grand Axe' towards the Terrasses de Nanterre.

Aerial 1:10,000

be a mere hinterland, despite being home to the large Université Paris Ouest Nanterre La Défense and its 35,000 students. Today, the situation has changed, and the sector contains a whole range of ongoing development projects, featuring a far higher percentage of residential uses than its eastern neighbour. The Parisian office Treuttel Garcias Treuttel (TGT & Associés), winner of a development competition in 2002, is responsible for the planning of a 120-hectare (297-acre) zone, which covers the entire 3.2-kilometre (2-mile) axis that spans from the Grande Arche to the Seine. The core and backbone of their scheme are the Terrasses de Nanterre, the slightly curved extension of this axis, organised in 20 terraced steps above the infrastructures'

tunnel. Asymmetric and filled with a multitude of public spaces and activities, they are designed as a democratic, playful and contemporary version of their more central and aristocratic neighbour. Most importantly they mark, paradoxically despite their position above a tunnel, a return to an urbanism of continuity that respects the nature of the ground in providing a functionally effective and simple solution for a 45-metre (148-foot) slope between the Grande Arche and the Seine.

ARCHITECTURAL TYPOLOGIES

The site's impressive size and its long development time span make it difficult to identify any clearly repetitive architectural typology. This is true even if we limit our

Urban plan 1:5,000

analysis to the high-rise sector. If the early towers such as Tour Nobel (now Tour RTE Nexity; 1966, by Jean de Mailly, Jacques Depussé and Jean Prouvé) and Tour FIAT (now Tour AREVA; 1974, by Roger Saubot, François Jullien and SOM) were in their elegance and austerity of clearly Miesian inspiration, the following generations offered some interesting and more playful alternatives. Still following international trends, a whole set of towers and mid-rise buildings of the 1980s and early 1990s, including Tour Elf (now Tour Total Coupole; 1985, by WZMH Architects, Roger Saubot and François Jullien), featured mirrored glass and established an ambivalent relation between the pedestrians, the buildings and the sky. Of the more recent constructions,

the Tour EDF of 2001 (by Pei Cobb Freed & Partners and SRA-Architectes) is considered to be a masterpiece of Neomodernism.

Often overlooked are the remainders of the 'Palais-Royals' typology. Seen in combination with the office towers, they are clearly reminiscent of Le Corbusier's Plan Voisin (1925) and Immeubles Villas (1922), even though their Brutalist exterior, the doughnut-shaped plan and the interior courtyard bear greater formal resemblance to his La Tourette Monastery (1960) or the Ahmedabad Museum (1957). Of 15 planned 'Palais-Royal' in the 1964 masterplan, only four have been built, one example being the Résidence Lorraine by Camelot & Finelli (1969). Symptomatic for the change of urban

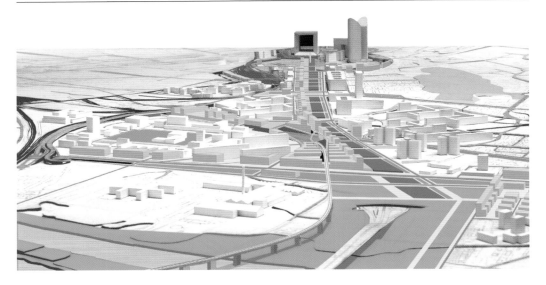

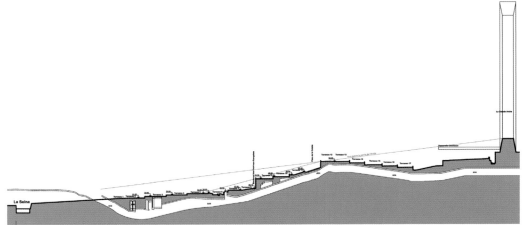

LEFT: Visualisation of TGT & Associés' Terrasses de Nanterre masterplan.

CENTRE: Amplified section of the Terrasses de Nanterre with the Grande Arche to the right. One of the project's main drivers is the provision of a certain continuity despite the significant variations in ground level, both natural and caused by infrastructural works. This strategy allows for the extension of the monumental axis to the west.

BELOW: View from the Terrasses de Nanterre, designed by TGT & Associés, towards the Grande Arche de la Défense.

paradigms, the living rooms of the apartments are oriented towards the building's green interior, contradicting the spatial logic of the traditional Parisian apartment buildings and their street-oriented enfilade of representative rooms.

CONCLUSION

Since 2009, the office of Dusapin Leclercq has been working on EPADESA's 20-year urban strategy, taking into account the multitude of existing sub-projects and the site's crucial relation to the neighbouring communities. The scope of this study is strongly linked to the still-open plans for 'Le Grand Paris' which try to provide a comprehensive development vision for the future of the Greater Paris region. Since its adoption by President Sarkozy through the organisation of an invited ideas competition in 2008, 'Le Grand Paris' has had a considerable impact on French society as a whole. It deals with the particularity of the political separation between the centre of Paris and its surroundings, the *banlieue*. After approximately three years of visionary studies, it became clear that transport connections will provide the key to the region's change, focusing on the suburb-to-suburb links much more than on the existing and fairly well-developed radial connections. In this planned network of 175 kilometres (109 miles) of an automated 'Grand Paris Express', currently in an advanced planning stage, La Défense and Nanterre will have a key position. These fairly new plans add to older ones for the extension of the RER E line from Saint-Lazare Station to La Défense and the construction of a new high-speed train station between the University of Nanterre and the Grande Arche. Taking into account the existing connections to the regional express train network through the RER A (since 1970), the conventional metro network through the number 1 line (since 1992), and numerous bus, tram and train lines, the territory of EPADESA will be the best-connected area outside the historic core.

These exciting prospects arise at the right time, supporting not only the multiple projects of the Seine Arche area, but also the latest renewal plan for the high-rise district, announced in 2006. This plan, well under way despite the global crisis of the end of the decade, envisages the renovation and construction of 450,000 square metres (4.8 million square feet) of office space and 100,000 square metres (1.1 million square feet) of residential space. Most of the new-built projects are based on the extension of existing development envelopes, necessitating the destruction of older and less efficient towers. In these plans, the residential component has gained more importance and, little by little, La Défense Seine Arche seems to be losing the status of an 'inhuman corporate' novelty while reaching the maturity of a dense mixed-use district. It releases development pressure from the historic core and increasingly builds bridges to its neighbours.

Who would have thought this in the late 1960s, when – in the shadow of the student protests – La Défense with its monstrous podium and few finished towers symbolised the failure of a technocratic and authoritarian post-war urbanism?

BELOW: Bird's-eye view of Seine Arche and La Défense, seen from the west. The two sectors follow blatantly different development rules.

Appendices

Timeline

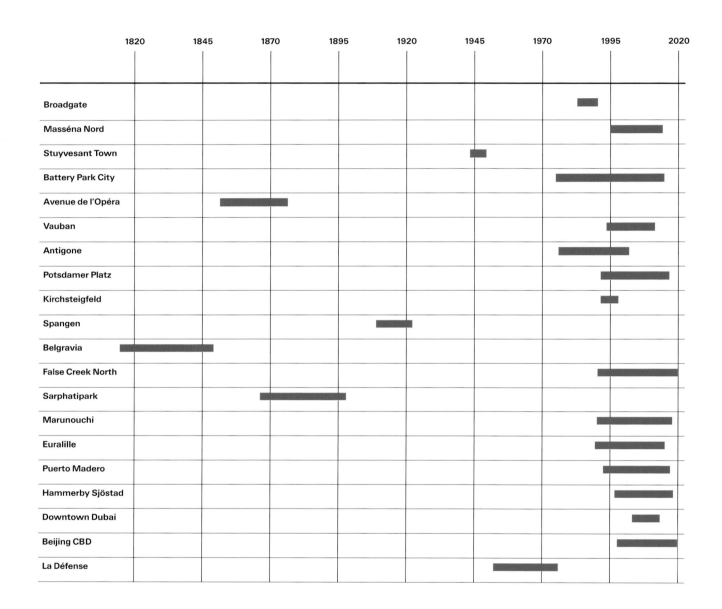

	1820	1845	1870	1895	1920	1945	1970	1995	2020
Broadgate							▬		
Masséna Nord								▬▬▬	
Stuyvesant Town						▬			
Battery Park City							▬▬▬▬▬▬▬		
Avenue de l'Opéra		▬▬▬▬							
Vauban								▬▬	
Antigone							▬▬▬▬		
Potsdamer Platz								▬▬▬▬	
Kirchsteigfeld								▬	
Spangen					▬				
Belgravia	▬▬▬▬								
False Creek North								▬▬▬	
Sarphatipark			▬▬▬▬						
Marunouchi								▬▬▬▬	
Euralille								▬▬▬	
Puerto Madero								▬▬▬	
Hammerby Sjöstad								▬▬▬	
Downtown Dubai								▬	
Beijing CBD								▬▬▬▬	
La Défense						▬▬▬			

Density Table

Project name *Location*	Site area			Development area		Floor area ratio	Population	Population/ ha	Predominant land use		
	ha	acres	m²	m²	ft²				office	residential	mixed
Broadgate [1] *London, UK*	11.7	29	117,000	422,900	4,552,500	3.61	0	n/a	x		
Masséna Nord (Paris Rive Gauche) [2] *Paris, France*	12.6	31	126,000	339,400	3,653,300	2.69	2,430	193			x
Stuyvesant Town *New York City, USA*	24.7	61	247,000	706,100	7,600,000	2.86	18,000	729		x	
Battery Park City *New York City, USA*	37.6	93	376,000	1,945,000	20,936,200	5.17	13,314	354			x
Avenue de l'Opéra [3] *Paris, France*	40	99	400,000	1,216,000	13,088,900	3.04	3,480	87			x
Vauban [4] *Freiburg, Germany*	41	101	410,000	n/a	n/a	1.40	5,300	129		x	
Antigone *Montpellier, France*	50	124	500,000	520,000	5,597,200	1.04	8,000	160		x	
Potsdamer Platz *Berlin, Germany*	51	126	510,000	1,100,000	11,840,300	2.16	4,500	88			x
Kirchsteigfeld [5] *Potsdam, Germany*	58.7	145	587,000	430,350	4,632,200	0.73	5,000	85		x	
Spangen *Rotterdam, The Netherlands*	64	158	640,000	550,000	5,920,200	0.86	9,800	153		x	
Belgravia [6] *London, UK*	80.9	200	809,000	1,068,400	11,500,000	1.32	6,300	78			x
False Creek North [7] *Vancouver, Canada*	83	204	830,000	1,370,000	14,746,600	1.65	20,000	241		x	
Sarphatipark *Amsterdam, The Netherlands*	101.5	251	1,015,000	1,863,450	20,058,000	1.84	23,850	235		x	
Marunouchi *Tokyo, Japan*	120	297	1,200,000	6,758,000	72,742,500	5.63	0	n/a	x		
Euralille *Lille, France*	126	311	1,260,000	1,029,400	11,080,400	0.82	8,000	63			x
Puerto Madero *Buenos Aires, Argentina*	131	324	1,310,000	2,615,800	28,156,200	2.00	21,800	166			x
Hammerby Sjöstad [8] *Stockholm, Sweden*	160	395	1,600,000	n/a	n/a	1.43	24,000	150		x	
Downtown Dubai *Dubai, UAE*	200	494	2,000,000	n/a	n/a	n/a	30,000	150			x
Beijing Central Business District [9] *Beijing, China*	399	986	3,990,000	10,000,000	107,639,100	2.51	62,500	157			x
La Défense Seine Arche [10] *Greater Paris Region, France*	564	1,394	5,640,000	4,700,000	50,590,400	0.83	25,00	44			x

Figures given here and throughout the book are approximate and do not include parking.

1   The density figures include the recent high-rise development on the northern edge of the site (Broadgate Tower and 201 Bishopsgate).

2   The 130 ha of Paris Rive Gauche as a whole have a floor area ratio of 1:86.

3   The figures for population and development areas are the result of a pro-rata calculation based on census information for a subzone.

4   The average FAR of 1:4 relates only to the plots of the development that have been zoned for residential use (excluding public spaces).

5   The figures for the total development area include the business park which is not yet developed.

6   The population figure is based on the census information from 2001.

7   Due to a lack of available information, the development figures are based on the False Creek North UDP.

8   The FAR of 1:43 relates only to the *c* 93 ha of the central residential sector. The overall density is lower.

9   The population figure is an estimate based on 25% of the total development area being reserved for residential uses.

10   The figure for the total development area excludes several existing uses.

Figure-ground Diagrams

Avenue de l'Opéra, Paris

Belgravia, London

Sarphatipark, Amsterdam

Spangen, Rotterdam

Stuyvesant Town, New York

La Défense Seine Arche, Greater Paris

Battery Park City, New York

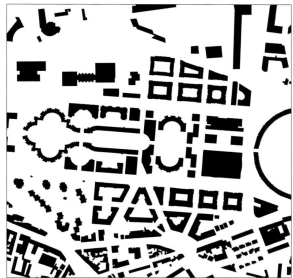

Antigone, Montpellier

Broadgate, London

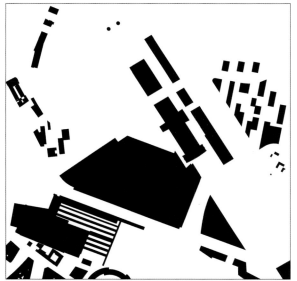

Euralille, Lille

Potsdamer Platz, Berlin

Kirchsteigfeld, Potsdam

Hammarby Sjöstad, Stockholm

Vauban, Freiburg

Masséna Nord, Paris

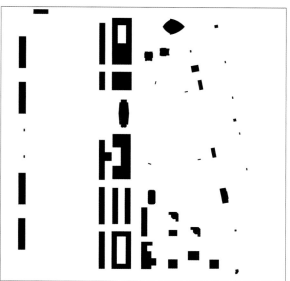

Puerto Madero, Buenos Aires

Marunouchi, Tokyo

Beijing Central Business District

Downtown Dubai

False Creek North, Vancouver

Scale Comparison of all Projects

Berlin
Potsdamer Platz
51 ha

Paris
Avenue de l'Opéra
40 ha

Montpellier
Antigone
50 ha

Stockholm
Hammarby Sjöstad
160 ha

Freiburg
Vauban
41 ha

Rotterdam
Spangen
64 ha

Potsdam
Kirchsteigfeld
58.7 ha

London
Belgravia
80.9 ha

London
Broadgate
11.7 ha

Grand Paris
La Défense Seine Arche
564 ha

Lille
Euralille
126 ha

Amsterdam
Sarphatipark
101.5 ha

Paris
Masséna Nord
12.6 ha

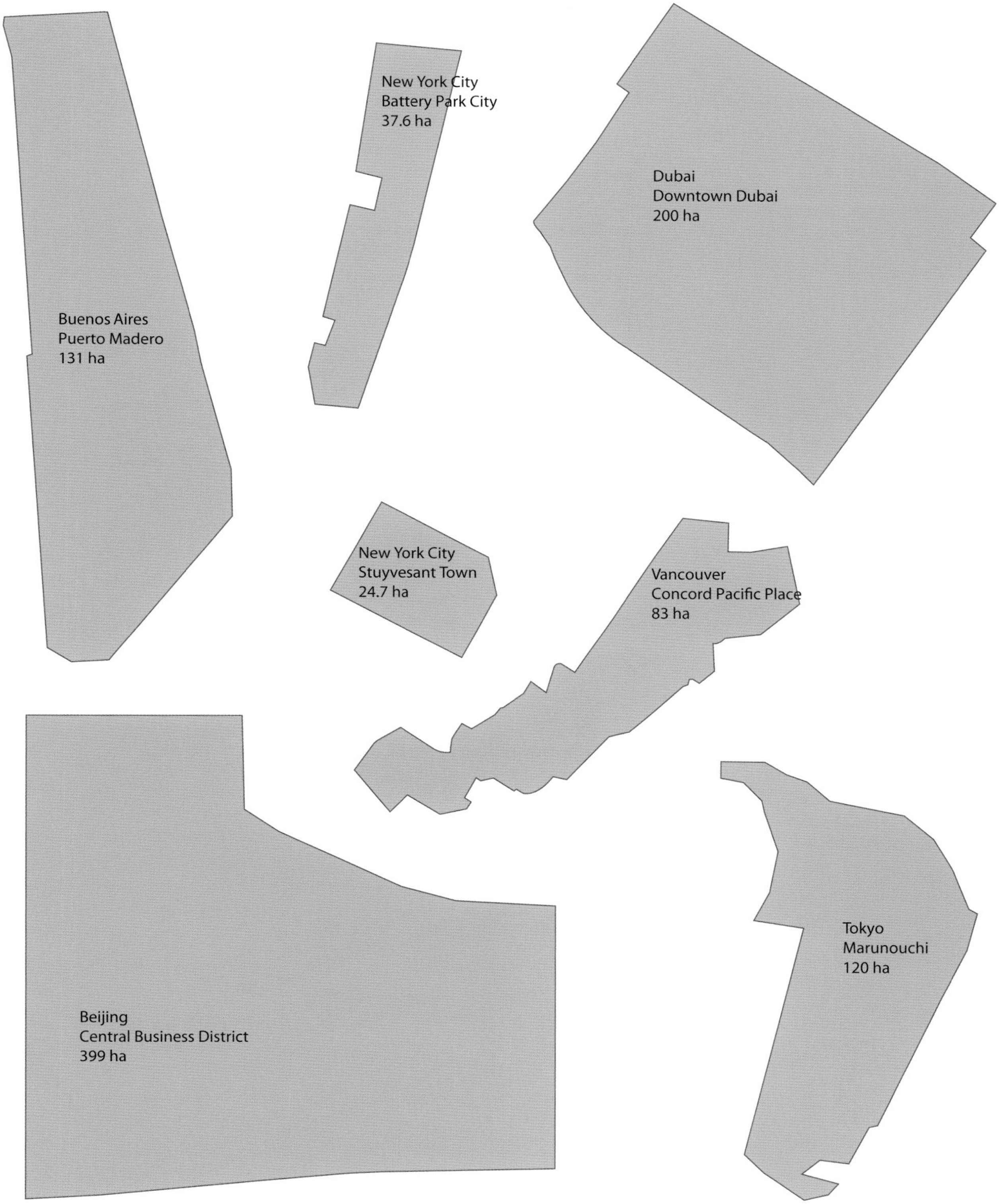

New York City
Battery Park City
37.6 ha

Dubai
Downtown Dubai
200 ha

Buenos Aires
Puerto Madero
131 ha

New York City
Stuyvesant Town
24.7 ha

Vancouver
Concord Pacific Place
83 ha

Tokyo
Marunouchi
120 ha

Beijing
Central Business District
399 ha

Bibliography

GENERAL REFERENCE

In preparing our study and writing the book's introduction, we consulted the following books.

Bassett, Edward M, *The Master Plan*, Russell Sage Foundation (New York), 1938

Benevolo, Leonardo, *The European City*, Blackwell (Oxford), 1993

Benevolo, Leonardo, *The Origins of Modern Town Planning*, MIT Press (Cambridge, MA), 1971

Billings, Keith H, *Master Planning for Architecture*, Van Nostrand Reinhold (New York), 1993

Branch, Melville Campbell, *Urban Planning Theory*, Dowden Hutchinson & Ross (Stroudsburg, PA), 1975

Bressi, Todd, *The Seaside Debates*, Rizzoli (New York), 2002

Campbell, Scott and Fainstein, Susan S, *Readings in Planning Theory*, Blackwell (Oxford), 2003

Catanese, Anthony J and Snyder, James C, *Urban Planning*, McGraw-Hill (New York), 1988

Cowan, Robert, *The Dictionary of Urbanism*, Streetwise Press (Tisbury), 2005

Cuthbert, Alexander R, *The Form of Cities*, Blackwell (Oxford), 2006

Erber, Ernest, *Urban Planning in Transition*, Grossman Publishers (New York), 1970

Firley, Eric and Stahl, Caroline, *The Urban Housing Handbook*, John Wiley & Sons (Chichester), 2009

Firley, Eric and Gimbal, Julie, *The Urban Towers Handbook*, John Wiley & Sons (Chichester), 2011

Hall, Peter Geoffrey, *Cities of Tomorrow*, Blackwell (Oxford), 1996

Hall, Peter Geoffrey, *Urban & Regional Planning*, Routledge (London), 1992

Hall, Thomas, *Planning Europe's Capital Cities*, Routledge (New York), 2010

Holland, Laurence B, *Who Designs America?*, Anchor Books (New York), 1966

Howard, Ebenezer, *Garden Cities of To-Morrow*, Faber & Faber (London), 1965

Jacobs, Jane, *The Death and Life of Great American Cities*, Vintage Books (New York), 1961

Krieger, Alex and Saunders, William S. *Urban Design*, University of Minnesota Press (Minneapolis), 2009

Krier, Leon, *The Architecture of Community*, Island Press (Washington, DC), 2009

Larice, Michael and Macdonald, Elizabeth, *The Urban Design Reader*, Routledge (New York), 2007

LeGates, Richard T and Stout, Frederic, *The City Reader*, Routledge (London), 1996

Levy, John M, *Contemporary Urban Planning*, Prentice-Hall (Englewood Cliffs, NJ), 1988

Lewis, Harold MacLean, *Planning the Modern City*, John Wiley & Sons (New York), 1949

Lim, CJ and Liu, Ed, *Smart Cities and Eco-Warriors*, Routledge (London), 2010

Lodge, Rupert C, *Plato's Theory of Art*, Routledge & Kegan Paul (London), 1953

Master Plan Delhi 2021, Rupa & Co (New Delhi), 2007

McConnell, Shean, *Theories for Planning*, Heinemann (London), 1981

Miles, Malcolm, *Urban Utopias*, Routledge (New York), 2008

Mumford, Eric, *Defining Urban Design – CIAM Architects and the Formation of a Discipline, 1937–69*, Yale University Press (New Haven, CT), 2009

Mumford, Lewis, *The City in History*, Harcourt Brace & World (New York), 1961

Panerai, Philippe, Castex, Jean and Depaule, Jean-Charles, *Urban Forms: Death and Life of the Urban Block*, Architectural Press (Oxford), 2004

Platt, Kalvin, *Master-Planned Communities*, Urban Land Institute (Washington, DC), 2011

Reps, John W, *The Making of Urban America*, Princeton University Press (Princeton, NJ), 1965

Roche, R Samuel and Lasher, Aric, *Plans of Chicago*, Architects Research Foundation (Chicago), 2010

Rowe, Colin and Koetter, Fred, *Collage City*, MIT Press (Cambridge, MA), 1984

Scott, Mel, *American City Planning Since 1890*, University of California Press (Berkeley, CA), 1969

Sutcliffe, Anthony, *The Rise of Modern Urban Planning 1800–1914*, Mansell (London), 1980

Vernez Moudon, Anne, *Master-Planned Communities*, University of Washington (Washington, DC), 1990

CASE STUDIES

The information in our 20 case studies is based on interviews with representatives of each city concerned, as well as with developers, architects, urban designers and building users. Some planning documents were supplied to us directly, while others are available on the Internet. Our research was further informed by magazines, academic journals and the following books.

Broadgate, London

Davies, John, *Broadgate*, Davenport (London), 1991

Duffy, Francis, *The Changing Workplace*, Phaidon (London), 1992

Fainstein, Susan, *The City Builders*, Blackwell (Cambridge), 1994

Hunting, Penelope, *Broadgate and Liverpool Street Station*, Rosehaugh Stanhope Developments (London), 1991

Powell, Kenneth, *London*, Academy Editions (London), 1993

Masséna Nord, Paris

Accorsi, Florence, *The Open Block by Christian de Portzamparc*, Archives d'Architecture Moderne (AAM) (Paris), 2010

Firley, Eric and Gimbal, Julie, *The Urban Towers Handbook*, John Wiley & Sons (Chichester), 2011

Ministère de l'Équipement, *Projets Urbains en France – French Urban Strategies*, Le Moniteur (Paris), 2002

Werquin, Ann-Caroll and Pélissier, Alain, *La Consultation Masséna*, Éditions d'Art Albert Skira (Geneva), 1997

Stuyvesant Town, New York

Heilberg, Frieda N, *A Study of the Rehousing Needs of Tenants who will be Displaced by the Stuyvesant Town Project in New York City*, Master's thesis, New York School of Social Work, 1944

Simon, Arthur, *Stuyvesant Town, USA*, New York University Press (New York), 1970

Zipp, Samuel, *Manhattan Projects*, Oxford University Press (New York), 2010

Battery Park City, New York

Fainstein, Susan, *The City Builders*, Blackwell (Cambridge), 1994

Gordon, David LA, *Battery Park City*, Routledge (New York), 1997

Krieger, Alex and Saunders, William S, *Urban Design*, University of Minnesota Press (Minneapolis), 2009

Stern, Robert AM, *New York 1960*, Monacelli Press (New York), 1995

Urstadt, Charles J with Brown, Gene, *Battery Park City: The Early Years*, Xlibris (New York), 2005

Willis, Carol, *The Lower Manhattan Plan*, Princeton Architectural Press (New York), 2002

Avenue de l'Opéra, Paris
Autour de l'Opéra, Délégation à l'Action Artistique de la Ville de Paris (Paris), 1995

Hénard, Eugène, *Études sur les transformations de Paris*, Éditions l'Équerre (Paris), 1982

Pinon, Pierre, *Atlas du Paris haussmannien*, Parigramme (Paris), 2002

Saalman, Howard, *Haussmann: Paris Transformed*, George Braziller (New York), 1971

Vauban, Freiburg
Lütke Daldrup, Engelbert and Zlonicky, Peter, *Large Scale Projects in German Cities*, Jovis Verlag (Berlin), 2010

Antigone, Montpellier
Cruells, Bartomeu, *Ricardo Bofill*, Editorial Gustavo Gili (Barcelona), 1992

Volle, Jean-Paul, Viala, Laurent, Négrier, Laurent and Bernié-Boissard, Catherine, *Montpellier – la ville inventée*, Éditions Parenthèses (Marseilles), 2010

Potsdamer Platz, Berlin
Nishen, Dirk, *Projekt Potsdamer Platz, 1989 bis 2000*, IPA Verlag (Berlin), 2002

von Rauch, Yamin and Visscher, Jochen, *Der Potsdamer Platz: urbane Architektur für das Neue Berlin*, Jovis (Berlin), 2002

Stimmann, Hans, *Von der Architektur zur Stadtdebatte – die Diskussion um das Planwerk Innenstadt*, Verlagshaus Braun (Berlin), 2001

Kirchsteigfeld, Potsdam
Basten, Ludger, *Postmoderner Urbanismus: Gestaltung in der städtischen Peripherie*, LIT Verlag (Berlin), 2005

Krier, Rob and Kohl, Christoph, *Potsdam Kirchsteigfeld*, awf Verlag (Bensheim), 1997

Spangen, Rotterdam
Grinberg, Donald I, *Housing in the Netherlands 1900–1940*, Delft University Press (Rotterdam), 1977

Peterek, Michael, *Wohnung, Siedlung, Stadt*, Gebrüder Mann Verlag (Berlin), 2000

Sherwood, Roger, *Modern Housing Prototypes*, Harvard University Press (Cambridge, MA), 1978

Steenhuis, Marinke, *Stedenbouw in het landschap – Pieter Verhagen (1882–1950)*, NAi Uitgevers (Rotterdam), 2007

Belgravia, London
Gatty, Charles T, *Mary Davies and the Manor of Ebury*, Cassell & Company (London), 1921

Hazelton-Swales, Michael John, *Urban Aristocrats: The Grosvenors and the Development of Belgravia and Pimlico in the Nineteenth Century*, PhD thesis, University of London, 1981

Hobhouse, Hermione, *Thomas Cubitt – Master Builder*, MacMillan (London), 1971

Olsen, Donald J, *Town Planning in London*, Yale University Press (London), 1964

Summerson, John, *Georgian London*, Yale University Press (New Haven, CT), 2003

False Creek North, Vancouver
Hutton, Thomas A, *The Transformation of Canada's Pacific Metropolis: A Study of Vancouver*, McGill-Queens University Press (Montreal), *c* 1998

Punter, John, *The Vancouver Achievement*, UBC Press (Vancouver), 2003

Sarphatipark, Amsterdam
Van Haaren, Marloes, *Atlas van de 19de eeuwse ring Amsterdam*, de Balie (Amsterdam), 2004

Komossa, Susanne, *Atlas of the Dutch Urban Block*, THOTH Publishers (Bussum), 2005

Prak, Niels L, *Het Nederlandse woonhuis van 1800 tot 1940*, Delftse Universitaire Pers (Delft), 1991

Marunouchi, Toyko
The Marunouchi Book, Shinkenchiku-Sha (Tokyo), 2008

Euralille, Lille
Carré, Dominique, *Euralille – Chroniques d'une métropole en mutation*, Dominique Carré éditeur (Paris), 2009

Espace Croisé, *Euralille – The Making of a New City Center*, Birkhäuser (Basel), 1996

Hayer, Dominique, *Fabriquer la ville autrement*, Le Moniteur (Paris), 2005

Simon, Michel, *Un jour – un train*, La Voix du Nord (Lille), 1993

Koolhaas, Rem and Mau, Bruce, *S,M,L,XL*, Monacelli Press (New York), 1995

Puerto Madero, Buenos Aires
Corporación Antiguo Puerto Madero SA, *Costanera Sur*, Ediciones Larivière (Buenos Aires), 1999

Corporación Antiguo Puerto Madero SA, *Puerto Madero – A Model of Urban Management*, Kollor Press (Buenos Aires), 2006

Liernur, Jorge F and Zalduendo, Ines, *Case: Puerto Madero Waterfront*, Prestel Verlag (Munich), 2007

Hammarby Sjöstad, Stockholm
The information for this case study was entirely from non-book sources.

Downtown Dubai
Al Manakh 2: Export Gulf, Stichting Archis (Amsterdam), 2010

Davidson, Christopher M, *The Vulnerability of Success*, Columbia University Press (New York), 2008

Elsheshtawy, Yasser, *Dubai: Behind an Urban Spectacle*, Routledge (New York), 2010

Kanna, Ahmed, *Dubai: The City as Corporation*, University of Minnesota Press (Minneapolis), 2011

Krane, Jim, *Dubai: The Story of the World's Fastest City*, Atlantic Books (London), 2009

Ramos, Stephen J, *Dubai Amplified*, Ashgate (Farnham), 2010

Beijing Central Business District
Campanella, Thomas J, *The Concrete Dragon*, Princeton Architectural Press (New York), 2008

Logan, John, *The New Chinese City: Globalization and Market Reform*, Wiley-Blackwell (Oxford), 2001

Wu, Fulong, *China's Emerging Cities: The Making of New Urbanism*, Routledge (London), 2008

La Défense Seine Arche
EPAD, *Tête Défense – Concours International d'Architecture 1983*, Electa Moniteur (Paris), 1984

EPAD, *La Défense*, le cherche midi (Paris), 2009

Lefebvre, Virginie, *Paris – Ville Moderne*, Éditions Norma (Paris), 2003

Index

Figures in italics indicate captions.

Image Credits

The author and the publisher gratefully acknowledge the people who gave their permission to reproduce material in this book. While every effort has been made to contact copyright holders for their permission to reprint material, the publishers would be grateful to hear from any copyright holder who is not acknowledged here and will undertake to rectify any errors or omissions in future editions.

Front cover photos © Eric Firley
Background cover line drawing © 2013 Katharina Grön and Eric Firley
Four back cover inset images © 2013 Katharina Grön and Eric Firley

t – top, b – bottom, l – left,
r – right, c- centre

pp 2, 6, 8, 9 (t), 10 (b), 11, 24 (b), 27 (t & b), 31 (b), 32 (photos), 33-5, 36 (b), 38, 41-2, 43 (b), 46, 48-9, 50 (b), 52-3, 56, 60-1, 62 (b), 65, 67-9, 72, 74-5, 76 (b), 80-1, 86-7, 88 (b), 91, 93, 96 (t), 97, 99 (b), 100 (t), 104-5, 106 (l), 110-13, 114 (b), 118 (b), 119, 122 (t), 123-25, 126 (b), 129, 130 (t), 132 (t), 133, 136-7, 138 (b), 141-2, 146-7, 149, 150 (b), 153, 156-8, 159 (section and photos), 162-3, 164 (t), 166, 168-9, 171, 173, 176-7, 178 (b), 181, 184, 188-9, 190 (b), 193, 195, 198, 199 (b), 200 (b), 202 (c & b), 204-5, 207, 210 (t), 211, 212 (b), 214, 217 (t), 220, 222-3, 224 (b), 229-31, 234, 236 (b), 237, 239, 241-3, 246-7, 248 (b), 252-3, 254 (b), 255, 258-9, 260 (b), 262, 264-5, 267, 270 (b), 274-5 © Eric Firley; pp 12 (r), 13 (t & c) Courtesy Eric Firley; pp 9 (br & bl), 10 (tl & tr), 24 (t), 26, 29, 30, 36 (t), 39, 40, 45, 50 (t), 54-5, 59, 62 (t), 64, 66, 71, 76 (t), 79, 82, 85, 88 (t), 90, 92, 95, 100 (t), 102-3, 109, 114 (t), 116-17, 121, 126 (t), 128, 131, 135, 138 (t), 140, 143, 145, 150 (t), 154-5, 161, 164 (t), 170, 172, 175, 178 (t), 182-3, 187, 190 (t), 192, 194, 197, 200 (t), 203, 206, 209, 212 (t), 215-16, 219, 224 (t), 227-8, 233, 236 (t), 238, 240, 245, 248 (t), 250-1, 257, 260 (t), 263, 266, 269, 276-81 © 2013 Katharina Grön and Eric Firley; p 12 (l) Courtesy New York Public Library, Miriam and Ira D Wallach Division of Art, Prints and Photographs; p 13 (b) © The Art Institute of Chicago; pp 16 (t), 127 (t) © Bavaria Luftbild Verlags GmbH (Archive Krier Kohl); pp 130 (b), 132 (b) © Archive Krier Kohl; p 16 (b) © Stockholm City planning Administration; pp 17 (t), 201 (t & b), 202 (t), 210 (b) © SPL Euralille; p 18 (t) Krier Kohl Architekten; pp 18 (b), 261 (b) © EPADESA; p 25 (t & b) © Courtesy Sir Stuart Lipton; pp 28, 160 © Blueskyworld.com; p 31 (t) © Skidmore Owings Merrill LLP 2011; p 32 (plan) © Arup Associates; p 37 (t) © SEMAPA; pp 37 (b), 271 Courtesy Air Images; p 43 (t) © Frédéric Borel; pp 44, 84, 108, 208, 268 Courtesy l'Institut national de l'information géographique et forestière (IGN), France; p 47 © Foster + Partners; p 51 © Bettmann/Corbis; p 57 © Courtesy Metropolitan Life Insurance Company; pp 58, 70 Courtesy USDA-FSA-APFO Aerial Photography Field Office/Public Domain; pp 63 (l), 73 (t & b) © Courtesy of Pelli Clarke Pelli Architects, All rights reserved; p 63 (r) © Cooper, Robertson & Partners; pp 77 (t & b), 83 Courtesy BNF; p 78 (t) © Ecole Nationale des Ponts et Chaussees, (b) © BHVP / Roger-Viollet; pp 89 (l), 94 © Stadt Freiburg im Breisgau; p 89 (r) © Kohlhoff & Kohlhoff Architekten; p 96 (b) © Hansen-Architekten; pp 98, 99 (t) © Architecten Böwer, Eith, Murken; p 101 Courtesy Ville de Montpellier; pp 106 (r), 107 (t & b)© Ricardo Bofill - Taller de Arquitectura; pp 115 (l), 120 Courtesy Senatsverwaltung fuer Stadtentwickung – Luftbildservice; p 115 (r) © Hilmer & Sattler und Albrecht; p 118 (t & c) © Renzo Piano Building Workshop; p 122 (c & b) © HGHI Leipziger Platz GmbH; p 127 (t) © Bavaria Luftbild Verlags GmbH (Archive Krier Kohl), (b) © Archive Krier Kohl; p 134 © GeoBasis DE/LGB (2011); p 139 (t) Courtesy Grote Historische Atlas Zuid-Holland, 2005. Uitgeverij Nieuwland, (c & b) © Municipal Archive Rotterdam; p 144 The aerial photograph was provided by the Public Works Department of the City of Rotterdam, the Netherlands; p 148 © Netherland Architecture Institute (NAI) Rotterdam; p 151 (l) Map designed by Sheila Waters; pp 151 (r), 152 © By kind permission of Grosvenor; pp 165, 174 © City of Vancouver; pp 166 (t), 167 © James KM Cheng Architects Inc; pp 179, 180, 185 © Amsterdam City Archives; p 186 © 2008 City of Amsterdam DPG, © Aerodata Int. Surveys, flight date March 23, 2008; p 191 © Mitsubishi Estate Co.Ltd; pp 196, 218, 244, 256 Courtesy Terraserver; p 199 (l) © Chiba Manabu Architects, (r) © Mitsubishi Jisho Sekkei.Inc; p 213 © Corporacion Antiguo Puerto Madero SA (CAPMSA); p 217 (b) © Estudio Arq. Mario Roberto Alvarez y Asoc.; p 221 (t & b) © Faena Group; p 225 (t) "Ice Skating at Hammarby Lake" (Issågning på Hammarby sjö) by Ehrenfried Wahlqvist 1864. Oil on canvas. Stockholm City Museum; pp 225 (b), 226, 232 © Stockholm City Planning Administration; p 235 plans © Mats Egelius, White Arkitekter, photo © White Arkitekter, Photo Åke E:son Lindman; p 249 (t) © Johnson Fain (b) © Pei Cobb Freed & Partners; p 254 (t) © Riken Yamamoto and Field Shop; p 261 (t) © Defacto; p 270 (t & c) © TGTFP.